NITRO: A DOG'S TALE

Eric A. Ewald

Dedication

To Trinitrotoluene George Ewald III

Known to those who loved him as "Nitro"

.

PROLOGUE

November 17, 2009, in Raleigh, NC started like most days that year: I was pretending to enjoy working on my office computer at my environmental consulting job. On this day, however, I began thinking that I really needed a dog in my life. As I scrolled through (mostly) unremarkable postings on Craigslist, a bold heading in oversized, capitalized, and bright red letters suddenly appeared: "All dogs will be euthanized!" This was the worst statement ever, and I needed to find out more concerning this posting from the Columbus County animal shelter in Whiteville, NC. Columbus County was at least an hour's drive from my office and I needed to take a very long lunch break anyway.

When I arrived at the animal shelter, most of the dogs had already been rescued. A few older dogs remained, and there was one litter of seven delightful "lab mix" puppies. They were clambering all over each other in a chaotic and messy mass of brown, tan, and black furry adorableness. One of them came over to the gate to greet me, and I knew this was my guy. I grabbed him up, plodded to the front desk, and paid $25 so I could take little Nitro home. I had no idea how memorable and meaningful the next eleven years were going to be.

CHAPTER 1

The Four O'clock Gang

"Dogs are not our whole lives, but they make our lives whole." — Roger A. Caras, host of the annual *Westminster Kennel Club Dog Show* and author of *Dog Is Listening: The Way Our Closest Friends View Us.*

Nitro was a happy and wondrous bundle of joy from the moment I met him. Our first adventure was a jailbreak from the Columbus County animal shelter, followed by a one-hour drive through the sandhills of North Carolina on a cold and rainy November evening. Once we reached the Triangle, Nitro was excited, cautious, and overwhelmed by all the sights and smells of his new Cary home. I showed tiny Nitro the dog door installed in the laundry room, and right away that fifteen-pound furball leapt enthusiastically through. We walked together for several minutes as Nitro explored his new backyard playground. Wood chips covered the ground where forty oak trees stood on a lot of one third of an acre. Once a year these tall timbers would offer him countless acorn snacks, as the canopy transformed and innumerable leaves glided earthward, forming a crunchy veneer. Nitro was thrilled with his new home and roommate arrangement, and he did not seem to mind walking around in the drizzly rain that first night. After he checked everything out, we returned to the warm, dry house to relax from our big day.

The drive to pick up Nitro had taken us through Lumberton, a town I had not seen for more than twenty-five years. I have called North Carolina home since 1980, when

I moved to Southern Pines from Bethesda, Maryland in the seventh grade. Lumberton was a rival to our Pinecrest Patriots, and during my high school years, we traveled there often to contend with their soccer players and wrestlers. I spent a brief time away from North Carolina to attend Auburn University (Alabama) from 1992 to 1993, and years later I survived a four-year adventure in Queens County, New York from 1999 to 2003. New York City is unforgettable and awe inspiring, but tends to be terrifying or infuriating on most days. After my bittersweet odyssey in the Big Apple, I moved back to North Carolina and bought a house in Cary during the summer of 2004.

Cary is in Wake County, adjacent to Research Triangle Park (RTP), and within the Raleigh-Durham-Chapel Hill triangle area. Cary is one of those towns that, for many years, consistently scores high in the "best places to live" category. Publications that prepare comparative lists recommend Cary for its education system, low crime rates, affordable and accessible housing, job opportunities, and health care availability. I like Cary mostly because it's a quiet town with verdant parks and greenways for dog walking. Even the traffic medians are beautiful, and the cost of living is reasonable when compared to other places I've lived such as New York City or areas surrounding the District of Columbia.

Cary began as a village in 1854 when an intrepid entrepreneur Allison Francis "Frank" Page developed three-hundred acres into a farm and sawmill. After the Seaboard and North Carolina Railroads formed a junction in Cary, Frank built a hotel in 1868 to provide meals and lodgings to train travelers. Cary was incorporated in 1871, and by 1880, there were three-hundred residents. By 1930, that number had tripled. The timber industry, cotton gins, and other manufacturing businesses ensured that Cary flourished for several generations.

Cary had a private boarding school by 1870, and in 1907, the private academy adapted into a public school when Cary became home to North Carolina's first public high school. As its population grew, Cary needed additional services and doctors, lawyers, merchants, churches, and many other businesses materialized. However, it was the creation of RTP in 1959 that caused Cary's explosive growth. Cary's population nearly doubled every decade from 1950 to 2000, and in 2010, the population of Cary was a little over 100,000. Of course, Nitro didn't care about any of this. One of the greatest things about dogs is that they really don't care where they live, as long as it's with you.

A couple of days after the jailbreak, we marshaled another patrol of the backyard so Nitro could relieve himself before his first vet visit. He bounded about happily, loving this new territory to explore, run amok, and scout for varmints or other potential threats to the food source. Nitro's visit at Cary Veterinary Hospital in northeast Cary went well, although he did have a case of heartworm. Dr. McCann told me this is not uncommon with shelter dogs and filled out a scrip to ensure Nitro would be on the mend in no time. Before we left, Dr. McCann took a moment to say, "He's going to be a really good dog." Not only did I enjoy hearing this, but the assessment aligned with my own observations. Even as a four-month-old puppy, Nitro demonstrated a noble combination of alacrity, empathy, and calm. I was certain that as soon as I could convince him to stop pooping in the living room, he would become a first-rate companion.

Nitro, a "lab mix" according to the index card hastily labeled with a sharpie on his kennel at the animal shelter, definitely had some hound in the woodpile. His soft, fluffy, tan fur was marbled with black etchings and a dash of white on the chest. He had oversized boxing gloves for feet and my neighbors and friends could not stop saying, "He's going to be huge!" Nitro also had a black speckled tongue, which led people to believe he was part chow. A speckled tongue is actually a recessive trait shared by many breeds including German shepherds, Labrador retrievers, and at least thirty others. These "freckles" are a result of extra pigmentation deposited in the tongue and were hardly noticeable until Nitro ran around for a bit and needed to cool off.

By the time Nitro joined in my errantry, I had become a well-traveled forty-year-old. My campaigns as an environmental consultant carried me hither and yon amongst the eastern seaboard states from 1993 through 2009. My job was to remediate soil and groundwater impacted by leaking gasoline and diesel underground storage tanks. By the end of the 2000s, nearly all the steel tanks in the nation had been replaced with double-walled fiberglass tank systems with leak-detection and overspill-protection devices. This was good news for the environment, but since my resume was completely centered around this type of work, it became a problem as the demand for remediation engineers decreased.

The previous two years at my job had been especially trying as the 2008 economy lugubriously loomed and lumbered along. The company I worked for had been regularly staging "Black Fridays" when half a dozen poor souls were sent home with their boxes of personal effects, never to be seen again. In retrospect, their fate was probably not so dark and terrible since the "survivors" became overloaded with work while still worrying about losing their jobs. Sure enough, in late November 2009, a week after adopting Nitro and just in time for the holidays, the environmental consulting firm I worked for let me go. I was actually quite relieved and wasn't concerned since I had previously never spent more than two weeks searching for a job.

The layoff occurred right before Thanksgiving and Christmas, so I didn't have high expectations to be rehired before the New Year. Nevertheless, I updated my resume and filled out innumerable online applications to get myself out there. I decided the best thing to do in the coming weeks was to work on training and socializing Nitro. Now free from the demands of work, I considered visiting several of my friends and family in the intervening weeks as well.

Training Nitro was a treat and not extraordinarily difficult. He learned the basics like "sit" and "down" and "heel" in no time at all. Perhaps he caught on so fast because he was smart, but it probably had more to do with his love for doggie biscuits. He did have a bit of a problem pulling on walks, so I bought him a tactical harness with pockets for cookies, bags, or spare change for the doggie deli.

There was a dog park about a mile from my house, and I was optimistic that Nitro would enjoy off-leash capers while exercising and making friends. I had never really been a dog park guy before, even though I've had three dogs since the age of ten. I would typically walk or run with them, and those constitutionals inevitably revealed areas to covertly romp unleashed. Particularly with a puppy, exercising is fun and promotes a healthy lifestyle on several fronts. A well exercised pup tends to train more easily, sleep better, and the likelihood that shoes, furniture, and flooring will be clawed or gnawed into itty little bits is greatly diminished.

Membership at the Town of Cary Dog Park (part of their Robert V. Godbold park campus) requires owners to fill out an application to include proof of their rabies vaccine and a $40 annual fee for a barcoded pass card. If one were to go to the dog park every day, it would work out to only ten cents per day. The dog park itself is a fenced-in area mantled with a tasty blend of shredded wood chips. The park has several benches, trees, and even overhead lighting so visitors arriving at 7:00 a.m. or 9:00 p.m. have some visibility. A five-foot chain link fence surrounds the park and divides it into two areas: one area for small dogs (about half an acre), and a larger, two-acre area for the big dogs. The laser reader at the entrance requires members to scan their membership card to unlock an electromagnetically controlled gate allowing access to a small waiting room, or "airlock" as I like to call it. The double gate system provides this small area in which to safely put your coffee down, unleash your dog, then open the inside gate without any escapees darting out.

There are a few trash cans with poop-bag stations that provide free bags so owners can pick up after their dogs. Only about 75 percent of members actually do so, and this remains one of a few enduring scandals that keep dog park parishioners perpetually perturbed. Water is delivered through two auto-filling livestock bowls; one on the large dog side and the other on the small dog side. These bowls feature low-voltage heating coils and insulation to resist freezing in the colder months.

Nitro's first dog park trip was between Thanksgiving and Christmas 2009. After entering the gate, Nitro's eyebrows immediately raised above his boggled eyes. His puppy posture bolted into a disconcerted ready stance under an invisible thought bubble which read, "Wha??" Another dog was already clocking him and had begun to bear down with his belly to the ground and feet pointed forward. This body language seemed to say, "I'm going to get you!" –and he did. Nitro was oft rolled during that first week; but he soon learned to give as much as he got. He was merely fifteen pounds around this time, but by mid-December he burgeoned to thirty pounds. I felt grateful in those early weeks, as Nitro's demeanor proved to be friendly and earnest. He wasn't hyper, dominant, or high maintenance, and although he embattled many, a real fight never ensued. My unruffled and tender-hearted puppy continued to be well-received by dog park guests, and despite a couple of messy picking points, this vivacious domain rapidly became our favorite destination.

We developed a habit of going to the park as soon as it opened at 7:00 a.m. Nitro was not one to let me sleep in, and his adorable 6:00 a.m. ritual was to half-jump on the bed, and then gently punch me in the face. On most days this meant, "Get up and feed me!" But sometimes it meant, "It's thundering out!" or "I have to poop." We were happy to discover there were several early risers enjoying the park before work (or a job search) each weekday. Numerous dogs would engage in spellbinding chaos during those cold November mornings, and with Nitro romping about, it was easy to make friends. One memorable pup was a spry and playful husky named Didi. Huskies are beautiful but way more mischievous than your average dog. Ace was another morning regular, and this winsome German shepherd was primarily interested in the big bag of toys his mom brought each morning. The Town has a "no toys" rule for the dog park, but it is common practice to bring Chuck-it balls, squeaky balls, or tennis balls despite the ivory-tower mandate. The park has a "member enforced" rule structure, and this clearly was one of those rules no one was interested in implementing.

The large canvas bag of squeaky toys instantly made all the pups go wilder than peach orchard hogs, and breaking the rules made it twice as much fun. It did become a little awkward sometimes, since Ace's mom was uptight about toy management and made a point to muster every coveted toy before she left each morning. Moreover, not every dog knew the toys were for everyone, and quarrels ensued as dogs wrestled over one toy or another. Ace's mom eventually grew fed up with the purloining puppies, and one morning she gathered her toys and hurled complaints of improper sharing into the air. I suppose she figured the winds of justice would carry culpability off her own shoulders somehow. She never returned, but folks still bring tennis balls or other fetching toys every day.

Plastic and rubber toys are not without their drawbacks. Dogs like to peel and chew on those delicious tennis balls, and after such a rendering, the husk and a dozen tennis ball parings are left behind. Some dogs eat those little bits and this is where Didi found trouble. She apparently ate a pile of shredded tennis ball fragments and her owner later told us about the $1,500 surgery to clear Didi's digestive system. Most of us couldn't believe the story since we've seen dogs eat socks, money, aluminum wrappers, and even bars of soap. Aside from worrying their owners half to death, dogs generally pass inappropriate objects without a problem. For a long time after Didi's mishap, I would pick up tiny shards from shredded toys around the dog park and exclaim, "Fifteen hundred dollars!" People who knew the story got a chuckle, but others just assumed I was nuts.

At least half the fun of going to the dog park derives from the interactions, conversations, and study of its many intriguing and quirky visitors. One morning regular, Karen, had a small boxer mix named Loco and a passion for diet and nutrition. Every day she would share a new detox smoothie recipe with us. They weren't anything mundane, either, like banana-strawberry or peaches and cream. Loco's mom imbibed celestial concoctions to evoke divine detoxification. Contentious components such as kale, spinach, or peas were part of her frighteningly effective detox program. Karen claimed she could "feel" the cheeseburgers and pizza she had eaten fifteen years ago emanating out of her pores during a detox. Consuming a blended beverage that tasted like lawn clippings was bad enough, but the reverse osmosis reports seemed singularly preposterous. Admittedly, I've enjoyed smoothies with specially marketed green powders, but I've never experienced Big Macs, Nathan's hot dogs, or burrito supremes springing from my pores.

One remarkable dog who became fast friends with Nitro was Finn, a Catahoula leopard dog and German shepherd mix that loved to bark and chase fetchers. When his owner, Stephanie, had her car windows down, we could hear Finn barking before they rolled into the dog park parking lot. Once in, he would bark continuously as if to say, "Hey! Hey there! Hey! Hey you!"

His favorite game was to stalk a dog playing fetch; then he would bark and wait (and bark) until the ball was thrown again. Then he would sprint after the dog chasing the ball (still barking). Even during those precious few seconds after the ball was dropped, and the owner fumbled with Chuck-it placement, Finn would continue to bark. Interestingly, Finn never went after the ball itself; like so many of us, he only lived for the chase. Most people got a kick out of this, but it could be shell-shocking if you were close to the picnic table under the gazebo when the chucker was nearby. The gazebo acted like an echo chamber, and those sitting at the picnic table would be jaw-jarred by Finn's mighty subwoofer. We never knew when we would see Finn because Stephanie worked marathon twelve-hour nursing shifts on different days (or nights) each week. Finn was quite a card and definitely one of the fastest dogs in the park.

Greta, a black lab puppy about four months older than Nitro, was Nitro's all-time favorite. Those two played nonstop, and Greta lent herself to a playstyle where she would initially engage and then feign an attempt to escape. Nitro chased her every time, but just before Greta allowed him to catch up, she would whirl about and conduct a symphony of bared teeth, crazy eyes, and a jeering growl that became known as "monster face." Needless to say, this sortie was only a bluff, and Nitro responded by hurling himself at Greta while nipping at shanks, sable neck fur, or whatever else his needly puppy teeth could gain purchase on. I learned that Jen, Greta's mom, was a data analyst and also between jobs. Greta's dad, Phil, is a Marine and an information technology (IT) genius. Phil was so smart that if you asked him what time it is, he'd tell you how a clock works.

After a morning dog park trip, I would go home and log in to Indeed, Monster, and several company websites to search the job postings. Internet technology had noticeably improved since my last job search in 2003, but application macros still had plenty of hiccups. Even after uploading a resume, online databases were unable to fill relevant data fields with the correct information. This meant that applicants needed to manually re-type their qualifications, which became tedious since there were dozens of environmental companies in the region. Sometimes we just get stuck with technology when all we really want is something that works. This was still an early battle in my job-search war, so perpetuating a plucky perspective wasn't an immediate problem. I hoped I would receive feedback soon and maybe land some interviews after the holidays.

Wondering if there were other peak times at the dog park, Nitro and I would venture out at various times of the day. We discovered a lunchtime crowd with several regulars whom we liked, including Nacho, a lab-shepherd mix. Since I had very nearly named Nitro Nacho, that became the icebreaker when meeting the noontime group. I had expected a name like Nitro would be easy to remember, but people I met sometimes called him Turbo, Astro, or Nigel. Another noontime regular was Vixen, a husky and evil genius that loved to escape from the park. Vixen was playful and vocal and she could deftly run up and over the fence like it was nothing at all. The transit was so rapid and inaudible, visitors wouldn't even notice she was gone. Joan, Vixen's owner, could recall Vixen as needed; but Vixen was a source of endless entertainment, and her frequent channeling of the great Houdini was something none of us would soon forget.

The fence around the dog park is at least five feet tall around three quarters of the perimeter. The relief and slope of the park provided a situation where rain runoff carried mulch which collected along the downhill portion of the enclosure. The section that faced the Black Creek Greenway effectively decreased in height over time as rain and erosion brought about this natural process. The Town of Cary later replaced the earthward section, increasing its height to eight feet, intending that no one should ever escape again. Vixen accepted this challenge, and a few days after the new installation, several of us witnessed her run up and over the eight-foot hurdle as if it were a trifling baby gate.

While learning the peak visitation schedule of the dog park, networking efforts yielded a few thought-provoking observations. I was meeting an inordinate number of taxpayers who were also unemployed and, for what it's worth, a large number of these folks were over forty. Most of the fifty-and-over people had been out of work for so long, they had resigned themselves to an early retirement after being mothballed by their former employers. Not everyone I met was an engineer, but we all noticed similar details about the job market. For instance, during our job search it was apparent companies expected candidates to have a great number of skills and experience (like that of a forty-year-old). They also required that contenders have the flexibility, verve, and energy of a thirty-year-old. Of course, the coup de grâce was when you found out the pay would be commensurate with someone in their twenties. I turned forty in 2009 but decided not to let my recent observations freak me out. Besides, there would be plenty of time to freak out later. For now, I was actually enjoying the respite from corporate dysfunctionalities such as unendurable and pointless staff meetings, long-winded memos stuffed with management-speak, and those infuriating eleventh-hour blame-game conference calls.

It turned out that four o'clock was the most popular time at the dog park. Even the normally vacant small dog park filled up with a herd of scrappy and dauntless little devils around this time. Nitro's afternoon girlfriend was Rosie, a white lab mix dappled with brown patches, including a prominent print painted symmetrically around her left eye. Rosie's mom is a gregarious older woman named Ellie, who did an impressive job of handling all seventy pounds of Rosie. Ellie is so old the Dead Sea was still sick when she was growing up. Ellie typically ambled in wearing a smile and pastel raiment bedecked with flowers, which belied her sagacious gaze and sharp tongue that could cast clever comebacks were anyone to crack wise. Ellie had raised at least six children, all of whom had three-letter, one-syllable names. Apparently, this was so she could holler at them with greater efficiency. Ellie, considered to be the matriarch of the park, was not one to tolerate any tomfoolery.

    Ellie liked to meet up with Jane and her dachshund mix, Bailey. Despite her diminutive size, Bailey ruled that park. Until this first year as a dog park member, I always thought toy dogs were just silly, but these Lilliputian companions are widely misunderstood. They have prodigious personalities, stout hearts, and do not consider themselves unimportant at all. As far as Bailey was concerned, this was her world, and we just lived in it. Jane worked for a major telephone company and is one of the most well-read and interesting people I've ever known.

    Diane and Jasper were also part of that group. Jasper, a brown-gray terrier mix, mostly loved simply to be left the hell alone. Diane was between jobs and enjoyed talking history and literature with Jane and other folks who warmed up to the gazebo gatherings. Bob and Rex rounded out the foursome. Rex is a black-and-tan lab mix, with perhaps some Doberman or Rottweiler in the woodpile. Rex loved to play fetch like it was nobody's business, and he would bring the ball to anyone nearby. In his mind, *everyone* loved to play fetch! Rex didn't like regular tennis balls, so Bob would bring brightly colored and squeaky Kong balls. Bob launched them throughout the park with his infamous Chuck-it ball launcher.

Although Chuck-its seem to be the only ball launcher on the market, Bob's spurious slinger was renowned due to his propensity to thwack people with a grimy spittle-bedecked ball when they least expected it. One time he hit a woman right between the shoulder blades, and it made a horridly hilarious splat sound as it thudded and squeaked on impact. Thankfully, she laughed it off because Bob is such a kind and good-natured soul. He hit me square in the forehead once, but I pretended not to notice. Attendees arriving at four o'clock learned to sit or stand behind Bob to belay friendly fire, but truth be told, it was never entirely safe. Bob could slice the ball at such an extreme angle, it would ricochet off the gazebo ceiling and hit targets behind him. The safest place was probably going to be another dog park, but people really liked Bob, so the risk was worth it.

The four to six p.m. window was popular since it attracted citizens striving to optimize daylight and temperature conditions. Individuals who needed to visit straightaway after work or school would also join the Fabulous Four, who were always there, rain or shine. Other characters we looked forward to seeing included Nick and MJ. Nick was a waiter and extraordinarily outgoing and charismatic. His dog, MJ, was a feisty wire-haired terrier mix. She loved to play hard, and if necessary, fight hard. Kelley brought her hound Lily nearly every day. Lily was somewhat shy but liked to steal fetch balls and bury them as far from civilization as possible. Lily didn't like to play with other dogs, but she was often chased regardless.

Kelley made the first leap to solidify the dog park

community by starting a Cary Dog Park group on social media. This forum served to keep dog park regulars "in the know" about matters such as muddy park conditions, mulch maintenance days, parking problems, or that strident team of landscapers our dogs dreaded. Mostly we used it to share dog memes and cute puppy photos, but when something important was abuzz, we now had a way to plan ahead. For some reason, the Town email distribution did not reach about half of the dog park members, and that left them out to sea on days the park was closed for maintenance. In addition, park regulars noticed there were situations the Town might not have been aware of or were otherwise unable (or unwilling) to do anything about.

Common concerns included vehicle break-ins, flooding of the water bowl area, copperheads, hawks, or skate park competitions. The adjacent skate park wasn't a problem on normal days, but during their weekend events, finding a parking space became harder than woodpecker lips. Not to mention, the public address system pegged the decibel meter so far in the red, dogs would tremble in terror.

Most of us had dogs less than one year old and members traveling to the park bereft of maintenance cognizance would have to scramble to find another playground for their crestfallen companion. Social media could prevent epic fiascos such as this and was initially a great success. We even used it to share that we could sneak in at 7:00 a.m. on maintenance days, before the Town workers arrived. These were followed by conscientious updates posted after 2:00 p.m. to let members know the Town was already done for the day. Once the dog park social media page became popular, Kelley added me as an Admin to the group because she didn't have time to approve new members or monitor posts. She also knew I was at the park multiple times each day and had already met nearly all of the regular attendees. We didn't want spammers and trolls eclipsing our precious puppy memes, so I was brought on board to weed out imposters and approve only genuine dog park posts.

The last peak time of the day is the 8 to 10 p.m. crowd. I

seldom went this late because Nitro and I were usually worn out by then. When I did visit, we noticed the late-night crew were comprised of a scrappier and mightier bunch compared to the daylight dogs. The early crowds certainly knew how to bend the rules regarding toys, treats, and beach chairs, but the late-night crowd truly knew how to let their dogs be dogs! It's perfectly safe, but not recommended for beginners.

Visiting during most of the peak times became a regular venture for Nitro and me. We enjoyed the fellowship, and the breaks served to clear the mind-numbing gloom that would befoul our morning and afternoon job searching efforts. We continued to meet new dogs and build friendships as those early months of 2010 rolled along.

Conversations in the dog park usually began by discussing where you adopted your dog, which vet you use, and what kind of dog food you prefer. These exchanges proved useful, since it generally behooves owners to share their experiences with training, grooming, or traveling with their dogs. We also shared war stories about problem behaviors and compared experiences with pet-friendly businesses around town.

The four o'clock group in particular liked to have fascinating conversations about books, classic films, world history, trivia, the origins of phrases, and a plethora of other topics. These confabulations repeatedly converged on cuisine since, for most of us, dinner was the next escapade after the dog park. One thing about Cary is that current residents are primarily from someplace else. A majority are from the northeastern US, but Chicago, California, and the United Kingdom are also well represented.

Regardless of their geographic origin, folks are passionate about the authenticity of their favorite cuisine. It goes without saying that New York City natives are regularly dissatisfied with pizza made anywhere outside of NYC. Pizza discussions inevitably led to considerations of whether imposter pizzas were inferior due to water, dough, sauce ingredients, or ovens. A pizza parley would become particularly heated if a park parishioner dared to profess that Brooklyn pizza was superior to that of the other boroughs. This was usually the cue for a Chicagoan to chime in, since their hefty deep-dish pizza crushes anything New York could concoct. Before things devolved into an Italian ancestry contest, the dogs customarily provided a timely distraction (thank goodness).

Pittsburgh peeps complained that there were no proper pierogies in the south. Buffalonians are peculiarly picky and purport that neither chicken wings, hot dogs, pierogies, nor mustard passes muster in Cary. Former residents of the United Kingdom did not consider Indian and Asian restaurants in Cary to be authentic. This clash of the titans would escalate whenever a Brit and a New Yorker decided to duke it out over which of their respective hamlets had truly authentic cuisine.

I strove to avoid these arguments, but I had experienced "authentic" Asian cuisine in Queens during the 2000s. I'll admit the dishes were exceptional and less oily than Americanized Chinese food, but I also recall there being a ghastly amount of fish heads and chicken feet on the table. Carolinians in the group would chuckle at all this, but one thing you did NOT want to do was claim that western barbecue was better than eastern barbecue.

Despite my best efforts and post-holiday optimism, the job search situation was fast approaching its six-month slump. I applied to jobs out of state, but only about one in twenty of those firms contacted me. They would ask, "Are you moving to Poughkeepsie?" I responded with, "Yes, I need to go where there's work." This was followed by a cumbrous conversation about the cost of travel and lodging for the interview. Then they would hammer the nail in the coffin with, "We already have hundreds of local candidates to consider, but thanks for your interest." Although I did prefer negative feedback to dead air, it was disheartening all the same.

At least I still had Nitro and my dog park support group. Nitro was not particularly clingy or needy, nor was he a cuddly dog. Even so, Nitro constantly emanated joy with his presence. His untroubled manner meant that the next nap, or "holding the world down" as I called it, was inescapable. He didn't nap just anywhere either. A nap location was only acceptable if I was in his line of sight. If that was not possible, he would pick a spot where he could observe every lane of egress. Not that I would go anywhere without him since his mere existence effectuated peace and calm.

Trips to the park worked to elevate my mood, but to be fair, it wasn't always fun and games at the bark park. Several negative and prickly personalities could harangue and hinder the habitual harmony from time to time. Hugh and his dog, Minerva, initially visited in the mornings, but would switch times after launching one epic altercation after another. Minerva, a golden retriever, was a splendid dog who only cared about her frisbee. Hugh, on the other hand, insisted on imposing unsolicited dog training advice with all the furor and temperament of a monster truck rally emcee. Two acres seems like a big area, until a beslubbering beef-witted canker-blossom like Hugh began blathering. You could try to ignore him, but the volume and shuddering awkwardness of his unwelcome advice and preposterous bragging was adamantly assured. One morning I actually laughed out loud when he trumpeted, "I just spent four hours at the gym." Dotards like Hugh aren't completely worthless, they can always be used as a bad example. Thankfully, vociferous blowhards were short-timers, so they never defiled the park experience completely.

Then there was Garth, who leeched on to the four o'clock group and, oy vey, this attercop may have loved dogs, but he surely hated people. Garth distinctly preferred to ordain political, culinary, and musical decrees upon unsuspecting visitors. He was about as relatable as a hubcap in the fast lane, and if you didn't agree with him, he let you know you were an idiot. Most of us were shunned for life from the get-go, but he could change personalities when he needed someone to listen.

Although odious, Garth was no dummy, and could drop a

crumb of astute levity once in a while. Garth was from Chicago and had been a lead singer in a rock band nearly forty years prior to his current tour of misery. An aficionado of food and music, Garth loved comedy, especially late-night shows. Garth needed to be the center of attention (lead singer's disease), and this enabled him to offend with maximum effect (an important strategy since he was so easily offended himself). He inserted his presence into the four o'clock group while masterfully ignoring (or indulging) the sighs and groans as gazebo attendees averted eye contact or just simply fled in terror.

Now and again, he would grow weary of the gazebo group and disappear from the park and social media. We referred to him as Garth the unfriending ghost during those much-needed breaks. Unfortunately, the dark lord of anguish would eventually return to twist and corrupt new matters in his prism of despair. We were the dog parkers he loved to hate. Garth had two wonderful dogs named Eddie and Beaches. They were both huge, fluffy, Bernese mountain dogs mixed with Saint Bernard, or something else that was fluffy and huge. His dogs didn't play; they just lumbered in and did their business and received pets. Interestingly, Nitro seemed to like Garth just fine, so maybe ol' Vexatus Maximus was not purely evil.

Aside from the few contumacious customers, the park itself could be troublesome at times. For some unknown reason, there was no drain associated with the water bowls. The area around the large-dog bowl perpetuated itself as a drenched trench and muddy mess. Big dogs liked to paddle in the bowl to cool off their feet, and others shook their jowls when they drank, so owners had to dump muddied water out to keep the basin fresh. The area around the small dog's bowl did not have this problem due to the significantly lower attendance rate, and because small dogs are too polite to engage in any sort of inappropriate paddling anyway. Members, on more than one occasion, attempted to point out the problem to Town employees. Yet Cary maintenance representatives would simply motion to the small dog side and say, "Well there isn't a problem over there," before walking away, apparently satisfied with a job well done.

Despite these sorts of anomalies, Nitro loved our daily visits and continued to help with my networking efforts. In just a few months, we already had over eighty dog park regulars in our social media group. I wondered how many visits the park received each day, and how many dog park members there were in total. Cary's population was around 100,000 citizens in 2010, so that meant there were nearly 8,000 dogs in town; but there was no way even half that many attended the Godbold Dog Park. Based on my observations, I estimated the park averaged about eighty visits per day in good weather. Nitro and I had met about 150 "part-timers" too. These were members that attended the park sporadically, or only on weekends. I found out later there were about 400 members of the dog park in 2010. Obviously, there had been a significant number of people who had joined, visited once, and ran for the hills.

Regrettably, my networking efforts weren't leading anywhere on the job front. I had even been looking for work outside of the engineering arena at temp agencies, hardware stores, fast food joints, and several local businesses. Local managers however, simply didn't see me as a good fit. If they were able to call me back, they would explain that it was too risky to hire someone out of their wheelhouse. Besides, they already had hundreds of resumes on their desk to mull over. It was around this time that I began to find out more about unemployment statistics and the U6 unemployment rate. I understood that the standard unemployment rate reported on the news measures the number of people who are looking for work and are collecting unemployment benefits. The U6 value however, includes those people, *and* the underemployed and unemployed who are no longer eligible to receive unemployment benefits. In 2010, the U6 was at a record high of nearly 18 percent.

Despite what some people may say, you cannot live off unemployment. Not only is it a fraction of what you used to make, it's temporary income. I received a few wisecracks from people who thought I wasn't getting a job because I was receiving "that mad unemployment money," and was disappointed to learn folks actually thought this way. A long-term unemployment situation and its compounding challenges is extremely frustrating and depressing. As if losing your sense of purpose while going broke wasn't bad enough, it worsens over time. I enjoyed rejections such as, "We just aren't hiring in this economy" or "We are evaluating at least 400 resumes for this position." Later, I would hear, "You're overqualified." or "You're from out of town." But I was truly fit to be tied when I began hearing, "What have you been doing for six months?" I've been applying for jobs you mammering, milk-livered, miscreant (I never actually said that, but I wanted to).

Before the internet, I would have tailored my resume to gain temporary employment outside my area of expertise. I did just that in 1998 when I worked as a forklift operator in a retail distribution center before moving to New York City. Once I moved to New York, I had a new environmental job within ten days. Nowadays, it's a whole different kettle of fish. Once you create an account with Indeed, Monster, temp agencies, and an unnumbered sum of environmental consulting firms, you are branded, and then buried somewhere in the dark web. Whenever I attempted to apply for a job at a bookstore, Bass Pro Shop, or the nearest TCBY, they just looked at me like I had three heads.

Once each and every career opportunity webpage became oversaturated with my unsullied qualifications, I was compelled to find busy-work to keep my sanity intact. Frequently asked questions on the dog park social media group quickly grabbed my attention. I enjoyed researching and writing about dogs and felt pride-of-place as an Admin contributing to the page. I had seen how rover revelry engendered a shared love for these knuckleheads and hoped that furnishing information might encourage the growing community. Since dog park members had so many good questions, I began saving my notes and observations in a Word document so I could copy and paste them later onto the forum. Over time, I would provide additional information and qualifications to subsequent write-ups. Many members had asked about safety and rule enforcement, so one of my first posts was about risk management at the dog park.

I had been attending Godbold Dog Park for about six months, and felt that a well-managed dog park that includes fenced-in areas for large and small dogs is an outstanding place to exercise and socialize Nitro. Going to the dog park does require risk management, because they CAN be dangerous, especially for tiny dogs. Membership dog parks are routinely safer than those open to the general public or unenclosed dog parks, and membership requirements cultivate a consortium of conscientious dog owners. Another major advantage of membership parks is the ability to report repeat offenders to the Town of Cary Parks Department. Even so, dust-ups are going to happen. Even when the two best dog owners in the world follow all the rules, dogs will vie for dominance over nearly anything (like a wood chip or a hole they've just started working on).

Children under the age of twelve, or anyone choosing to run and scream through the park are definitely putting themselves at risk. Dogs, whether they like this behavior or not, will engage and push, nip, or jump on the target. Of course, sometimes dogs jump on folks just because it's fun. Ideally, owners have already corrected this habit, but particularly at the park where everyone is new and the party is nonstop, jumping is going to happen. Inattentive attendees are mainly the ones at risk, and Murphy's Law dictates dogs will hit them in a sensitive spot. I maintain constant vigilance at the park because nothing will send you ass over tea kettle faster than a pack of dogs with the zoomies. When this happens, I remind people to use trees, benches, or their spouse to shield them from the scampering scoundrels.

Breaking up a fight is a natural thing to do because no one wants to see their dog suffer a stressful and expensive injury. In a perfect world, both owners are paying attention and are able to grab their own dog right away. I had learned that the best approach was to grab the collar and rear leg(s), but this is easier said than done, particularly when a whirlwind involves more than two dogs. I've seen folks knocked over and stampeded by a brouhaha that's grown out of control. Prevention is the best medicine and I encouraged other members to stay engaged with their dog and to be mindful of overcrowding.

Territorial dogs (most dogs) may sometimes develop what I call "gate envy." This is when dogs become barky, growly, and snappy-faced when a new dog approaches the entrance gate (humans behave in a similar fashion when separated by a computer screen on social media). The best thing to do is simply open the gate and come in. Removing the barrier douses the furry and furious flame war and everyone is in the same boat again. The *worst* thing to do is stand there, not open the gate, and wait.

I made it a point to let the small-dog owners know when birds of prey are checking out the small dog park. I've never actually seen a hawk swoop down to grab a dog, because they are usually clocking varmints or dainty birds in the adjacent woods. Even so, I liked to remind folks to keep an eye out for those regal and ravenous raptors. Whether we saw them or not, our dog park visits commonly included snakes, deer, toads, turtles, and other wildlife ambling through. You'd think they would be afraid of dogs, but no, they are not. Not noticing wildlife was one thing, but there were plenty of people who didn't bother to pay attention to their own dog. This is because they are in love with their phone, their own voice, or the puppy of the day. The best way to manage this situation is to remain patient, gracious, and stay cognizant of the disposition of those ignored dogs.

One of the top things to look out for are the owners who keep their dog leashed after they've entered the park. Reading the body language here may reveal if they are indulging poor judgment to use a public space to "test the waters" for an unsocialized dog. Socializing and rehabilitating a dog is a wonderfully noble thing to do, but folks shouldn't impose this sort of surprise party on unsuspecting dog park members. Of course, this owner could also be a beginner who feels unsure about the dog park. These folks are low risk and should be encouraged to let their pup run free. Talking to new owners served to assuage their fears and I would mention to them that the benefits of Godbold included learning about playstyles, joining the local pet network, and making new friends. I would also mention the social media page since most posts and comments were helpful and informative.

One of the positives to being jobless is that you can finally catch up on correspondence. As the summer grew long in the tooth, I contacted the rescue volunteer, Julie, who had helped me adopt Nitro. I told her how great Nitro was doing and was curious about the rest of his litter. She informed me that his entire litter had found forever homes and that her rescue group, Julie's Dogz, had driven a few of them to homes in faraway lands such as Pennsylvania and New York! I was relieved to hear that, and I wondered if Nitro's siblings were as Zen and wonderful as he was.

A favorite memory from that first year with Nitro was taking him for swimming "lessons." We drove over to Lake Crabtree and met up with Greta and Sam, two of Nitro's favorite friends. Lake Crabtree isn't an official off-leash park, so we had to walk along the tree-lined greenway for a short bit to find an appropriate place to let the dogs loose and take the plunge. We found a good spot that we judged was far enough from the greenway so that the dogs wouldn't be distracted by walkers or joggers. We had also serendipitously chosen a time when there weren't a lot of people at the lake anyway.

After unleashing the hounds, I tossed a ball into the lake and was very surprised to see Nitro sprint, jump, splash, and begin swimming as if he'd been doing it all his life. Greta and Sam were right there with him, even though I had fully expected them to stall, sniff, stare, wade, or procrastinate in one way or another. Those three were having the time of their lives and we threw frisbees, tennis balls, driftwood, or whatever else we could find to keep the game going.

Technically, we were breaking the rules because you aren't supposed to have dogs off leash in Town, but Nitro, Greta, and Sam were entirely too spellbound by this new and exciting lake to bother anyone nearby. One great thing about swimming, is that it wears the dogs out significantly faster than walking or running. We told several dog park friends about our maverick swim sessions, and within a few weeks we had our very own "Lake Crabtree Swim Club" going. This was a huge hit for several late summer weeks, but eventually the dogs acclimated to the routine. As the excitement of swimming waned, our dogs became more interested in patrolling the shore. After a couple of awkward altercations with bicyclists and then a pack of screaming kids, the swim club was kaput. Later, when no one was watching, I still took Nitro to local lakes for swimming adventures (it was perfectly acceptable as long as I didn't tell anyone).

Wake County has several special doggie events to look forward to each year. The Town of Cary sponsors the Dog Days of Summer every June in the Fred G. Bond Metro Park (a.k.a. Bond Lake), their most popular park. It may be best described as a "county fair" for dogs, or a wonderful excuse for everyone to take their dog to Bond Lake at the same time. In addition to the entertaining frisbee fetch competition, dozens of local businesses fill small tents around the greenway and softball fields near the lake. Vaccinations are discounted, doggie day camps are represented, and numerous foster groups also attend. Nitro's favorite kiosks, of course, are the ones where delightful people hand out homemade dog biscuits and cookies. It isn't an off-leash experience, except for one frisbee competitor at a time, but it is a very doggie afternoon, and Nitro and I love attending every year.

Another crowd favorite is a fundraiser held by the Neuse River Golden Retriever Rescue group in south Cary. The popular

Montague Pond event is held two or three times per year and it draws in at least 300 dogs every time. The dogs are able to run, play, and swim until everyone is saturated, sunburnt, or both. Montague Pond swims are the kind of days where your face hurts from smiling too much. They even have a snack bar with grilled foods and dog treats. If Dog Days at Bond are like a county fair, Montague Pond days are the Super Bowl.

Finally, after eight months of torturous rejections and dead air, I received an email from a local environmental consulting firm inviting me to an interview. I was more excited than a mule in a corn patch. The interview went well despite how rusty and useless I had been feeling. They even walked me around the office to meet several folks, which, although terribly awkward, may have been a good sign. Unfortunately, I never heard from them again. I followed up in a polite manner, but the situation would remain a mystery forever more. Did they hire someone else? Are they too busy? Is life just one kick in the pants after the next? I was extremely frustrated and realized I would have to create my own job, but I really didn't know how.

A couple of my dog park friends were teachers, and they suggested I try tutoring math and science. I could put an ad on Craigslist and meet students at the public library. While doing this I also contemplated bartending, or becoming a limo driver, and I even priced out what it would cost to open a brick-and-mortar business, like a pet supply store. I wondered too if it would be difficult to fake my own death so I could create a new identity on Indeed, Monster, and other websites.

The most exasperating part about a long-term job search is seeing a great number of the same job postings repeated ad nauseum. Those ads were deceiving, and I wondered why these punishing replications persisted. Surely, the nice people in Human Resources were not evil geniuses bent on tormenting the unemployed? Since I wasn't able to respond to duplicate postings (career databases did not allow this), I would apply instead to other jobs within the same company, just to make sure

NITRO: A DOG'S TALE

the internet was still on.

The most annoying aspect of this was when my friends or family would report seeing these perma-posts. Based on the derision and disdain delivered in their observations, I deduced they were not well-versed on repeat postings. Instead of strangling my ignorant and arrogant friends, I calmly explained that companies maintain posts for positions so that their HR department always has a collection of resumes on file or because they need more than one person to assign to a role. Moreover, companies purchase these postings to run for a year because that's cost effective. Furthermore, this strategy accommodates a situation when they might need to replace the original applicant six to twelve months later due to attrition or promotion.

Regardless of what was going on behind the scenes in the corporate world, no one was calling my number, and my professional network contacts continued to report the same dismal situation where they worked. The U6 unemployment rate kept climbing, so at least I didn't feel completely alone. Several folks I knew had been unemployed so long, they defaulted on their mortgages and moved back in with their parents. One vital update I was saddened to receive was an account of an old college roommate who had taken his own life. He had been unemployed about a year longer than me. Although there probably were some personal conditions I didn't know about, the direness of the situation was undeniable. When things are going well for us, we may think that depression is an excuse that other people use, or that some things just "won't happen to me." Unfortunately, 2010 was the year I learned what depression really felt like.

Despite having been drained to the dregs this cup of woe, I still had Nitro and I cannot overstate my gratitude for all the goodness evoked by this four-legged furry generator of joy. He was a little over a year old at this point and had effectively become my emotional support dog. Nitro understood that I wasn't okay, and he would come over to me and look at me with those Nitro eyes that said, "I love you, Dad, what can I do?"

This was the moment this hairy dog changed my life. Perhaps I was anthropomorphizing or delusional with despair, but all aggrandizing confirmation bias aside, I truly felt Nitro cared, and it lifted my spirits. I knew things had to work out because Nitro needed me. The ramifications of this sudden recognition of symbiosis would stay with me for a long time, but in the short term, I kept my mind occupied with my writing hobby. You would think that, by now, I would have figured out what I was going to do for a living, but sometimes we don't see the forest for the trees.

After nearly a year of regular dog park attendance, I had observed remarkable and sometimes hilarious patterns of behavior that were too exquisite not to share. I really needed a laugh after reaching the end of the internet on the job search, so I crafted a write-up describing the many personalities of the people that enjoyed the dog park. There were numerous types of personalities, but my favorites included the Phoner, Stepper, Meddler, and the Hall Monitor. The Phoner has absolutely no intention of poo cleanup nor canine cognizance. They often have a tablet or laptop and camp out on the bench with their notes (while shouldering their phone) because they are very important and extremely busy. I was just grateful they let me use their office as a dog park! I have to admit, I am one of the Steppers (Fitbit addicts). We're those kooks that walk circles around the park during most of our visit. People would often ask me if I've lost my keys or dog tags. While stepping circuits, I observed many piles of abandoned poo, and I would pick them up (preferably with a bag, and not my shoe). A Meddler doesn't start arguments, he arranges them. They like to sow discord, and will blurt out whatever they're thinking as if they have some sort of Special Edition Tourette's. These folks are unpopular and frequently get cussed out. Meddlers are also famous for creating the exhausting paradox of imposing rule call-outs while pretending not to notice violations by their own dog. A Hall Monitor visits the park to tell other people their dog is pooping. Also, kids are not allowed and, by the way, your dog is digging. You will have less than 400 milliseconds to take corrective action when this micromanager is around.

Despite my tongue-in-cheek lampoon, our first year at the dog park was teeming with great memories. Nitro was loving life and I don't think I've made so many friends since, well, ever. I mean, if it weren't for the helpless feelings of uselessness, the lack of purpose, a tailspin towards bankruptcy, and the paralyzing depression, I was completely content. Then, as so often times it happens, we find the key.

The holidays were coming up and Stephanie (Finn), Jen (Greta), Ellie (Rosie), and Bob (Rex) were all asking me to keep their dogs at my house during the holidays. "We'll pay you," they said.

Great Mother of Pearl! Why had I not thought of this? If brains were leather, I couldn't saddle a flea. I could, however, be a pet sitter since I knew so many people with dogs by now. All this "career networking" really worked, but in a way I had not at all expected. I was reeling with excitement. That evening, after responding that yes, I would watch Finn, Greta, Rosie, and Rex all at once, I went to grind out some spreadsheets to complete schedule and revenue forecasts. I searched online for information about starting a small business and read the North

Carolina General Statutes relevant to animal care. I even scripted several questions to ask my accountant (then I wrote a note to myself to find an accountant).

The process of changing my career required vital self-examination since committing to this endeavor might resign my engineering journey into the annals of history. I recalled that 98 percent of engineering work required that I perform as a project manager, and owning a small business is just that. Although I still knew Pi to a dozen decimal places, I hadn't used calculus, differential equations, or any of the formulas from physics since college. However, my grounding in environmental consulting assured that I was well versed in critical matters like scheduling, cost tracking, communicating with clients, and business development.

This assessment was tempered with a realization that tutoring wasn't going to work out. Although I'm a math whiz, I was having a difficult time with the methods used in 2010, nearly thirty years after I began my own training in algebra and calculus. Moreover, there was no way I could afford to open a brick-and-mortar business, and the other ideas I had regarding bartending, limo driving, or interpretive dance instruction, simply made little sense as compared to becoming a dog walker. Nitro was not only going to love this idea, but he would prove to be a vital business partner. Without a dog who plays well with others, becoming a full-time pet sitter would be extremely difficult. Nitro was just as good with the other dogs as I was, and he loved it when playmates arrived for puppy parties.

I needed to find more information and knew one of ladies that visited the park around 2:00 p.m. on weekdays was a dog walker. Nitro and I hopped in the car one afternoon and found Sheree in the park with Ace, a very well-postured black standard Poodle. Sheree knew the real deal and I asked how feasible it would be to pet sit, dog walk, and house sit to make a living. She was enormously helpful, and the main thing I remember from that talk was when she said, "Make no mistake, it sounds like fun, but pet sitting requires long hours and hard work. It's true that anybody can walk a dog, but not everybody can walk a lot of dogs every day, regardless of the weather. Not to mention, not every dog is nice like Nitro."

I asked her about accounting, registering a business, insurance requirements, and what she charged per walk. Sheree also shared info about setting up a website, printing business cards, obtaining pet CPR and first aid, and even busted a few myths about tax deductions and the local animal regulations. More than anything, I was grateful to finally have goals and a sustainable purpose. Caring for pets was something I truly felt confident about. From then on, every time a park friend asked me that interrogative I had grown to dread: "How's things on the job front?" I finally had a real answer.

I couldn't believe it. Finally. I hadn't found a job; I was creating one. I looked over at Nitro on the couch that night and said, "Nitro, we're going to be dog walkers!" He looked back at me with his kind, knowing, and slightly sleepy eyes, as that invisible thought bubble read, "It's about time you figured that out."

CHAPTER 2

Walk Away

"It is amazing how much love and laughter they bring into our lives and even how much closer we become with each other because of them." — John Grogan, author of *Marley & Me.*

I knew that eventually I would need to setup my pet sitting small business officially and formally, but I wanted to begin a trial run for a time to make sure I could consistently fill a full-time schedule with hairy clients. On the one hand, there was a part of me that thought an engineering job opening could still occur at any time. Besides, major life changes, with all their uncertainties and opportunity costs, are scary. On the other hand, the idea of becoming my own boss and no longer having to endure soul-corroding head games and corporate dysfunction was very appealing to me. Regardless, I knew any great journey must begin with the first step, and my initial pet undertaking became the 2010 Thanksgiving weekend with Nitro and four guest dogs. Greta would be there along with Finn, Rosie, and Rex. All five of them had been playing at the park together every day for a year, so I didn't anticipate any problems on the harmony front. I was, however, a little worried that a noisy backyard could trigger complaints from the neighbors. I also suspected this long weekend would test the limits of what I considered to be a puppy-proof home and an escape-proof yard. Dog hair, muddy paws, and sleeping arrangements were also matters of concern. Then, the doubts and questions began colliding. Would I be able to feed five dogs at once? Should I take five dogs to the park at the same time? It all seemed a little crazy, but I told myself everything would work out. It had to.

Rosie was the first to arrive on the Tuesday before Thanksgiving and Nitro and Rosie were overjoyed to see each other outside the dog park. Rosie probably thought, "Look, Nitro is at this random house we've just visited!" Ellie walked Rosie to the front door, and as I let Rosie in, Ellie tossed in a bag containing dog food, a blankie, and numerous treats. She then said, "Ok, we'll see you Sunday," and left. Ellie wasn't one to fuss about with small talk.

After crashing into Rosie in the living room, Nitro rushed around the fireplace and over through the galley kitchen to the laundry room doggie door. Rosie chased him but slammed on the brakes before reaching the laundry room door. She had never seen a doggie door before. I walked over to her and opened the door flap a little so she could nose around a bit. Rosie cautiously sniffed, then stepped back wondering what sort of witchcraft was afoot. She looked up as her head-tilt imparted, "What's happened to poor Nitro?" Just then, Nitro barreled in through the mini-door and made Rosie whirl around and bolt through the kitchen again. I would have to show her the dog door some other time since Rex would be arriving soon and it would be best if Nitro and Rosie were in the backyard so that Bob and Rex could enter the house unmolested. This was going to be interesting. Not only would I need to teach four dogs how to use the doggie door, they would also all need to learn the protocols for arrivals and departures—not to mention meals, bedtime, dog park trips, unscheduled noises, and everything else I hadn't thought of yet. Nitro and I were going to be busy.

Bob and Rex pulled into the driveway an hour after Rosie was dropped off. Before Rex even entered the front door, he was overwhelmed with euphoria seldom seen and began wailing gloriously when he detected Nitro and Rosie behind the house. While Bob handed me Rex's ginormous canvas bag of food, Chuck-it gear, and dog bowls (thank goodness because I only had two), he explained he would return "sometime Sunday" but would text when he knew exactly when. Bob didn't like to fly and loved to read so he took a train each time he visited his family in Michigan. While Bob explained his travel agenda, Rex was champing at the bit to join Nitro and Rosie as they leaped about in anticipation. Bob said, "Well, I'll leave you to it," and returned to his MINI Cooper.

Rex then experienced that bittersweet numbness somewhere between "Where did my dad go?" and "I want to play with Nitro and Rosie!" I caught his attention as I walked to the laundry room and removed the plastic shield blocking the dog door. Nitro came barging in, ramming into Rex, then turned around and flew through the dog portal again to find Rosie outside. She was still refusing to use the terrifying door from *any* direction. Rex understood right away and dashed through the contraption and began zipping around the backyard with Nitro and Rosie as if they hadn't seen each other in a dog's age. This was going to be the craziest Thanksgiving ever.

After an hour of playtime, Nitro, Rosie, and Rex were down for a nap. Then Finn arrived. Holy Lazarus! Everyone abruptly rose from a comfortable rest and began barking, cartwheeling, and scratching at the doors and windows like they had just spotted a herd of cats. Stephanie and Finn wriggled their way in and we took everyone to the backyard expediently using the sliding glass door. As the zany quadruplets zoomily zigged and zagged between the azaleas, Steph smiled and said, "You're going to have a busy weekend." She was so right, and we talked a few minutes regarding this revolutionary, if not ludicrous, pet sitting idea.

Steph is really good at asking questions, and she began with, "How many dogs will you walk each week? How many will you have for doggie daycare? How many different dogs will you have each day? Will they be the same dogs every week? How many dogs can you watch at one time?" Then she pointed out that most people will want dogs walked in the morning and evenings, or maybe at lunchtime. I replied, "Those are good questions and I'm going to have to figure it all out."

My main concern was whether I should take all four of these knucklehead monsters to the park at once. I knew it was against park rules to take more than two at a time, but Nitro and the gang knew everyone at the park and weren't contentious dogs to begin with. Greta would arrive tomorrow, so I decided to attempt an excursion with just four to see how it went. Nitro, Rosie, Rex, and Finn were having plenty of fun in the backyard, but I needed to be seen at the park, so people will know that I'm their friendly neighborhood pet sitter. After Steph left, I let the pack play, investigate, and fool around for a short while. As 4:00 p.m. approached, I began to gear up the dream team.

One thing I love about dogs is that no matter how much activity they've had in a day, as soon as you grab their leashes and head toward the door, they become ecstatic all over again. Keeping charge of multiple dogs may have drawbacks, but their unending and infectious positive energy is nothing short of therapeutic. Once everyone was leashed (and then tangled and untangled again), I carefully opened the door and quickly prayed for the five of us to perform a catastrophe-free egress. I was amazed when they naturally walked together to the car and when I opened the rear passenger door, they rapidly piled in and found their own places to sit. I was relieved we actually got into the car without a single door smash, squirrel dash, or face-bash.

Driving with four dogs is a bit surreal, but they did a magnificent job of sitting still with smiles on, as they seemed to know exactly where we were going. Upon entering the Godbold parking area, I used a gruff but enthusiastic "Hold up now" voice to ensure they didn't all blast out of the clown car before I had a grip on everyone's leash. After everyone was unraveled and on to the tarmac, it was time for the two-hundred-foot march through the parking lot and into the airlock entrance. We were already having the time of our life and we haven't even entered the park yet.

On the way through the parking lot I heard comments such as, "You've got your hands full!" or "Here comes the party!" The dog park suddenly felt new and sensational again. I smirked to myself and thought, "Yep. First day at the new office," and wished I had started doing this years ago.

The pack stormed into the park and played for nearly half an hour before settling down a bit; it had been such a stimulating day already. I talked to a few people to share that I was giving pet sitting a whirl, but I didn't want to overdo it since this was only my first journey. Besides, I couldn't possibly add any more dogs this weekend anyway. I acted like the whole thing was no big deal and my goal was to appear calm, assertive, and professional during this early phase of pet sitting. Even so, my face hurt later that night from all the grinning.

One pleasant surprise about that first trip with a pack was how all four of my charges were highly tuned in to me. They followed, kept an eye out, or moseyed over to perform a "check in" when they temporarily lost sight of me. Generally, most dogs do not do this. Nitro, for example, didn't perform check-ins because he stayed within three yards of me at all times. Other dogs prefer to run amok at the park and completely forget who brought them in the first place. Finn loved to chase and run hard, but as I watched him closely, I noticed he was keeping an eye on me as well. One time, as he chased after a fetcher, I snuck behind a large tree and out of sight for a moment. Sure enough, as I peered from around the tree, Finn appeared visibly nervous and, forsaking the game of chase, began searching for me. The look on his poor little face was too much, and I returned to a spot where he could see me. Apparently, Finn does *not* like to play hide and go seek.

After an hour at the park, I grabbed up the leashes to leave, and Nitro, Rosie, Rex, and Finn immediately rushed to me. This day was becoming one of the best first days I had ever experienced. I was both astounded and pleased as the pack and I left the park and hopped into the car. At this point I steeled myself for the next test: dinner for four.

Everyone in the group had a similar feeding situation: one cup of dry kibble in the morning and another in the evening. My strategy to prevent crossfire was to prepare all four bowls in the laundry room, then place them on the kitchen floor simultaneously so that I was standing in the middle of a four-way intersection. It wasn't a problem though because all four of those hungry hippos immediately focused on their own kibble. Except Finn. Finn looked up at me after I put his bowl down, then looked at the food, then looked away. Puzzled, I wondered what sort of dog doesn't immediately scarf his food down? Maybe he was upset that Stephanie had left him here and had begun a hunger strike! I decided to try again later, and picked up his bowl so none of the other piggies would polish off his dinner.

During the evening wind-down hours, each guest dog spent some time sniffing and studying my home while they policed up any crumbs Nitro may have overlooked (highly unlikely). My house or, rather, the doghouse, is a 1,200 square foot ranch that was built on a slab on grade in 1984. With only three bedrooms and two baths, it didn't take the boarders long to complete their curious combing. Nitro, as usual, hopped up on his "observation post" in the living room. This is a spot on the couch next to the large front window where a section of the couch backrest is missing. From this vantage point, Nitro had a full view of the front of the property, the front door, my bedroom door, the kitchen entrance, and the sliding glass back door. I couldn't possibly leave or grab a snack without Nitro knowing.

Rosie found a spot on the comfy couch near Nitro, and Rex plopped down on the bed in the guest bedroom. On this night, and through most of his stay, Finn liked to lie down on the linoleum floor by the front door, since that was the last place he had seen Stephanie. By the time I went to bed, all the dogs were already in Palookaville and none of them bothered to hop on my bed, which was fine by me.

When I woke up the next morning, Rosie had magically appeared by my side, the sneaky devil. I served breakfast using my four-way traffic cop routine, and Finn ate a few bites of kibble this time, but not all of it. I intended to arrive at a solution to Finn's hunger strike situation soon, although I knew he would grow hungry eventually. After breakfast, the dogs and I enjoyed

35

the backyard while awaiting Greta's arrival.

It was a cloudy Wednesday morning in November, and I was worried it might rain. However, I didn't want to bring the dogs inside because it would be nearly impossible to hold four dogs back when Greta tried to enter through the front door. This was my first conundrum as a pet sitter: I needed to make sure owners told me when they would arrive, and within a reasonably narrow window of time, so I could manage arrivals and departures efficiently. Little details like this are important because an escapee situation may be dangerous due to the cross-street traffic. Even worse, it would be embarrassing.

Luckily, fate was on our side and no rain fell before Greta disembarked one hour after breakfast. I didn't show Greta the dog door, but instead just released her via the sliding glass access to be outside with the pack. I then asked Jen and Phil when they would return to pick up Greta and Jen said, "Late on Sunday afternoon, and good luck with 'monster face!'"

During that first Thanksgiving as a pet sitter, I established several routines. I would take three to five dogs at a time to the park, and despite this being an outlandish move, the surprise party was well received. When there was only one dog in the park, owners were happy to have an instant puppy party. Sometimes there would be a large group in the park, and this bode well for my street cred as a dog sitter. Finn remained a stubborn eater until I thought to place a few pepperoni slices in the bottom of his kibble bowl. This was a game changer and completely guaranteed he would eat all his kibble and forget about Stephanie, at least for a few minutes.

Thanksgiving dinner itself was low key. My brother, Doug, and Dad (a.k.a. Big Bad Bill or Billdad) visited, and we had Cornish game hens with several traditional side dishes. Dogs love Cornish game hens, but they enjoyed backyard time while the humans ate inside.

Brother Doug is twenty years younger than I am and was a junior and the University of North Carolina in Asheville (I refer to him as "Brother Doug" because one of the four o'clock regulars is also named Doug). Brother Doug was a biology major, just like Billdad, and he would return to Wake County a few times a year for holidays or school breaks. Doug grew up in Apex, a town adjacent to Cary, in the house where my wicked stepmother still lives. Over the years, I have always maintained a good rapport with Brother Doug since we both enjoy reading books about history, listening to the same kinds of music, playing videogames, and most of all, spending innumerable hours discussing the Star Wars galaxy or the ages of Middle-earth. I wouldn't say Doug is a huge fan of dogs, but he likes them. He keeps cats as pets because, as he says, "They are much cleaner than dogs, but it's possible my cat is planning to murder me."

Billdad was a biologist in civilian life and worked for government agencies such as the National Institutes of Health (NIH) and the Environmental Protection Agency (EPA) as a biologist or air quality specialist for forty years. Big Bad Bill also served in the US Army for most of his adult life. Many years ago, after several prep schools and colleges had asked him to leave, Dad joined the Army in 1962 and served as a military policeman until 1966.

After his honorable discharge, he attended Middlebury College in Vermont where he met my mother. They were soon married and I was born in Burlington, Vermont on July 28, 1969. We moved to Bethesda, Maryland, and from 1970 through 2008, Dad served in either the Army Reserve or the Army National Guard as a noncommissioned officer in several units. These included Nuclear Biological and Chemical (NBC), Armor, and Special Forces units. After 9/11 he was in a military intelligence outfit and, obviously, was unable to reveal anything about that duty station. This was just fine with him because Billdad didn't like to talk much anyway.

By the time Sunday evening rolled around, Rosie, Rex, Finn, and Greta had all been picked up and I was $700 in the black. Hands down, it had been the most extraordinary, and the most profitable, weekend I had had in a long time. I expected the same lineup for Christmas, but in the meantime, I needed to perform enough business development to fill my weekly schedule with day campers and dog walks. I knew it was feasible to care for six dogs per day, but actually loading that schedule is easier said than done. Initially, only Finn and Greta became three-day-a-week regulars, but it was only a matter of time before the dog park provided more charges.

There were, however, several other facets to this endeavor that I needed to examine. I had been researching state, county, and town laws regarding animals and couldn't find a statute that explicitly prohibited dog visitors. However, having too many dogs on a residential property could violate laws regarding noise, poo cleanup, or leash requirements. My neighborhood does not have a Homeowner's Association (HOA), and therefore, it had none of the by-laws that would limit the number of animals permitted per household. Cary does not allow kennels in residential zones, but I promoted myself as a dog walker, and not a kennel service. This was a bit of a marketing tightrope, since I wanted word to get out about my day camp and overnights, but I didn't want nosey Nellies to tattle on Nitro's playmates.

I was mindful that there would be wear and tear on my car, carpet, and furniture, but the jury was still out on those deliberations. The main item of concern was whether neighbors would notice (or care) about all the barking and roughhousing happening in my backyard. My neighborhood has at least one barking dog per house already, so I hoped it would be unlikely that anyone would notice a few more. Having nonstop puppy shenanigans could, eventually, drive me bananas, but I needed the money. Besides, if twenty years of corporate dysfunction hadn't sent me to the funny farm, surely I could handle running a doggie day care. One thing I was NOT worried about was Nitro. He never missed a beat when it came to all the new pilgrims and extra dog park visits. Nitro was such a Zen dog and friendly to everyone.

As 2011 unfolded, I continued to notice new people at the dog park and kept my eye out for ways to be helpful and target potential clients. It felt good to be a money-grubbing capitalist again. One morning, a fella with a long and wildly hairy German shepherd puppy stopped in the dog park entrance gate. They both looked taken aback by all the gate envy. "You guys can go in the small park to let him warm up if you'd like," I offered. The young man returned my comment with an expression that seemed to say, "Don't tell me what to do, dork." I just smiled and kept walking. Later, I got to know Justin and Kaiser well as they became regular attendees. Kaiser had a lot of personality, loved to chase the ball, but he hated rakes and raking. When somebody tried to smooth over a hole in the dog park mulch, Kaiser didn't hesitate to have a little talk with them. I know dogs can't talk, but Kaiser would vocalize in such a manner that you would have sworn he was making a citizen's arrest. I watched Kaiser now and again when Justin took long weekends to visit family.

My favorite new guy was a very old man named Pete. Pete rolled up to the park in a Jeep Wrangler with a cigarette dangling out of his mouth and his dog Lulu dangling out the roll bars. Pete's emaciated frame couldn't stay vertical without a cane, but he ambled into the park every day despite this. Lulu was a tan, wire-haired terrier mix who loved to run around with all the other dogs. A few of us maintained earnest intentions to help Pete out if Lulu were to land in any trouble, but that never happened.

Over time, I grew to be familiar with several of the small-dog park regulars. If unchecked, small parkers and large parkers would naturally develop enmity since their respective dogs barked at and chased each other along the fence dividing the two areas. We kept things cordial to each other's face, but the outgroup hate was palpable. Sometimes, when I was sitting for a small dog, or if Nitro was being harassed by a ne'er do well, I would sneak him into the small dog side. Nitro was so calm and cool that the small parkers gave little heed to his presence.

Keira was an outgoing and interesting lady who attended the small park with Lamont, a tan Westie mix, and her other dog, Mable. Mable can best be described as a Yorkie mix that strongly resembled Master Splinter from Teenage Mutant Ninja Turtles. They were both sociable dogs and didn't become scrappy or fussy concerning Nitro's presence on "their" side. Making friends with Keira was important because she shared the scuttlebutt that went on over there in tiny town.

From the sole central bench in the small dog park, members had a commanding view of the entire dog park, and the acoustics were such that they could hear nearly everything that was said in those front thirty yards. The small parkers enjoyed this view and liked to predict the next fight in the large-dog area. Their vantage point also enabled them to spot poo pickup failures, something they discussed at great length apparently. I laughed when Keira shared this useful information and made sure to minimize derision toward the small parkers in the near future. Keira also told me that many of the small park people thought I worked for the Town of Cary since I was always at the park and was the Admin on the dog park social media page. This also cracked me up, and I wondered why more people didn't speak up and ask me directly.

The Town of Cary, in public-spiritedness no doubt, did not assign a park ranger for Godbold. In fact, aside from mulching twice a year, they did not maintain a presence other than to empty trash cans and refill doggie poo-bag dispensers a couple of times a week. Due to this maintenance void, I started to complete a number of minor housekeeping duties during my daily visits. This began with the unbearably disorganized and photo-degraded bulletin board with broken thumbtacks, obsolete notices, and business cards jammed in such a crowded way that no one could view them.

After organizing and making the bulletin board usable again, I provided rakes so owners could easily backfill holes made by their dogs. I also installed eight hooks for leashes (or coats) in the wooden four-by-fours that provided vertical support for the gazebo. I disposed of small pieces of debris when needed ("1,500 dollars!"), along with countless abandoned piles of poo each day. Completing these sorts of chores felt completely natural and made sense to me since the park was essentially becoming my workplace. I truly enjoyed doing whatever I could to remedy paltry problems and to add value to a Town park that was already special in many ways.

One nice lady I met, Natalia, was from Siberia, Russia. She visited the park with Nazer (pronounced Nah-zeer), a Russian wolfhound (a.k.a. borzoi, which is Russian for "fast"). Russian wolfhounds were originally bred as a type of hunting sighthound. They resemble other sighthounds such as Afghan hounds, greyhounds, and saluki. While hunting, these breeds rely on keen vision and speed more than their sense of smell. Nazer stayed over several times when Natalia traveled to see her family in Russia. Although he was lanky and awkward, Nitro loved him just the same.

Rigby became a regular dog park attendee in the early months of 2011, and it was difficult to miss her because she loved to eat anything and everything! When Rigby was at the park, members who hadn't learned to keep their gloves, phones, or scarves out of reach usually lost at least one of these items. Kristine often had to take Rigby to the vet for a dose of hydrogen peroxide so that Rigby would urp up the various soggy belongings she had consumed. It became difficult to determine which was more fun: watching Rigby run around with something unusual in her mouth, or watching Kristine running after her screaming with arms flailing. I never had Rigby over for day camp, but if Kristine had asked, I had intended to report that I was "too busy" in order to prevent my remotes, cupholders, and silverware from going missing.

Zeus and Apollo were a pair of vizslas owned by Crystal and Patrick. These guys were nuttier than a squirrel turd (referring to the dogs, of course, although Crystal and Patrick are characters in their own right). I was able to pet sit for them now and again, and they were notably the craziest pair of hounds

I knew, particularly while riding in the car. This dynamic duo could inadvertently roll down windows, change gears, and one day Apollo even turned on the interior lights. To this day, I have no idea how he did that.

Mark and Janice co-owned Boomer, a large, kind, and rascally yellow lab. Both Mark and Janice were active, athletic types who could be spotted walking or running with Boomer all around town. We saw them so often that Kelley (Lily's mom) liked to say, "Did anyone see Boomer on his perpetual walk today?" The four o'clock gang laughed out loud since most of us had seen Mark and Boomer walking all times of the day in locations that were miles apart from one another.

Jan brought Bacchus, a ginormous German shepherd, only on Friday afternoons at 4:00 p.m. Jan and her husband John were really nice people and had recently retired. Bacchus, although huge, was kind and calm but park members always looked twice whenever one of the several giant breeds frequented the park. The giants were mostly Great Danes, Newfoundlands, and the occasional great Pyrenees. Nitro's favorite giant was Jade, who visited with Carole and Gary. Jade was a beautiful blue Great Dane who loved to fend off Nitro's advances.

We watched their terrifying antics with glee as Jade, who was at least twice Nitro's size, would bend Nitro in half, backward, so that his little chicken neck was thrown back when these titans clashed. Nitro grew to be sixty-four pounds in 2011, and I was so proud of my hirsute little contortionist buddy.

Pet sitting in the first several months of 2011 was slow at first, but by the middle of the year I was watching pets for twenty households. That translated to thirty dogs, seven cats, and two fish. Cat sitting is easy, unless you have one that objects to oral medication. I had heard that can be a little tricky, but thankfully none of my charges fell into that category.

Life as a pet sitter was snowballing in a positive way because more people were seeing me with different dogs each day. Likewise, it was obvious my charges were having the time of their lives. I have never been able to explain why, but dogs follow me around like I was the Pied Piper of Hamelin. Ellie accused me of smuggling treats, but the most likely explanation is that the dogs detected the scent of numerous other dogs on my clothes. Even dogs outside of my charge tended to follow me around, and once one or two began to follow, it would rapidly grow to be four or five. Perhaps they thought I was leading them to a magical spot in the dog park that had a trove of tasty treats and tempting toys.

The dogs also listened to me, which was conspicuously useful when preventing or disrupting doggie squabbles. Dogs who had stayed with me for day camp, and specifically those who had spent long weekends, perceived "crazy uncle Eric" as their pack leader. Even dogs who barely knew me sensed that something fun was going to happen. As this momentum of doggie goodness compounded, my confidence and client base increased, and as summer roiled along, I had to pace myself because demand began to exceed capacity. The whole situation was surreal, but also satisfying. I felt grateful, not only for stumbling into this walk of life but that this path felt so natural. I wondered if all pet sitters felt this way, and I also wondered why in the blue blazes had I ever become an engineer in the first place?

Even so, mistakes were made and while learning the ropes, I occasionally would agree to watch a dog who I didn't know well or who tended to be too dominant. I pushed the envelope a few times that year during my pet sitting "pre-season," and I took on several challenging dogs with intense energy or a propensity to be pugnacious. I knew I could handle them, and those owners were expressly thankful since they had already been booted out of the "big box" doggie day cares around town. Although this worked in the short-term by greatly improving my reputation (while teaching me a few lessons), dogs requiring close supervision incurred opportunity costs. The most rambunctious dogs made it so I couldn't turn my back for even one second to grab another poo-bag or, if at home, check my mail or answer the door. As the year unfurled, I found that filling the roster with playful, sociable, or lazy pups bestowed a more efficient, harmonious, and safer workplace.

The social media page for the dog park was still going strong with regard to sharing park maintenance dates and other pertinent information. Although I did not use it overtly for business development, my contributions to that group proved to be mutually beneficial. My favorite observation concurrent with becoming the resident dog park pet sitter was when dog park members started forming a real community. Parkgoers connected here and there during visits, but the social media page and my pet sitting service markedly improved connectivity. Dogs who visited only in the morning, or only on weekends, were now meeting and becoming friends with dogs who visited at other times of the day or week.

My client dogs spent a lot of time with Nitro, and the dogs who stayed with us maintained a pack mentality. This positive side effect fostered community among owners as small groups began meeting for Saturday cookouts or Sunday night dinners. By the end of the year, I was watching numerous dogs from each of the peak times at the park. I do not take credit for this serendipitous entropy, and prefer to consider fate the fundamental orchestrator of these circumstances. Perhaps it was a function of recession recovery, or maybe the commending chemistry occurred for other reasons. Regardless, I had unintentionally contributed to improving the park dynamic, and I ran with it. As my venture began to function as a focal point of a freshly forming fellowship, the symbiosis benefited everyone.

As familiarity and friendships developed, birthday parties for dogs became a regular occurrence. Both the dog park parishioners and their dogs particularly loved these special days. I had a birthday party for Nitro when he turned two on July 17, 2011. For doggie birthdays, we typically brought in treats, balloons, cookies, donuts, or cupcakes. After the great cake catastrophe in the spring of 2011, owners learned that handheld treats were a much smarter option. Balloons are irresistible, but also bittersweet since at least half of the dogs tended to freak out when those floating mylar demons hovered by. Nitro liked balloons and would even let me clip one to his collar. He gave me the side eye at first but would quickly forget it was there. In an attempt to one-up my party, Ismail (Misha's dad) bought two twenty-four-packs of Krispy Kreme donuts to share with everyone on Misha's first birthday. Misha was a yellow lab who was about as friendly, clumsy, enthusiastic, and plump as anyone could stand.

She loved everyone too, and her Krispy Kreme day was a huge hit, but we just couldn't finish the last two donuts. Ismail thought it would be safe to precariously place the leftover donuts, in their broad lightweight box, on a boney crossbeam above the park bulletin board. When the next light breeze blew the box down, it was Vixen with her husky-like reflexes who snarfed down the remaining two donuts in the blink of an eye.

Despite the wondrous year 2011 was turning out to be, there were still a small number of fussy characters who guaranteed a shadow would fall upon the joy of Godbold from time to time. The worst were the tattletales. Members did expect that dangerous situations or injuries should be reported, but there was one couple that wouldn't let anything slide. Gilroy and his grumpy wife, Natasha, brought his friendly boxer nearly every day for a while. These curmudgeons emanated doom and despair as they grumbled over everyone else's dogs. Granted, their boxer was a paragon of obedience, but most of us could have done without the judgmental leering and scathing commentary.

Another mope I'd nominate for the groaner hall of fame was an IT fella named Benedict. He would ignore his cranky dogs while bragging about his knowledge of computers and smartphones. Of course, if anyone asked him a question about their device, he would only mock their ignorance and failed to provide any assistance. We couldn't discuss our favorite television shows around this guy either, because he would instantly blurt out vital spoilers; it seemed as if his sole purpose on this planet was to poo on everyone's parade. His wife, Lucinda, was no prize either as she maintained a bubbly and manic veneer that belied an insidious and aggressive psyche. She loved it when people "got into it," and made it her full-time job to ensure this would happen by tattling on one member to another.

Aside from the obnoxious or histrionic owners, there were others who managed to come up with new and inventive ways to stress out parkgoers. Although rare, there were those who insisted on bringing all three and a half pounds of their mini-baby toy dog into the large-dog park area. Large-dog owners would then politely hold their dogs back, so the little lunch pockets wouldn't be trampled or treated like a plush toy. Visits like these effectively hijacked normal park operation while large-dog owners watched helplessly as the gerbil-sized canine did his or her business.

Though evil deeds they had wrought did injury to the designs of Godbold, no permanent damage was ever done. These folks just came and went, and besides, nobody's perfect. Even Nitro had an incorrigible trait where he would go out in the wee hours and howl at the owls. I'm not sure what those arguments were over, but his reign of terror would have gone on all night if I had let it. It reached the point where part of my goodnight ritual was to bring Nitro and everyone inside and block the dog door so no one could go out after 11:00 p.m. Whenever I forgot to do this, I was certain to be awakened by a 3:00 a.m. symphony of howls and hoots as the unrelenting twins of tomfoolery deliberated yet again. I often wondered if it was the same owl every time.

Later in my first year as a pet sitter, I developed a rhythm where I was watching four dogs in day camp each day and would walk two other dogs a few days of the week. I took in overnight campers as needed, and soon realized that Easter, the Fourth of July, Thanksgiving, and Christmas commanded the highest demand for overnighters. Throughout this first year, many folks asked me about what it's like being a pet sitter, so I completed a comprehensive but concise write-up that I would email to subsequent inquirers. Many dog park members were still unemployed and wanted to hear firsthand about the pros and cons of pet sitting. Only two out of those twenty or so people actually attempted pet sitting, since the thought of changing careers was so indeterminate. Not to mention, managing six or more dogs per day was just too much for most folks.

I had learned so much in this first year, but the most important lesson was the confirmation that I could actually make a living as a full-time pet sitter. The demand for pet caretakers is significant when you consider that in most towns the pet population is 8 percent dogs and 6 percent cats. Cary's population of 100,000 citizens meant that there were approximately 8,000 dogs who needed exercise and relief breaks every day.

In the United States, the pet sitting market manages a revenue of $2.6 billion nationwide, and it's growing. I knew that if I charged $20 per walk, and if I walked one dog per day, five days per week, that would generate $5,000 per year. It is feasible and sustainable to care for six dogs a day and make $30,000 per year. Dog walking isn't "hard" work, but it is time consuming. A half-hour walk actually takes an hour with setup and travel time, and I established a service radius of three miles to safeguard my daily capacity. Most clients wanted me to walk their dogs at 6:00 a.m., noon, and 6:00 p.m. This meant I still had plenty of time for dog park trips and backyard playtime.

The days ahead were going to be long, and I now understood what Sheree meant when she told me last year that full-time dog walking is onerous. My strategy to reduce the risk of burnout was to manage mostly day campers and overnighters. These charges were more lucrative and served to shorten my days. Another way I would pet sit was to house sit for a couple of my clients. House sitting often included a cat (or three) and I charged $60 a night for this service. However, I could only pull this off on weekends when I didn't have a lot of overnighters already.

Determining my rates wasn't difficult since the competitive rate of twenty dollars per walk had been established by the local market. I noticed some sitters charged sixteen or eighteen dollars per walk, but they always had petty add-ons that ensured it resulted in twenty dollars anyway. I strove to establish a regular blend of sitting, walking, and overnights to make scheduling easier for myself, but demands changed often.

As holidays, school breaks, or severe weather rolled through, I would experience peaks followed by valleys. I made sure to visit the dog park at least twice a day since it imparted the luxury of previewing potential clients and served as an impromptu, but ongoing, "meet and greet" session. All dogs are wonderful of course, but I had learned that excessive barkers, escape artists, and overly dominant dogs were not optimal charges. More often than not, I observed dogs who were just fine; but it was the fussy and difficult owner that I needed to know about.

The bottom line is that pet sitting was proving to be a great way to earn a living by providing a service where I would not only be valued, trusted, and appreciated but could finally be my own boss. The end of 2011 brought the completion of an encouraging probationary period of my new venture. Since dog walking was becoming a marvelous success, I felt ready to officially say farewell to engineering. For 2012, my goals included registering as a small business with the Town of Cary and State of North Carolina. I also needed to obtain pet sitting insurance, kick off a website, and otherwise completely commit to pet sitting as my very own small business entity. Although driven by fate, new circumstances brought a sense of pride and confidence in my ability to be a reliable and faithful caretaker. This blessing stood in stark contrast to my grounding as an environmental consultant and offered an optimal lifestyle for my best buddy, Nitro.

CHAPTER 3

Eric's Pet Sitting

"Everyone thinks they have the best dog. And none of them are wrong." — W.R. Purche, author of *The Canine Commandments* and other works.

Nitro and I were determined to make 2012 a memorable year by establishing our pet sitting service as a legal, state-certified small business. There were several steps to this process and I expected it may take a couple of months to figure a few things out and actually seal the deal. More than one of my clients had told me, "Bah, you don't need a license, you can just be 'Under the Table Pet Sitting.'" That wasn't really my style though, and besides, I knew founding a company would confer several advantages. Becoming an officially registered business would add legitimacy to my enterprise, facilitate tax deductions, and permit access to business checking. A business checking account would be useful to minimize banking fees, enable payment by credit card, and provide a method to separate my personal and business holdings.

My dog walking friend Sheree had recommended I visit the Small Business Center at Wake Tech Community College (WTCC) to gather resources on how to start a small business in North Carolina. Sure enough, WTCC provides potential entrepreneurs with an instructional small business packet (which was incongruously quite large), and this information is made available free of charge. I eagerly began tailoring WTCC's catchall business setup formula to match my needs as a dog walker operating out of my own home. I boiled it down to fewer than ten tasks that included meeting an accountant, creating a name for my company, crafting a business plan, applying to the North Carolina Secretary of State (NCSOS), and insuring the business.

I love making to-do lists and this one was a doozy because most of these tasks were interrelated. I could already tell that there were going to be subtasks to tackle, therefore I prudently prioritized duties so everything wouldn't unfold all at once. Additional undertakings included creating a website, joining a pet sitting organization, and taking a class in pet first aid and CPR training.

After the trip to WTCC, Nitro and I elatedly set off to the dog park to update the four o'clock gang with our rousing progress report. One of the newer attendees, Dog Park Doug, had been operating a small business out of his home for many years. His black lab mix, Boomer, was a cheerful, outgoing pup and the main thing we looked forward to with Boomer was when he repeatedly made three-foot vertical leaps in front of his dad to say, "I'm hungry and it's time to go home!"

I began referring to Doug as "Dog Park Doug" to avoid confusion since eavesdroppers had misunderstood numerous stories about Brother Doug. The funny part is that Brother Doug is about forty-four years younger than Dog Park Doug and lives four hours away in the mountains around Asheville, North Carolina. Moreover, why would folks think Dog Park Doug went to Buckethead concerts or engaged in futile arguments with my wicked stepmother?

In any case, Dog Park Doug proved to be a good source of small business advice and was one of my first allies while busting several myths about tax deductions, corporate indemnification, and other legends. I love my dog park peeps, but when it comes to tax exemptions, "e-rumors," or urban myths, they say the darndest things. Even Dog Park Doug did not have all the answers because tax laws change every year, and his technical recruiting business was very different from a dog walking service. These dog park conversations were great when one of us needed to process matters of concern and helped me craft several relevant questions for the upcoming meeting with my new accountant. As soon as Boomer began his pogo mime routine, it was time to get organized and prepare for the imminent consultation.

I knew things were going to work out well with Drew, the accountant, because as soon as I entered his office, I was mugged by two adorable beagles. I gave them a couple of treats from the cookie jar on the reception desk before sitting down in the small conference room. I wasn't sure where to begin, so Drew started by asking questions about my vision for the small business. I explained that my venture would be service-based and that I could manage up to six dogs per day, but that I did not wish to expand operations beyond that. The thought of managing a commercial facility with employees made my face twist like a bulldog chewing a wasp, and I'd sooner be beaten by a sack of wet catfish than become ensnared in another corporate trap. Drew, appreciating my folksy comparisons, knew right away that a Limited Liability Company (LLC) was the way to go.

He explained that LLCs were invented in Wyoming in 1977 and that within the following twenty years, LLC statutes had been adopted in all fifty states to encourage small business growth. LLCs are the most popular and the most flexible business structure for business owners, entrepreneurs, and real estate investors because they offer a "have your cake and eat it too" condition compared to sole proprietorships. LLCs also offer "pass through" taxation which means I would not pay myself a salary and my pet sitting income would "pass through" my individual tax return.

A sole proprietorship is when a person operates their business as themselves. These owners risk losing property assets if their business loses in litigation, since courts can hold them personally responsible for debts and liabilities. Advantages of a sole proprietorship include pass through taxation, ease of setup, and flexible management. A corporation is best suited for companies that need to raise a significant amount of money to run a large company with shareholders and investors. Corporations must also elect a board of directors and corporate officers. Aside from being complicated and costly to maintain, corporations must pay taxes at the federal level, and the owners pay taxes again on their dividends (double taxation).

One essential point that Drew made sure I understood was that although LLCs are designed for liability protection, serious violations involving fraudulent use of company funds, or negligent practices that cause third parties to be injured, could pierce the corporate veil. Drew answered my prepared questions as we discussed numerous topics including LLC setup, tax deductions, frequency of filing, and why I would not be required to charge sales tax.

Drew also explained how the Federal Insurance Compensation Act (FICA) tax would be different as a business owner. FICA is 7.65 percent of gross taxable income for both the employee and the employer (6.2 percent for social security and 1.45 percent for Medicare). Employers pay a matching FICA tax, but self-employed individuals are considered both the employee and the employer and are responsible for paying the full 15.3 percent. However, the IRS allows self-employed individuals to deduct the employer portion of self-employment taxes from their taxable income (but are still required to pay the employee and employer tax for Medicare). Finally, he explained that my single-member LLC would not pay unemployment insurance or workers compensation—because employees would not be involved.

I was certainly impressed by the way Drew efficiently addressed my concerns as he effortlessly deciphered nebulous and nefarious tax codes. During the next tax season (it was only January 2012 when I met Drew and the beagles), I planned to return with my tax documents in good order so he could complete an IRS 1040 with a Schedule C attachment to include my business expenses.

As I left, and doled out a few more treats to the guard

dogs, he reminded me that the actual tax reduction from claiming deductible expenses varies from year to year and is tied into reported taxable income and the advanced premium tax credit used for health care (which I would now obtain through the HealthCare Marketplace). My crash course in business economics had taken less than an hour, but I knew it was going to save thousands of dollars over the life of my business. Now that I was chockfull of answers, it was time for me to begin overthinking a business plan and submit my application for a single-member LLC.

Before I did anything serious, however, I needed to take Nitro, Finn, Aesop, Molly, and Greta to the park again. On regular days, even with my current roster of concordant canines, I didn't like to leave the dogs unsupervised at home for more than an hour. Some days however, I just needed to rush out to complete an errand or set up a small business. On those days, the best strategy was to make appointments in the midmorning or midafternoon in order to sandwich engagements between peak playtimes.

It was a cold and cloudy Tuesday that January when the pack and I arrived at an empty park without seeing the usual noontime crowd. I wasn't too surprised since park attendance was typically highest in the spring and fall when the weather was more conducive to outdoor play. Moreover, an empty park isn't really an issue when you bring your own entourage of five happy hounds.

Aesop was a frisky and good-humored black lab mix, and although he wasn't one of my regulars, I agreed to have him stay over whenever his owner, Nancy, traveled to Florida to stay with her retired parents. There was never a question about which pile of poop belonged to Aesop, because you could see the chunks of carrots from at least twenty feet away. It is a strange and little-known fact that pet sitters, given just enough time, become forensic experts in feculence. I had already reached the point where I could discern the age of a pile and knew exactly which one of my charges it belonged to.

Molly was a tan-brown pit bull mix and fantastically enthusiastic about life. She loved Nitro immensely and was one of those dogs who wiggled her entire body when she wagged. When she came over to greet Nitro, the king of calm, she would flop down on her back and slink under him, wildly waving or kicking her legs about as she wriggle-nudged her way close enough to kiss his face. Nitro liked Molly but was often annoyed because she constantly disrupted his carefully crafted and comfortable stations of repose.

It was actually nice to have the park all to ourselves, at least for a little while. I decided today was a good day to make a weekly call to Mom since she would want to know her son was about to be the CEO of his very own company. Technically, my legal title would be "owner," but CEO made me sound more important.

Mom had retired to Key West back in 1996 with her husband, Bill, a former corporate tax lawyer (not to be confused with my father, his name was Billdad). Mom and stepdad Bill had always been huge fans of cruise ships and had discovered Key West in the 1980s, as it was a common port of call for those journeys to Bermuda or the Caribbean islands. They fell in love with Key West (Mom called it "paradise") right away since it was such a luxurious and picturesque island with perfect sunsets, performing arts, live music, scrumptious seafood, and sociable oddballs.

Unfortunately, after fourteen years of retirement, stepdad Bill passed away, and Mom had been on her own since then. Mom and I hadn't always had weekly calls, but I noticed, since 2010, that she was grieving and found that check-ins every seven days or so provided a good balance of support and connection. As usual, Mom was thoughtful and encouraging as I described the meeting with my new accountant. As a Key West resident who was only sixty-six years old in 2012, the concept of changing careers was something Mom considered to be totally natural, and she revealed that it was much more common than I had expected. The good advice she shared that afternoon included anecdotes about a surprising number of office professionals who had moved to Key West to become performers, artists, dive instructors, personal trainers, or small business owners.

The next phase of my small business initiation comprised of four steps that I intended to leap over in a single bound. I had been brainstorming about the business name, but the critical issue was picking one that wasn't already in use by another venture in North Carolina or by another web host customer on the internet. For now, I only desired to bookmark a URL (Uniform Resource Locator) for future use. I aimed to develop and launch a website later in the year when I was able to give that project the time and attention it deserved.

Although optional in North Carolina, Drew recommended I craft a business plan, since it's an excellent way to map out my very own concept of an optimal work/life balance. A business plan would be useful in case I needed a business loan or sold the business, or if sponsors, partners, or third parties were ever to become involved. A business plan describes the services that will be provided, the advantages of using my business, an overview of market competition, and business development strategies.

Before I visited the NCSOS website, I had an amusing time conjuring clever names exploiting wordplay using endearing doggie references. One regular at the dog park, George (he owned Petunia the basenji), insisted I name my company "Doggie Style." He thought this name was so hilarious he used this phrase every time I ran into him for the next five years. "How is Nitro doing with his Doggie Style?" became one of George's favorite interrogatives. Although I love to be hilarious, I preferred to choose a name that engendered a sense of responsibility and safety. I could always save my off-color dad jokes for one-on-one conversations that needed an injection of levity to break the ice; but potential clients ought to be introduced to a thoughtful name that left a positive impression.

The name I finally chose was Eric's Pet Sitting (EPS). A few folks razzed me for this "unoriginal" name, but most seemed to like it just fine. Even grumpy old Ellie said to me one day, "That's a good name because you want people to think of Eric. We trust Eric and that's a good name." Although Ellie's compliment reminded me of a Yogi Berra quote, I appreciated the kind word and was glad I hadn't chosen something like "The Fuzzy Farm" or "Boneyard Bonanza."

Once a name was decided upon, I went to the NCSOS website to apply as a single-member Limited Liability Corporation. In North Carolina this form is called the Articles of Organization, and it serves to provide the NCSOS with the name, registered agent, and address of the LLC. It also includes the effective date and duration of the LLC, and whether the LLC is member- or manager-managed. A registered agent is an individual designated by the LLC to receive service of process notices, government correspondence, or compliance-related documents on behalf of the LLC. I wanted Nitro to be my registered agent, but I ended up designating my lawyer (my Aunt Carol) to take on that role.

After submitting the Articles of Organization electronically, it took the NCSOS only one week to approve my application, and Eric's Pet Sitting, LLC, officially began to exist on February 9, 2012 (a.k.a. National Pizza Day). I did wonder briefly if I could get in trouble for conducting business the previous year, but Drew assured me that a short-term setup or trial period was not uncommon and that I hadn't made enough money to be at risk for tax evasion. The only drawback to conducting business prior to the LLC designation was that I hadn't put any income toward social security in 2011.

The next step for my brand-new LLC was to write an operating agreement. North Carolina is not one of the five states that require an operating agreement, but Drew recommended that I complete one anyway. This legal document defines the business, lays out how proceeds will be allocated, and provides other descriptors of how the business will be managed. A lawyer, or an online legal technology company, could provide this legal document for around three-hundred dollars; but to save money, I began a search for free operating agreement templates on the web. I discovered that online legal tech companies that claimed to have free operating agreements require that you sign up for a "free trial" of their ministrations. The catch is that getting out of those trial subscriptions is harder than chicken lips. Free legal sites are sneaky, crookeder than a snake on a hog wire fence, and *not* free!

I reached out to my Aunt Carol again, and she was able to send an operating agreement template without a problem. Although there is some overlap between a business plan and an operating agreement, they are distinct records. A business plan describes the services a business will provide and details how it will do so. An operating agreement determines the internal operations of the business, pursuant to my requirements as the business owner. In other words, the business plan is about pet sitting, but the operating agreement is about the LLC. Pet sitting isn't even mentioned in my operating agreement (aside from the company name). The primary advantage of establishing an operating agreement is to prove that the LLC structure is separate from that of the individual owner.

Setting up a small business was exhausting. In between checking the necessary boxes, Nitro and I continued to look forward to dog park communion for playtime and fellowship. The day after drafting my operating agreement was a heap of fun because several of our favorites were in the park all at once. Sue was visiting with Coco, a red-brown basenji mix with tall and pointy ears. Sue is a kindergarten teacher and definitely one of the most positive people in existence today. She loved talking to everyone and had a natural gift for making friends. It is a rare treasure and pleasure to encounter someone as genuine and bright as Sue. She may have seemed a little nosey at first, but she quickly disarmed park members as they embraced her shining personality and affable exchanges.

Salvador (also a teacher) and his English springer spaniel, Gallant, were milling about in left field. Unlike Sue, Salvador liked to listen to his headphones and keep to himself, but he was certainly friendly when you caught his attention. One day, a twentysomething-year-old female did just that. This enthusiastic dog park member clearly recognized Salvador and began waving and hollering and exclaimed, "Oh my goodness! Mr. Kilroy do you remember me? I'm Myrtle McGillicuddy! You taught me in first grade all those years ago!"

She then went on to explain her life since the first grade for several minutes—although I have completely forgotten those details. I do remember however, that she told him at least five times that he hadn't aged a day. Everyone in the park overheard and very much enjoyed this raucous reunion; but I knew Salvador was probably thinking, "Oh great, she's making a scene *and* everyone knows I'm at least fifty years old now." Even so, he spoke with Myrtle for several minutes while Gallant continued to explore the park and left messages for the other dogs to find later. I had watched Gallant one weekend late in 2011, and every time I see him, he still charges toward me and completely mugs me as though we had spent a lifetime together.

The dog park party truly started when Nick and Buzz arrived. Buzz was the perfect name for this ginormous yellow lab, because he behaved as if his whole brain were abuzz as he sprinted and hurled his one-hundred-pound frame at every dog he saw. I took Buzz on as a weekday regular for a while, and that proved to be rather interesting on the days I also had Nazer, because Buzz made Nazer mad enough to eat barbed wire and spit nails. The feud between those two made the Hatfields and McCoys look like a ping-pong match. I don't know why they hated each other from the get-go, but I haven't seen anything like it before or since.

Thankfully, Natalia and Nick worked things out so they could steer clear from visiting the park at the same time. It was so bad that if I had Nazer, and Buzz was already in the park, Nazer would begin bucking and growling as soon as we got out of the car. The opposite was also true, and I was flabbergasted that they could sense each other from such a distance. The lesson conferred by the Buzz vs. Nazer saga was that some dogs just have bad chemistry. I never witnessed Buzz or Nazer behave that way with any other dogs, and I would manage this pair by keeping their day camp dates mutually exclusive. I even learned Nick and Natalia's park schedules so I could avoid conflicts at Godbold.

Nitro never had any feuds and carried on like the happiest dog in the world. When Greta wasn't there, he would find Rosie, or Buzz, or maybe a new dog he had never met before. Nitro habitually introduced himself with a play bow, and he then used his signature side-leap and hop to express elation and eagerness to engage. This maneuver was also seen frequently at home, when dinnertime was imminent.

The side-leap and hop began with a crouch, followed by a jumping action that launched his butt one way while his front paws executed a rapid one-two punch or sometimes a high five. This smiley and ear-flappy move was beyond a doubt one of the most adorable dance moves I've seen a dog perform. After the side-leap and hop, Nitro pounced at his quarry, implementing a love-bite and hump-attack combo. This made his playmate flee with glee, with Nitro in hot pursuit, of course. Several dogs nearby customarily joined this mad dash around the playground until it ended at the water bowl, which dogs had tacitly maintained as a "hump free" zone.

In between dog park visits, I still had a few setup tasks to knock out before my journey to self-employment was formally complete. I visited the Internal Revenue Service website to apply for a Tax Identification Number (a.k.a. Employer Identification Number). The main reason I needed this was to open a business checking account. Establishing a property tax account with the Wake County Revenue Department took no time at all, but this step was important in order to establish home office dimensions required for tax deductions. I also listed my computer and desk as taxable business property. Making a trip to downtown Cary to obtain a privilege (business) license seemed like an unnecessary hoop to jump through, but rules are rules. Besides, I didn't want to be caught walking a dog around town without a license! The penultimate checklist item was to confirm whether there would be any local or state permits, zoning, or inspection requirements for Eric's Pet Sitting, LLC. There is certainly a long list of commercial and industrial activities that are not permitted in a residential zone, but establishing a home office for a dog walking business was not one of them.

Feeling accomplished and rather proud of myself, I still had one more task to make my small business completely legit: insurance. Procuring business insurance for pet sitting is unusual because you cannot simply dash over to the nearest Progressive or State Farm office and sign up for this type of insurance. Pet sitting insurance is obtained by joining a pet sitting organization like the National Association of Professional Pet Sitters (NAPPS). I was initially annoyed that I had to fork out one-hundred and sixty simoleons to join a group to acquire insurance, but joining NAPPS proved worthwhile on several fronts. Aside from being something that responsible caregivers do, additional benefits of joining NAPPS included networking opportunities, health insurance, certification programs, continuing education, and professional development through annual conferences, publications, and resources.

Particularly in the beginning months of 2012, tuning into the NAPPS forums was surprisingly helpful. Members regularly discussed relevant topics such as how to manage schedules, track revenue, or deal with difficult clients. There were recurring threads about subjective matters such as expanding a pet sitting business and comparisons on whether to hire employees or use independent contractors. Forums are monitored closely by NAPPS staff, so they don't devolve into a kettle of fish over a dumpster fire like on most social media sites.

Interestingly, there is a strict policy on discussing rates in these forums. Communicating pricing is not allowed because the Securities and Exchange Commission (SEC) knows that conniving caregivers will collude, and once in cahoots, this coalition of canine control will begin charging customers four-hundred dollars for each thirty-minute dog walk (they actually monitor this, I'm not kidding).

Pet sitting organizations are also useful to pet owners searching for quality sitters in their locality. Pet owners do not have to pay these organizations in order to search for pet sitters, since their websites feature "nonmember" sections. After joining NAPPS and obtaining insurance, my six-week mission to establish Eric's Pet Sitting, LLC, was finally accomplished. The running total for the setup costs was about $1,500 (all tax deductible), but I expected renewals to only be about $1,000 per year.

It had been a long while since I had looked forward to those social gatherings where humans feel obliged to tell family or friends what they currently do for a living. The honor of proudly claiming ownership of a small business was diluted somewhat since experience proved that it was, in fact, mostly monkey business. This was particularly evident on days when Gary and his exuberant hound mix, Briggs, visited Godbold Dog Park. This entertaining pair was easy to spot since Gary was eternally chasing his dog with a spray bottle in an attempt derail Briggs from serial humping every dog possible. Incidental humping with your friends is expected, but serial humping becomes problematic, and this preposterous playstyle is only funny until it mounts to a pugnacious predicament with an overreactive dog park member. We had seen Gary use spray bottles, e-collars, timeouts, and even good old-fashioned obedience training to belay his relentless rover, but Briggs' war on loneliness never seemed to end.

On special days, if we were very lucky, we witnessed the ludicrously bizarre "air hump" in one of its many forms. An air hump occurs when a humper continues their gesticulations after separation. If used as an approach tactic, the air hump will mesmerize any target as dogs and onlookers alike are rendered helpless by this implausible display of absurdity. Air humpers use a blend of mirth and dismay that serves to epoxy their victims into a state of inaction.

To be fair, most dogs who went to Godbold were nowhere near this mischievous. Nitro had too many favorites to count, including Dave and Sadie, who visited the park each morning. I recognized Dave from several years ago when I had attended Hope Church in Cary. He had been on staff as a pastor, and folks around the dog park liked to refer to him as "Preacher Dave." Sadie was a brown dog mix who was full of beans and very strong and fast. Dog parkers liked it when Dave was around since he wielded knowledge effortlessly and earnestly. He could talk about history, dogs, the history of dogs, and a great number of other interesting topics. Later in the year, we learned he helped out as a substitute teacher the high school his son attended, and we called him "Teacher Dave," a moniker that took for a while.

Talking to Maria, a friend of Natalia's (the Russian lady with Nazer the Russian wolfhound), proved to be another pleasant encounter Nitro and I looked forward to. Maria was one of those infrequent visitors who attended a few days a week at different times. Maria's dog, Tuoma, was a hound mix, mostly white with splotches of gray, brown, and black here and there. Tuoma was what I referred to as a "State Trooper" because he didn't like speeding. When his watchfulness disclosed a runner, he would immediately pull them over. This engaging and quirky reaction often served, but some dogs liked to speed and would argue about it. "State Troopers" WILL knock over a running child, and it's one of the reasons whippersnappers under twelve years of age are warned to stay away from the dog park.

Humping, rough housing, or suspicious contact was not tolerated by Tuoma either. If he witnessed one dog harassing another, he would jump out of nowhere flying faster than a toupee in a hurricane. I was never certain how you pronounce Tuoma, but when Maria said it, it sounded like "Chooma." One day I asked her, "Is it pronounced 'Chooma'?" Maria replied, "Chooma." So I said, "'Chooma'?" And she said, "CHOOMA." I just smiled and said, "He's a great dog." To this day I am not sure how to pronounce Tuoma, but I understand it to be the Russian equivalent of Thomas.

Jeannette visited regularly on the weekends with Lily and Charlie. Lily was, for lack of a better description, a female rendering of Nitro. She was an exceptionally lovable, red-brown lab mix who fancied a romp with anyone. Charlie was an old, black-haired cocker spaniel who cherished people but absolutely did not want another dog messing with her. Charlie's remarkable trait were the large, red growths on each of her eyelids. Jeannette explained to me that these were meibomian gland cysts, caused by blocked oil glands and therefore not contagious. While there are many treatments for these cysts, they tend to go away on their own. Regardless, Charlie freaked most everybody out as she lumbered toward them with those crimson devil eyes. Lily and Charlie were vacation clients and stayed over for several long weekends in 2012.

This was also the year when the dog park bloomed with at least a dozen dogs named after *Game of Thrones* characters. They weren't all direwolf names, but most of the pups brandishing names borrowed from Westeros were definitely huskies. One afternoon regular, Natalie, named her husky Winter (an homage to Summer, the name of Bran Stark's direwolf). Winter had a full white coat, and like most huskies, was mostly up to no good. Natalie also had a Chihuahua mix named Cinnamon who was cuter than a basket of puppies. Winter loved to splash her paws in the water bowl, and owners promptly indulged in the debate over the cause of this behavior. Some said that the water bowl paddle had a cooling effect on dogs. Others claimed it was a vestigial instinct from when their ancestors enjoyed ice fishing in Beringia. My theory is that water bowl wallowing satisfies two of the all-time doggie favorites: triggering exuberance and making an enormous mess.

Other names I heard that year included Nymeria, Arya, Shae, Sansa, Ghost, Lady, and one was even named Renly Baratheon. I already treasured meeting dogs on a regular basis, but *Game of Thrones* served as an excellent icebreaker as I met and talked to new folks. When I told Natalie that I am now officially an LLC, she chuckled and said, "But are you licensed,

NITRO: A DOG'S TALE

bonded, and insured?" She was joking because she thought there is no way a pet sitter would need to use such an awe-inspiring tagline. Much to her surprise, I answered her fully since the details regarding this greatly misunderstood topic were fresh in my mind.

The main thing about the phrase "licensed, bonded, and insured," is that it's important to qualify what it means in the context of the business. When a pet sitter is licensed, it means they are registered with the secretary of state or that they have obtained a privilege license to do business in their local municipality, or both. This is somewhat counterintuitive since "licensed" is a term used by doctors, engineers, teachers, real estate agents, psychologists, and so on. These "traditional" businesses are licensed by a state-sanctioned authority and have requirements that may include training, years of relevant experience, referrals from licensed peers, and an eight-hour examination to test their knowledge (and patience).

Even though pet sitters are motivated, caring, and wonderfully hairy people, states do not have a board of professional pet sitters that requires them to obtain a license. There are, however, several national (and state-level) associations that offer pet sitter certification programs. These are not compulsory, but small business owners who complete a certification process certainly benefit from that training; and kudos to them for demonstrating their competence and commitment to their craft.

I also explained that bonds are different from insurance but may be provided with an insurance policy. Bonds are one of those things that seem deliberately designed to be more confusing than necessary (like tax law or Stanley Kubrick films). Bonds are a pledge to provide contracted services when the pet sitter is unable to do so. For example, if I break my leg and cannot walk a dog, a surety bond is issued to pay for the replacement dog walker. However, I would have to pay that money back to the bonding company, and the dog owner would still pay me for the pet sitting. This is different from insurance because there are three parties involved, there hasn't been a financial loss, and the premiums I've already paid to the bonding company are used as surety. A bond may also compensate an owner's loss in the event there is a theft by a pet sitter's employee.

Insurance for pet sitters covers the costs of damage or injury incurred while the sitter is in charge of the client's pet. Insurance is different from a bond because there are only two parties (the insurer and the insured) in the deal. Also, if the costs of the damage or injury exceeds the premiums paid, the insurance company covers these losses. Conditions apply of course, and there are so many eventualities, exemptions, and exceptions that these insurance policies are probably best described as tedious. Clients rarely asked to actually read this wearisome charter.

The bottom line is that a small business that is "licensed, bonded, and insured" is exhibiting a conscientious effort to achieve excellence. Despite the measure of licensing requirements or meticulous details of insurance coverage, pet owners like to know the people working in their home have legally established surety and safeguards, particularly when their beloved pets are involved. Having these safeguards in place indubitably reduced my perceived and financial risk as a small business owner.

After nearly two years of caring for pets, I finally cultivated a full schedule every weekday. Clients would often ask, "How do you do it?" since they couldn't believe it was possible to tire out their relentless rovers. I explained that when you have all day, it's not such a big deal. I'm sure that some folks just assumed I left the dogs in the backyard while I went to a "real job" or hung out at the bowling alley. However, a typical day at Camp Ewald, or Eric's Boot Camp, as some liked to call it, typically looked like this:

Ante Meridiem
5:58 – Wake up and gear up with the cargo shorts
6:00 – Feed Nitro and overnighters Greta and Lily

6:15 – Drive to Sam's house and walk Sam for thirty min
7:00 – Rex and Finn are dropped off at my house
7:30 – Take Nitro, Rex, Finn, Greta, and Lily to dog park
9:30 – Bring the pack back to my house
10:00 – "Breaktime" for Eric (laundry, mowing, etc.)
11:00 – Drive to Grizzly's house and walk Grizzly

Post Meridiem
12:00 – Take the pack back to the dog park!
2:00 – Lunchtime for Eric
3:00 – Drive to Bailey's house and walk Bailey
4:00 – Dog park! Rex and Finn picked up from the park
6:00 – Return home with Nitro, Greta, and Lily
6:15 – Drive over to Sam's house and walk Sam
7:00 – Dinnertime for Nitro, Greta, and Lily

A common question I heard was, "How many crates do you have?" But there were no crates at EPS. Day campers and overnighters had the run of the house and the "on the bed" record was six dogs (thunderstorms usually). The regular schedule was typical for fair weather only. During the summer heat, more hours were spent under the cool, sun-dappled canopy of oaks in my backyard. Sometimes I would get a break because most owners canceled walks or day camp on rainy days. This didn't impact my average income too much, since rescheduling occurred (often causing an overload on another day that week) and there was always at least one camper in the rotation who wanted to play in the rain anyway.

Another familiar question was, "Why don't you just spend the entire day in your backyard?" The predominant motive was that *going somewhere* is adrenalizing to the dogs. Three trips to and from the dog park depletes heaps of that pesky and disagreeable furniture-gnawing energy dogs very stubbornly store each night. Additionally, I needed owners to see me at the park, which did wonders on the business development front. I strove to maintain a roster of at least six dogs per day, and there are four membership dog parks in the area (Cary has two, and the Town of Apex also has two). The dogs loved it when I mixed it up, although I would seldom go to one of the three Raleigh dog parks due to a higher risk of incident or injury. The free, nonmembership dog parks open to everyone inevitably lead to run-ins with anonymous and irresponsible dog owners.

Clients changed their schedules all the time, but having the house, doggie door, and fenced yard facilitated flexibility on my part. Owners who were chronically late picking up or dropping off became a challenge since they made me late for a relief walk or they hijacked those narrow windows of time I needed for chores and meals.

This point right here is the most difficult part of pet sitting: balancing my ability to be there for clients without overloading myself. I grew to love the dogs I cared for and felt strongly about being there for them. I understood how much clients loved their dogs because I knew how much I loved Nitro.

Dogs are family, and I endeavored to be patient and empathetic when clients encountered travel delays or were otherwise tied up with work. I learned early on that it is impossible to completely prevent overloading since I couldn't leave gaps in my schedule due to the opportunity costs. I would say "no" to people from time to time but ran the risk of losing those clients. Pet sitting isn't hard work from a physical standpoint, but it is tremendously insistent and will test your emotional resolve as you budget your time and attention. The silver lining was that the abundant demand for EPS left me the leverage I needed to pick and choose who I would work with.

Regardless of my growing popularity, not everyone liked me. Bad days and cantankerous characters still found ways to harsh our mellow now and again. One noontime regular, whom I called Cruella, was a "pet sitter" with an English accent and fake bleachy hair. I often caught her leering askance as I entered the park. Cruella wasn't really a dog walker; she was more of a know-it-all who watched one dog (an intact yellow lab named Henly) for one of her neighbors. As a self-proclaimed expert in dog training, Cruella's burden was to impose her impudence onto each new park member who entered Godbold. Cruella's gift was that she knew they were doing it wrong before they even had a chance to put their leash down. Been throwing tennis balls for forty years? Nope, you're doing it wrong. Cruella excelled at unnecessary corrections, casting unwanted advice about spouses and jobs, and making tedious interruptions.

During the first two years of canine custody, I experimented with many tools to distract, correct, or otherwise stop dogs from damaging belongings or injuring others. The lynchpin example was a popular and effective product that used compressed air and produced a PSSHHH sound that made dogs stop digging, fighting, jumping, or even humping. These air cans were relatively expensive however, so after a few months (and ninety dollars' worth of air), I realized I could just make that PSSHHH sound all by myself. Electronic collars were another popular choice for owners to use as a remote correction method. These collars featured a tone, vibration, or mild shock function. Cruella, of course, sanctioned zero percent of these "ghastly and dreadful" devices—until one fateful afternoon.

On the day in question, Henly had just stolen a bright,

shiny, and recently purchased squeaky toy from another dog park member. Cruella, in spite of all of her divine gifts, could not coax Henly into releasing that ball. She tried the gruff voice, hand signals, finger pointing, and even a "This is your last chance, buster!" or two before her hands left her hips and flew into the air. No one could see an end to this unbearable standoff, and Cruella was becoming desperate. She brought Henly over to where I was sitting, then asked if I could spray Henly in the face. Obviously, she thought I still carried the compressed air cans. I said, "No. Wait, what?? It isn't mace, you know, it's just air. You don't spray it *at* them, it's the sound that breaks their focus."

Then she said, "Spray him in the testicles."

Struck speechless by her ludicrous request, it took all I had to not laugh in her face. I finally replied, "Why don't you pretend you aren't interested in the ball and wait a minute for him to drop it." She was beyond reason by now and only continued to huff and wrestle with Henly for several more minutes until the owners of the ball became too embarrassed by the situation and left the park. After they were gone, Cruella stopped fussing with Henly and, sure enough, about nine seconds later he dropped the ball. Using my catlike pet sitting reflexes, I grabbed the ball and put it on top of the bulletin board (a.k.a. my work cubby) so I could retrieve it later when I saw the original owners again. Cruella left only a few minutes later and, for better or for worse, we never saw her again.

There was one fella, whose name I never learned but whom I called Batman because he wore a large Batman belt buckle; and his dog, Pennyworth, was obviously named for Bruce Wayne's butler, Alfred. Batman was what I call a "Helicopter Parent" because he was always hovering over his dog. These newbies truly have the best intentions. However, their inability to recognize valid escalation effectively thwarts playtime and frustrates other owners. I'm not sure what he was expecting from the dog park—perhaps that the dogs would light up some cigars and deal poker like in those old timey Coolidge paintings. One time one of my charges, I believe it was crazy ol'

Buzz, was attempting to play with Pennyworth. In order to stop this engagement, Batman began hollering, leaping, and flailing his arms and legs about in an unusually senseless manner. I called Buzz back to me and quietly prayed that Batman would never return to this park ever again.

Nitro didn't have enemies at the dog park, but one character who came close was Piper, a white, intact pit bull mix. All Piper wanted to do was hump Nitro and—jeez Louise—was he persistent. Piper's owner, Pauline, did very little to assuage our fears or intervene on behalf of Piper's poor choices. My solution to the Piper situation was to take Nitro over to the small dog park to prevent the pending escalation. I still had charges in the large dog park, so I returned to that side to manage them while Nitro mingled with the small dogs. Nitro may have felt like he was in timeout for some reason, but thankfully we didn't see Piper too often.

I had seen Piper get into it several times with dogs who did not appreciate obsessive humping, and Pauline wasn't exactly a superstar about managing these outbreaks. She tried, but the simple fact was that she couldn't handle Piper, and people would get so upset by the appalling dog fights that broke out, that a vicious argument between owners ensued. As a result, Pauline and Piper were eventually banned from the park.

The Town of Cary did not ban a member until they had been reported for at least six egregious events. Although considered to be too many strikes by some, it made sense to me since there were a lot of poofy one-timers who did not understand that dogs have different playstyles. Seasoned parkers had to be careful around sensitive types because they liked to tattle on people for essentially no reason. The fact is, dogs are going to hump, jump, scratch, nip, chase, get vocal, and, well, be dogs. In Piper's case, however, it was a circumstance where he was so self-possessed, combat was certain.

Despite their ban, we still noticed Pauline and Piper now and again. It isn't too difficult to approach the park entrance and say to someone, "I forgot my pass, can you let me in?" Park members were generally agreeable to helping other participants, but owners who let Piper in usually ended up with a case of gatekeeper's remorse. The lesson for Nitro and me was that intact dogs are much more likely to get into a scrap because dogs still carrying their suitcase will be challenged by neutered males who compulsively dominate dogs with those coveted cobblers. Piper certainly demonstrated that the opposite is true as well.

One of the most remarkable characters to grace the dog park was Fredo and his gray Akita mix, Jackie. Despite being seventy-five years old and married, Fredo asked every lady in the park to come home with him. When they said no (they always said no), he would turn to the next woman he saw (usually the mother or daughter of his previous strikeout), and then proceed to inflict his clumsy charisma upon her. To be fair, Fredo was a friendly person with a great sense of humor who enjoyed working to improve conditions at the dog park. He was what I would call a "Cruise Director" because he orchestrated many dog park dinners and happy hours in his home. Despite the wincing inelegance of his inescapable invitations, his cookouts were actually quite enjoyable. At the park, he loved to gabble and prattle while we were sure he had no idea what Jackie was doing.

Jackie was a good dog with a uniquely colored coat, and we loved how he had one ear pointing straight up, while the other was always flopped over. Jackie, like the best of us, had a tendency to sometimes get carried away during play initiation. He would paw at other dogs to get their attention, and if that didn't work, he was certain that nipping their hindquarters would. He became a weekday regular at EPS for several months in 2012, but he was one of those dogs I had to watch closely. Jackie was not so bad when you stayed engaged and managed his behavior, but that was apparently something Fredo preferred not to do.

Notwithstanding the various kooky and prickly characters, Nitro and I made way more friends than enemies. A circumstance beloved by many was the way Rex recruited new people into the four o'clock gang. During Rex's marathon fetching sessions, he broke the ice by encouraging a new friend to throw his filthy, slimy, and frequently peed-on projectile for him. Rex loved this particular game but sometimes he *had* to bring his Kong ball to someone besides Bob in order to avoid an "I want what you're having" fetcher. These dogs had every intention of stealing the desirable toy to bury it somewhere for themselves. Rex met April and Feynman this way.

When April was new to the park, she tended to mind her own business and sit on a bench away from the gazebo. Feynman, who was named for the American theoretical physicist known for his work in the superfluidity of supercooled liquid helium, was a superbly friendly golden retriever. Feynman minded his own business too, as long as everybody understood that his business was for you to pet him.

Worried that April might take out a restraining order on Rex, Bob invited April over to the gazebo to introduce her to the four o'clockers. April, as it turns out, is a motivated young woman who wrote an appealing book called *Gourmet Cooking for One or Two*, and she also maintains a delicious blog called Girl Gone Gourmet. There were so many outstanding, savory, and delectable recipes on her blog, everyone in the four o'clock gang bought a copy of her book.

When these types of enriching engagements transpired, it epitomized just how exceptional the dog park experience could be. Between the times we had to cope with the cranks or scrape the poop off our shoes, making new friends made all those incidents worthwhile. In fact, this very moment served to inspire me by recharging my earlier idea to fire up a website for Eric's Pet Sitting. I had never made a website before, and I knew it would be enjoyable for clients and anyone else who might stumble into my little corner of cyber space.

Meeting April was unquestionably a catalyst to creating my website, but I had been reminded of this task often by one of my clients, known to the park as "Flip-Flop John." John was currently a salesman of light-emitting diode (LED) overhead lighting systems and therefore very passionate about sharing his business development skills. He had recently been encouraging me to set up a professional and sharply presented website to foster the growth of my business.

I called him Flip-Flop John because he *always* wore flip-flops to the dog park, even if it was thirty degrees outside. John was from Minnesota, so thirty degrees probably felt like late spring to him as he wandered through the park in the tan cargo shorts and gray Bemidji hoodie he also wore every day. His dog, Kasper with a K, was a lab-shepherd mix so similar in color and size to Nitro that I had to examine digital photos carefully before texting images to Flip-Flop John while he was on vacation. I often sent photos to clients—so they knew their pup was having enough excitement at Camp Ewald each day—but I'm not sure ol' Flip-Flop John ever noticed the difference.

John's background in sales and marketing was useful as I sought sound website advice, and he also tried to help out by talking up EPS to every dog park member he met. His heart was in the right place, but one day I had to tell him that I didn't necessarily want every new member to know I'm a pet sitter. I reminded him that I was already checking out new owners and dogs to gain a measure of how wild, dominant, or high maintenance they might be. In fact, we had just met a new couple who brought a huge Great Dane and an old basset hound to the park. Bruce and Margaret were nice enough, but I wasn't ready for a Great Dane since they take up the space of three dogs in my car. Also, that basset was so old, he might have keeled over at any minute. The bottom line is that I didn't expect a website to serve as my primary instrument of business development. My presence (and hysterical dad jokes) in the dog park with friendly and likable Nitro completely covered that requirement.

After a five-minute internet search to determine the "best" web hosting service on the web, I decided to sign on with a provider called iPage and eagerly commenced the creation of ericspetsitting.com. My goal was to have the EPS website mimic my business plan, but I replaced most of the boring words with puppy pictures. Creating a website proved to be a rewarding diversion and, since I already had experience with Microsoft Power Point, building a webpage was incredibly intuitive. Even though most of my business derived from word of mouth, the website would enable a few more potential clients to consider EPS when they searched online. I also liked the idea that an internet site added to my legitimacy and conveyed dedication as a pet caregiver.

Dog owners, by and large, are picky about their pet sitter, so I included an "about me" section describing why and how I chose to become a pet sitter. I added how long I've been sitting, and some information about Nitro, my yard, and other clients. I included a "services" section so people knew EPS could also care for cats, fish, bunnies, and ferrets. There were exclusions such as birds, snakes, quokkas, and others, since exotic pets did not complement my risk management profile. I also included my service radius, and other functions like administering medications to pets, house sitting, and trips to the dog park.

I posted my base rates so people could know what I charge as a minimum and have a ballpark figure to work with. Although I was tempted to develop a chart capturing the innumerable permutations of pets, fees, and services, I decided against it. A chart that size is difficult to read, and I wouldn't catch every eventuality anyway. I had a contact form, but Bob and Rex were the only clients who used it. A contact form seemed like a good idea to serve as a way for tire-kickers to send me a message while I was on their mind, but in practice it only became a spam trap. My theory on contact forms is that they're better suited for larger companies to efficiently sort large numbers of inquiries.

The last section was about "policy," which I loved because I could (politely and professionally) describe all of my pet peeves. Things like cancelation fees, late pickups, and eleventh-hour reservations were covered here. I also presented important rules regarding keys, entry codes, third parties, and arrival confirmations. A recurring nightmare for pet sitters is the situation where we are instructed to leave a dog at their home only to find out later that the client's return flight was canceled. Throughout the site I pasted the most adorable client photos I could find, along with certification badges for memberships and training, social media links, and my contact information.

I was exceedingly proud of my website and how much I had learned about web hosts, web builders, and managing a site. I was relieved, too, when I discovered it was barely going to cost twenty dollars per month to keep it going. A website can be an outstanding way to support a small business, but when asked, I recommended that people spend some time researching web host provider reviews before launching their own site. In retrospect, when I consider what EPS really needed regarding an online presence, I could have just utilized free social media sites. Even so, websites have great flexibility since business owners can always edit or improve them as service conditions change over time. Websites or blogs may also be monetized or converted into e-commerce sites to significantly increase income.

Nitro and I reached our business goals and overall, it had been another successful year. I even stepped up my dog park maintenance game too. One recurring problem began when the dog park entrance gate failed to unlock for members after they scanned their membership card. This inconvenience usually occurred right after rainstorms, and members postulated that thunderstorms had caused voltage fluctuations that tripped a relay breaker in the programmable logic control (PLC) unit. The immediate and temporary fix was to jump the entrance gate and press the manual release button to unlock the outer exit gate, but not everyone had the ability or the gumption to do this. Those who were able to hop in, would then place an object (we used sticks, bricks, or whatever was handy) to leave the exit gate ajar for the next person. Of course, new arrivals had a tendency to immediately lock themselves out by removing the suspicious shim without thinking about why it was there. My favorites were those who kicked the object away from the exit gate on their way out, as if they were thinking, "Well *I* got into the park, but I'll be doggoned if I'm gonna let anyone else in!"

Managing the gate-propping wars was too tedious for everyone involved and the only other option was to leave a voice mail with the Town of Cary Parks Department and wait for someone downtown to reset the gate remotely. This could take anywhere between two hours to two days, so I began a search for another solution to the lockout-tagout conundrum. I already knew there was a Town of Cary mini-office in the adjacent skate park, only a couple hundred steps away from the dog park entrance. I nosed around and discovered that their computer was, indeed, connected to the telemetry network for the PLC at the dog park entrance.

The skate park usually had two employees (Billy and Lauren) working during regular business hours; their job was to rent skateboard or BMX gear, sell snacks, and ensure that visitors followed the safety rules in the skate park. I ended up buying a lot of Gatorade and Snickers bars in my quest to build a rapport with Billy and Lauren, but this was a win for everyone, since resetting the dog park gate was easy for them—and I love Snickers bars.

There were several stubborn patches in the dog park, where mushrooms, grass, or an epically strange, orange, vomit fungus appeared. Members took turns calling the Town about managing these issues, but the Town had bigger fish to fry and never did anything. Mushrooms and vomit mold just seemed to come and go, and the dogs knew better than to eat that stuff anyway. Grass patches, however, grew and spread, and several members became concerned about snakes. There were plenty of opportunities to see copperheads in and around that park already, but a couple of times a year (when no one was watching) I would remove the swaths of green tussocks to allay the fears of my clients and friends.

This was the year I more or less became the "go to guy" regarding minor dog park maintenance. The Town was responsive about major things like fallen trees, overhead lights going out, or if there was a problem with one of the service gates (these were padlocked but sometimes maintenance personnel forgot to replace the locks after a visit).

We still had a rill emanating from the water bowl in the large dog area and on several occasions frustrated members tried to take matters into their own hands. Many vain attempts were made to rake dry mulch or soil onto the shoals of the "Godbold River," but the syrupy mudflow continued. Other folks even attempted to excavate a narrow trench to divert water away from the water bowl's concrete pad. I lost count of how many citizens claimed they knew "someone" with the Town of Cary and could convince "somebody" to fix the drainage problem, but a solution to the water station wetland did not present itself this year.

The dog park was not without its flaws, but by the end of 2012, I felt that if life were to get any better, I'd have to hire someone to enjoy it. To put the icing on the cake, I invested a few hundred dollars for business cards, tee shirts, fridge magnets, and even pens emblazoned with "Eric's Pet Sitting, LLC." My logo featured Nitro's silhouette, and we printed this on every marketing item. That particular image was derived from one of my favorite photos of Nitro standing tall as snow fell around him in our backyard.

Below this airing of great esteem and vigilance, my new website URL and phone number were printed in bold lettering, so everyone knew we were too legit to quit. I had even become so adept at preventing and stopping dog squabbles that I was nicknamed "Sheriff of the dog park." Nitro, of course, was the "Mayor of the dog park" because he was perpetually greeting people with his noble vibes and Nitro smile. I suppose we were experiencing a "big fish in a little pond" situation, but one thing's for certain and two things for sure: everyone there cherished the slobbery ragamuffins who shared their short lives loving us and charging our homes with happiness. Granted, the barf eating and carpet poo is a little weird, but nobody's perfect.

CHAPTER 4

Southernmost Dog

"Petting, scratching, and cuddling a dog could be as soothing to the mind and heart as deep meditation, and almost as good for the soul as prayer." — Dean Koontz, American author.

Nitro and I began 2013 with a heap of optimism and anticipation. We loved our furry playmates and guests for several reasons, not the least of which being their astonishing range of invigorating personalities. Dog park visits were amusing and thought provoking when we noticed the diverse dynamics that develop within pairs or groups of dogs in neutral territory. These adorable knuckleheads always knew whether it was time to gang up, chase, bark, or just get that ball. Over time, I had developed nicknames to describe the classifications of playstyles exhibited by different dogs. A brown boxer mix named Josie became a day camp regular early in the year, and she earned the label "Equalizer," which is actually a special and rare type of "Scrapper." Scrappers are the ones who play on the fringe of a fight. They growl, snarl, nip, leap, and hurl their bodies at their challengers. Admittedly, I needed to watch Josie closely at the park because some owners attain anxiety from this deranged method of play. Scrappers who have the ability to successfully engage even the most submissive, or dominant, dogs in the park are called Equalizers. They compel timid dogs to play and clash with the dominant dogs without escalation. From a pet sitter's standpoint, these are ideal charges because everyone goes home exhausted.

NITRO: A DOG'S TALE

If things seemed too slow at the dog park, I would grab the leashes and feign egress, so my charges would then sprint about in protest (they are willful creatures). I could get away with this twice in one visit to the park, but if I tried it again, they just glared at me with contempt and derision for insulting their intelligence. Learning new tricks such as this persisted as a perpetual process and included a myriad of situations I wish I had known about before beginning pet sitting. For example, most dogs develop what I call "first-night-itis" even if they already knew Nitro and had visited often for day camp. Common symptoms of "first-night-itis" are marking in the house, pacing, and not eating or sleeping well.

Another lesson, gleaned from monitoring the NAPPS forum, was that if someone wants you to keep their dog for more than a month of overnights, only do this if you know the owners well. Sadly, many dogs are abandoned in this manner. Other lessons were learned the hard way, like when I agreed to have Dru drop off Jackson, her maniac German short-haired pointer mix, in the evening after work one Friday. I soon deduced that Jackson had been in the crate all day, and no one was able to sleep on his first night staying over. This never happened again.

Owners and clients continued to ask me for advice, mostly about exercising their dog but also for other tips, particularly for dogs who choose to be willful and crafty with pill snubbing. Even if medicine is camouflaged with a seductive dollop of peanut butter or other goodness, dogs are conniving and can consume conventional concealment with surgical precision. Then they spit out the pill and glare at you with that "Nice try, buster" look on their face. However, I have yet to meet a dog that can resist peer pressure. Dole out a couple rounds of treats to their buddies and the target dog will *not* be able to resist the next treat you give him. I helped owners and clients as best as I could, but most remedies only worked for pet sitters surrounded by dogs.

I've also been asked whether it's possible to over-condition a dog. Clients had expressed concern that doggie day care will acclimate their dog to some level of Olympian renown. I found that this was unlikely to happen. When dogs tire out, they simply plop down and chill. However, I did take care with dogs who were bedeviled by Chuck-it ball-fetching, since they would become overheated if I didn't make them take breaks. I did not use laser pointers either because dogs lose their little doggie minds chasing a laser dot, and I've seen them run into trees, fences, or other dogs. Additional advice that I offered included mixing it up (dogs love new places) or playing hide-and-seek, which dogs find to be fun and stimulating game. Finally, my favorite nugget was to reveal a little-known secret: that dogs love it when you dance with them and sing "Peanut butter jelly time!"

By early 2013, Nitro had reached three and a half years of age and had calmed down a lot from his puppy days. I didn't have to worry that he wasn't exercising enough because he was always tired from constantly entertaining guests and making multiple trips to the park each day. Despite the hundreds of hours we had logged at the dog park, new experiences continually found a way to present themselves. One morning in early March, Cary animal control surprised us with an unannounced visit to the park. I thought they might be there to enforce the two-dog rule but, much to my relief, everything isn't about me. It turned out they were only there to remind parkgoer's about safety, canine first aid, and microchipping our dogs.

When it was time for the officer to leave, I lollygagged near the airlock because I predicted she might not know how to use the exit. First-time visitors typically aren't aware of the button that disengages the electro-magnetically sealed dog park (despite the fact it is a large and bright red button with a sign that reads: "PRESS TO EXIT"). Sure enough, the officer entered the airlock, then tried to push the outer gate and became trapped. As she began looking for a clue to find a way out, I was tempted to pretend not to notice what was going on. Maybe the officer would leap over the gate, or shoot the lock, but I politely pointed out the exit-release button and she was able to safely leave.

        After the visit from animal control, I began thinking again about taking the classes required for pet cardiopulmonary resuscitation (CPR) and first aid certifications. The class had already been recommended by my pet sitting friend Sheree and nearly every NAPPS member I knew. I expected that I may never actually need this training, but for some reason I remembered what my Calc II professor loved to say: "The more you know, the better off you'll be." I have found this to indeed be true (and ironic, since I haven't used calculus in 25 years) and besides, a first aid certification would be a confidence booster for everyone involved.

        Both the Red Cross and Pet Tech provide CPR and first aid courses that include basic pet care, checking vital signs, preventative care, and critical care for breathing and cardiac emergencies, wounds, bleeding, and seizures. I took the eight-hour course with Pet Tech, and they provided certification cards and useful reference materials to regularly brush up on my knowledge of first aid (but mostly to arbitrate those persistent arguments at the dog park). After two years of pet sitting, I had already learned that the frequently used first aid supplies included the tick remover tool, styptic powder to stop bleeding (usually from nicked ears), antiseptic wash and wipes, antibiotic ointment, and Diphenhydramine (Benadryl) for stings and allergic reactions. Little did I know that my first aid training would serve as a segue to an epic health caretaking tour that I will never forget.

In late March 2013, I received a call from my mother's good friend and next-door neighbor, Robby. He explained that my mom had called him late the previous night after she collapsed in her den. Robby and his partner, Mark, went over to help Mom and call an ambulance for her. There wasn't an official diagnosis at this point other than Robby's report that "She isn't doing well and you'd better come down here right away." This stunning bolt from the blue was so unexpected, I could barely fathom what might have happened. Did she have a stroke? Was she dehydrated? When did she eat last? Mom hadn't reported any health issues during our weekly calls, but as her authorized health surrogate, power of attorney, and only family member within 1,000 miles, I needed to respond right away. Emergency protocols would take over until I arrived in Key West, and by then her doctor would be able to fill me in on what was going on. After canceling my charges for the week, I hopped in the car (there was no way I was *not* taking Nitro) and began the fourteen-hour drive to Key West.

In the past, I had only ever flown to Key West, but the thought of making such a long drive wasn't daunting. I could break it up into two seven-hour trips, which was no big deal. Ewalds have a long history of completing incredibly long driving events; to the point that I firmly believed driving had somehow been imprinted into our DNA. My Aunt Carol regularly made the fifteen-hour drive from Charlotte, North Carolina, to her second home in southern Vermont several times a year.

Upon entering Jacksonville, FL, about half the distance from Cary to Key West, Nitro and I navigated to my preferred motel chain. Known for its cheap rates and pet-friendly policies, the Motel 6 had been my go-to during the 2000s when I traveled extensively for work. That night, however, Nitro was unremittingly vigilant thanks to the steady slamming of vehicle and room doors. I'm sure he could also sense my unease as I continued to worry over Mom's fate. Needless to say, neither one of us slept much at all during that overnight "rest" stop.

I must have finally dozed off because a minute later, the morning light arrived with unrelieved cacophony as Motel 6 customers reloaded their trucks, slammed more doors, and cranked up their diesels. I fed Nitro and took him out for a relief walk, and we loaded up for the day's drive. I checked my phone to see if there were any messages, but there was no news from Key West. Mom did not have a cell phone since she was a bit of a Luddite when it came to using a computer, checking email, or acquiring smart devices for home or personal use. Shoot, Mom didn't even own a microwave. The reason, she maintained (since 1982), was that "They just dry out the food and take up way too much space on the counter."

Traveling I-95 through Florida went well, but once we passed through Miami, our average speed decreased as we journeyed along scenic Route 1 from Florida City across the overseas highway into Key Largo. The next one-hundred miles on Route 1 was particularly slow as drivers negotiated several thirty-five-mile-per-hour zones and two-lane bridges. The slower driving wasn't so bad since we were able to enjoy clear blue waters, tropical foliage, and all the salty maritime trimmings on shops and restaurants along the way.

One thing about sustained drives is the high opportunity cost of each pit stop. Small time delays add up in due course, so my strategy was to stop only one or two times in order to fuel up and allow Nitro and me to both "use the restroom." There are two hazards inherent with gas-and-go breaks in Florida: heat and gators. The stifling Florida heat was bearable for a short walk but the hitch was during those few minutes I had to go in to the store to use the restroom and leave Nitro in the car. I left the car running with the air-conditioner on so he wouldn't overheat, but I was worried someone might steal the car, or worse, pitch a fit that I had left my dog in a "hot" car. As far as gators, I was relieved to find that surface waters at rest stops and gas stations were bounded with fencing affixed with warning signs. Presumably, these measures worked to keep the gators out of the small ponds while keeping small children and pets out of danger.

When I arrived at Mom's house a little after noon, Nitro and I grunted out of the car and went straight to Mom's tiny, fenced-in front yard so Nitro could do his business. I hated to do this, but I needed to leave Nitro in this "strange" house by himself after driving nearly 1,000 miles from home. It's possible the hospital was pet-friendly, but I needed to find out what the Sam Hill was going on right away. After verifying the house was puppy-proof, I made sure to adjust the air conditioning for Nitro (Mom typically set the thermostat to eighty degrees Fahrenheit). Next, as I left through the carport door to depart for the hospital, Nitro very earnestly attempted to leave with me and was quite displeased when I told him to stay and be a good boy. He didn't want to do any of those things, but I dashed out the door anyway. Poor Nitro.

The Lower Keys Medical Center (LKMC) is located on Stock Island, the municipality just to the east of Key West. Since Key West is only one by four miles in size, the drive to the hospital took just a few minutes. I entered the hospital lobby and signed in as a visitor for Keith McCausland (my mother's name was, in fact, Keith and she changed her last name after divorcing Dad in 1979). Once armed with a lanyard and visitor badge—and relieved to discover Mom was not in the intensive care unit—I made my way up to the room she had been assigned.

Mom appeared to be asleep when I knocked on the open door to the small and clinically furnished room. I waited briefly to observe whether she would stir, but she was deep in Palookaville. She was mostly under the covers, but I could tell she was awfully thin, which worried me a bit. I walked over to the nurse's station, asked for Mom's doctor, and after a brief wait, Dr. Carlos greeted me in the hallway then invited me in to his office. With an equal measure of empathy and brevity, he explained that Mom had metastatic stage four breast cancer. I knew what this meant, but I obeyed an instinct to delay the direness of the situation and asked him to expound on what he had just told me.

As I listened and silently hoped that further elucidation might improve her condition somehow, Dr. Carlos clarified that when cancer is not detected, secondary malignant growths may propagate throughout the body. As the metastatic condition worsens, a patient may experience vital organ failure. The doctor also explained that since Mom had arrived in the hospital, they had run a computed tomography (CT or "cat") scan and magnetic resonance imaging (MRI) to determine the extent of metastases. While we looked at a selection of those images, he shared that she already had surgery to remove the largest mass, and that while she was stable for now, they wanted to keep her under observation for a few days.

The scans revealed a growth in Mom's brain, and Dr. Carlos suspected she had had a "mini stroke"—which was probably why she had collapsed the night the ambulance was called. As bad as all this news was, Dr. Carlos wasn't finished. He said she probably wouldn't live through the weekend (today was Thursday) and that she may only have two weeks at the most.

This was too much information to receive all at once. I was speechless. I remember briefly thinking that the precision of his forecast seemed a little weird. Two weeks? After a few moments, I was finally able to muster five words: "What can we do next?" Dr. Carlos recommended that we meet with an oncologist to make a judgment based on her biopsy results. I liked the sound of that since it was the only bit of his report that heralded a hopeful outcome. Still stunned by the diagnosis delivered, I withheld further questions. I would need a few minutes to process all this while I steeled myself for the visit with Mom once she woke up.

By the time I returned to Mom's room, she was sitting up in her bed and a nurse was trying to administer several pills to my freshly awakened and grumpy mother.

"Keith Ann, you have to take your medicine," the nurse said.

"What are all these pills?" Mom asked.

"We've been over this. There's a vitamin, a blood pressure pill, a blood thinner, an antibiotic, and an anti-inflammatory since you've just had surgery."

"I don't have high blood pressure! And I'm not taking a blood thinner. My friend died from taking blood thinners. They make you hemorrhage."

The nurse appeared relieved that I had just arrived. She sighed heavily and asked me, "Can you please help her take her medicine?"

"Sure," I replied, noticing her nametag that read "Matilda" as she briskly huffed out of the room.

I smirked after Matilda left, then looked at Mom and said, "They call you 'Keith Ann?'"

"Oh Eric, I'm so glad you're here," Nikki replied. Mom's name was Keith because my grandfather wanted to name his firstborn Keith, and, by God, it didn't matter that she was a daughter. To her friends, Mom went by Nikki, a nickname she earned in high school. The nurses, apparently, did not know this so they called her Keith Ann (her middle name was Ann).

I placed the tiny souffle cup of pills on the table next to Mom's bed and leaned over to very gently give her a hug. She looked emaciated and frail, and her hair was much thinner and grayer than the last time I had seen her. This dramatic change in appearance was something I wasn't prepared for; her eyes no longer had her intelligent and sharp look to them, they looked scared and a little drunk. Her voice wasn't quite right either, and I assumed it was the "mini stroke" that affected her speech. She could speak clearly, but her cadence was deliberate and measured in a way that wasn't ordinary. It was not unlike how we speak to our parents when we're drunk, but don't want to sound drunk. She looked at me and said, "Did they tell you my days are numbered?"

I said, "Of course not. Dr. Carlos is referring you to an oncologist so we can find out what your options are."

Mom most assuredly knew I was lying but didn't care. Holding back a tear she said, "I love you so much, Eric."

The next few days while Mom was in the hospital were a little precarious, but my presence as her son and advocate made matters much more manageable. I would visit Mom's room around eight in the morning and talk to her for a few hours until she became tired again. By then, it was time to return to the house and let Nitro out anyway. While walking with Nitro through Old Town, I had crucial and cathartic phone conversations with family and friends as I continued to process the ordeal life had suddenly presented to us. The primary operative for these ongoing calls was my Aunt Edie (Mom's sister), a retired recovery nurse who provided insight into how deeply Mom had been grieving the loss of my stepdad Bill (no one else had any idea). Edie lived in Massachusetts however, so she didn't know the details that I was now able to provide about Mom's medical condition. It would take several calls to Edie and a couple of Mom's close friends before I was able to triangulate the data and figure out that Mom had known she had cancer many months ago but had stopped seeing her doctor. I ascertained that losing stepdad Bill was too overwhelming, and the ensuing depression, along with her pride, had been holding her health hostage for some time.

Calling each and every one of my friends and clients would have been time prohibitive, so I maintained a short list of contacts in those first few days Mom was in the hospital. One important friend was Stephanie (Finn's mom), who was a nurse and a key link to the four o'clock gang at the dog park back home. My best friend in Cary, Chris Gooding, heard from me at least once a day. Chris had been a caregiver for his mother in the 2000s, and his wisdom, empathy, and listening skills proved to be vital during this harrowing time.

There were a great number of Mom's friends, not to mention family members on my dad's side, who cared about Mom and wanted to know what was going on. I promptly realized that being a health surrogate in the course of a crisis is no easy task. The flood of emotions, questions, opinions, and uncertainty rapidly tested my mettle during those early, and somewhat frustrating, days. Thankfully, most enquirers demonstrated grace or forbearance as they presented questions or waited for answers.

After our therapeutic walk through Mom's verdant and tropical neighborhood, Nitro and I would return to the house for a quick lunch. Nitro rapidly acclimated to the routine of my leaving him in his "new house" while disappearing for a few hours to revisit the hospital. My second daily trip to the hospital would happen a little after lunchtime to bring Mom things to read, crosswords to puzzle, and most essential of all, snacks.

Key West is a small island, and as our disquieting news spread, several of Mom's friends visited the hospital to see how Nikki was faring. Tom Luna, a singer, actor, business owner, bartender, and total character, had been one of Mom's best friends in Key West for at least fifteen years. Mom and Bill met Tom years ago when he owned Peppers of Key West, a hot sauce and novelty shop in Old Town about a block away from Duval Street.

Carol and Fran knew Mom from attending The Waterfront Playhouse, a performing arts center adjacent to the Market Street pier and the Key West Aquarium. They were also retired and missed stepdad Bill enormously. Carol and Fran clearly cared about Mom and lamented the absence of their frequent dinners, shows, and walks with their favorite couple.

Robby and Mark were Mom's next-door neighbors and had become instant friends with Mom when she moved to Key West in 1997. Robby played piano and sang at several of the local hotels and country clubs, and Mark was a personal trainer. Mom had been a long-time client of Mark's, who had introduced her to Pilates when she was about fifty years old. Mom had never been much of an athletic type, but Pilates turned things around for her and was soon added to that short list of things she never stopped talking about. Mom loved receiving visitors but was, understandably, withholding with regard to her dreary diagnosis. There was too much ambivalence anyway, and she didn't want anyone (including herself) to worry unnecessarily.

After about four days, Mom's doctor determined that she could leave the hospital and return home. We were still a few days away from the oncologist appointment, and Nitro was eager to bring the caretaking effort to his new house full-time. Upon arriving at the house, Mom was finally able to meet Nitro, who enthusiastically smiled and wagged as I helped her in from the carport through the kitchen door. This was one of those times everyone was appreciative that Nitro was not a jumpy greeter. Mom said, "Good doggie. My, he's enormous!" Nitro was only seventy pounds, but most of her retired friends had toy dogs so he seemed comparatively large in her eyes.

In the past, Mom had not been a big fan of dogs, and we never had one while I was growing up. Whenever neighborhood dogs even came near our Bethesda house back in the 70s, Mom would become annoyed and say, "Shoo! Shoo dog!" I didn't even have my first dog until I was eleven years old, when Dad and I adopted a female black lab who I affectionately named Fang. Mom and Dad were already divorced by then, so Fang stayed at Dad's house in North Carolina through the 1980s. I never really understood why Mom didn't like dogs. I suppose it was because they are so messy and hairy and noisy.

After Mom sat down, it took less than one minute of petting a calm and cheerful Nitro before she became hopelessly hooked. Nitro was quiet, relaxed, didn't climb on her furniture (when she was looking), and had a soft fluffy coat that she loved to pet. It also didn't take long for Mom to deduce how much Nitro loved food. He wasn't a drooling beggar, but he certainly knew when nibbles were nigh and strategically placed himself so as to not miss anything tendered by gravity or fate.

Nitro was also one of those dogs blessed with the appearance that someone had spread a generous application of dark eyeliner around his puppy dog eyes. He knew just how to put those Egyptian eyes of Horus to work, too. Mom even said, "He seduces you with his gaze. How can you not resist him?" Another interpretation she frequently offered was, "Oh look, it's Nitro coming over to say, 'I'll have what you're having.'" I loved that phrase. Mom had a gift for delivering forgiving and humorous zingers that concisely captured the waywardness of others.

Mom's house was a four-bedroom Victorian-style home near the center of Old Town. It featured two two-story wings joined by a great room she furnished as a living and dining room. Mom's bedroom was on the second floor of the south wing, while the spare rooms on the first floor functioned as a den (TV room) and a library (stepdad Bill's old office). The second floor of the north wing housed the spare bedroom where Nitro and I stayed. Behind the living room, separated by a wall, was a spacious single-story kitchen, with an outdoor hot tub off the north side and the carport off the south. Like most properties in the Keys, the house took up at least ninety percent of its lot. There was a large porch along the front of the house (the west side), and beyond that was a tiny fenced-in yard where Nitro could snoop around and relish his relief breaks.

Mom was still too weak and wobbly to manage the staircase up to her room, so I arranged for a hospital bed to be delivered from one of the many local medical supply businesses that served Key West. They had no problem persuading me to rent additional items like a wheelchair, a walker, and a shower bench to assist us in the journey to recovery. The hospital bed and other equipment arrived during a visit from Carol and Fran, and they helped to rearrange the furniture in the spacious living room. As Mom fussed with the remote control for the bed, she groaned about the unattractive collection of institutional clutter but took things in stride since she was happy to be finally home. She wryly stated, "All this geriatric gear is marring the feng shui of my living room, but it will be fun to camp out with you and Nitro for a while."

Several curious and well-wishing friends dropped by to visit throughout Mom's first day back home. Dennis, who looked just like George Clooney, was a singer and dancer Mom knew from The Barn, a popular performing arts center along Duval Street. Dennis was one of Mom's favorites not only because he was hilarious but because he was a genuine and kind soul. Numerous other folks ambled through; some brought flowers or food, but all lavished her with well-wishes. Nitro assumed the food was for him and spent the entire afternoon beaming and wagging as he greeted everyone. As the day wore on, the homecoming visits tapered off about the same time Mom's energy faded. Then Mom reclined in her new bed, and Nitro and I surveyed the food situation.

Robby and Mark had brought a ginormous lasagna so Mom (with a little help from Nitro) happily enjoyed a home-cooked Italian dinner on her first night back. Mom definitely didn't want to discuss cancer that night, so she tactfully changed the subject by asking how the pet sitting business was going. She still knew how to be an excellent listener and communicator (and mom), especially during difficult times. We laughed a lot that evening as I shared choice anecdotes about the peculiar pets or obstinate owners I had encountered. "Some owners actually make a decision to skip monthly flea and tick medication or their Bordetella (kennel cough) vaccine in order to save money," I told her.

Mom thought this was ironic since she knew Cary was such an affluent town. "Cheap is expensive," was her reply. She asked if I was afraid the dogs would escape from my yard and run amok in the neighborhood. I told her that dogs do, in fact, have an uncanny ability to find a weakness in the fence well before I notice it. Then they scratch, dig, and punch at it like they were auditioning for the sequel to The Great Escape. I went on about going to client's houses, and that sometimes a teenager, grandma, or cleaning crew was in the house as I arrived. This was a little awkward sometimes, so I would offer a friendly greeting as I let myself in (and muttered a quick prayer, since Carolina grandmas, more often than not, are packing heat).

I droned on to explain that preventing dog fights had developed into an art form, and that I had learned how to use my voice or various noises to distract the dogs from instigating an altercation. Staying engaged and removing sources of conflict served best, but I had also discovered that dogs become fascinated and completely distracted when you speak gibberish to them. All in all, however, the best fight stopper around was a quick spray with the ol' garden hose. I'm not sure when Mom fell asleep, but by the time I had mentioned "garden hose" she was snoring. Nitro had been snoring for some time already. The last thing I remember about that night was feeling exhausted and a little overwhelmed by everything.

The next morning, as we savored some scrambled eggs and toast I had whipped up, Mom said, "What's your secret to these eggs, Eric? They're so good!"

"It's your recipe, Ma," I replied from the kitchen, making a second pan for myself.

I could already hear Nitro crunching on toast. I rolled my eyes and thought to myself, "Nitro's gonna get fat this spring!" I walked back in to the living room with my plate of super-fluffy and extra cheesy scrambled eggs as we began our first day of waiting for the next medical assessment. Between appointments and naps, Mom and I talked about family, my dad, football, movies, books, and shared stories about the various fools who had recently been complicating our lives.

Inevitably, our conversations steered towards those stories about my carefree antics as a kid in Bethesda, MD. There was the time I went "missing" for a couple hours one Saturday when a neighbor was having a birthday party a couple of blocks from our house. I may have been about eight at the time and had innocently wandered up to an irresistible blend of music, brightly colored balloons, screaming kids, and, of course, cake. I was happier than a cow in a cornfield because nobody knew, or seemed to care, that I hadn't been invited. When I finally returned home in a daze of sugar-induced glee, I was met by a pair of crabby parents hollering things like, "We were worried sick! Where did you go? Don't take off like that!"

Parents seldom suffer from a shortage of fears. Mom had always been afraid of heights, and my tree climbing tales still gave her the heebie-jeebies thirty years later. We had a seventy-five-foot pine in the yard of the Bethesda house that was easy to climb since the sap-soaked branches were so close together. Aside from being drunk on adrenaline, the height didn't bother me because I felt secure having a huge tree all around me, and all that sap improved my grip. Mom spied me when I was near the treetop one time and began shrieking, "Eric Andrew Ewald are you trying to kill yourself? Get down from there this minute!"

My most treasured recollection of my misspent youth includes the stories with my best friends Scott and Marcus when we would escape into the stormwater drain on Windsor Lane and travel to the Navy Medical Center under Maryland Avenue and Jones Bridge Road. Now, these weren't paltry twelve-inch storm drains; these circular pipes were four-feet in diameter in our neighborhood, and the section under Jones Bridge Road leading to the Naval property was an eight-foot-square culvert. We needed flashlights for the first few blocks underground; then we could follow daylight from the larger section that opened onto the medical grounds. What an adventure! I wish I had had Nitro when I was a kid. Needless to say, our parents were not pleased when Dan Goldman tattled on us and everyone found out. I remember Mom saying, "There are rats and poisonous gases down there. You could have died!" Even at nine years of age, I knew that Bethesda did not have a combined stormwater and sewer system, but I also knew not to argue with my mother.

The legends of yesteryear worked well to keep our minds occupied. When the elephant in the room is terminal disease, you want to keep that huge herbivore concealed as best as you can. Before we arrived at an uncomfortable silence, someone rang the doorbell. Nitro leapt up from his nap and howled as if the Russians were coming while I answered the front door.

Linda, a blonde and exceptionally tan native Key Westerner about ten years older than Mom, introduced herself as a physical therapist from the LKMC. She had a friendly personality and lots of energy. She opened with, "I love what you've done with the living room," noticing how we had obviously converted the great room to be, quite simply, the only occupied room in the house. Mom explained to Linda that she was able to get around, but had poor balance and was usually unable to stand up by herself. She asked Linda about one of those "stand-up" chairs but Linda replied, "No, no, no. You're going to get stronger so you can do it yourself."

I figured it was best to leave them alone for a bit, so Nitro and I geared up for another walk around the historic district.

As we departed, I noticed Linda unpacking her magic bag of small weights, resistance bands, and numerous tools of the trade including a boom box because, apparently, music was a vital part of physical therapy. You gotta love Key West.

When we returned from our walk, I was relieved to see Linda and Mom were becoming fast friends. They were listening to golden oldies, talking about Pilates and drinking iced tea together like they'd known each other forty years. I joined the conversation hoping I could somehow interleave an in-home nursing discussion. I asked whether in-home nursing was covered by insurance and Linda explained, "No, any sort of full-time care won't be covered. The going rate for the in-home nurses is twenty dollars per hour and the go-to lady in town is Francesca. I will ask around and find her number for you."

She went on to explain that in-home care was a widely misunderstood concept. LKMC provides nurses for short home visits only. They can check your vitals, provide physical therapy, administer medication, and a number of other duties covered by insurance, but they can't station a nurse at your house twenty-four hours a day. She added that a lot of folks assume that hospice care means people will come stay with you full-time until the end but that isn't true. Hospice doctors and nurses only complete short appointments, and it's up to the patient to have their own in-home providers of care.

We thanked Linda for the information and her extremely helpful visit. After she left, it was time to wait for another follow-up from LKMC staff while we also waited for the day to sit in the oncologist's waiting room to finally hear what he had to say. In addition to the physical therapist, LKMC would send a nurse to fulfill a wellness check and another professional to conduct a psychological assessment. Waiting was not easy when so much was on the line. I asked Mom whether it was Tom Petty or Homer who said, "Life is largely a matter of expectation," and that made her laugh.

When Mom was ready for a nap, or if one of her good friends visited with another box of ludicrously delicious Key

West Cupcakes, that was my cue to take Nitro for another constitutional around sunny and breezy Old Town. Key West is a small island, and the Old Town historic section is only eight by ten blocks. The area east of Duval Street is densely packed with historic homes, including several shops, cafes, pubs, churches, and offices peppered throughout. Many of the Victorian-styled homes had been converted and now billed themselves as inns, resorts, or bungalows—what folks in other parts of the country might brand as "bed and breakfasts." The Town of Key West has done a great job camouflaging the neighborhood to look like a great collection of Victorian houses all gathered together. It is difficult to tell whether a house was a commercial or residential property, and buildings are all nestled organically into the tropical foliage.

The Atlantic side (the south side) of the island is bordered by a bike trail and beaches. It is interesting to note that structures along the south side of Key West hold their ground at least one-thousand feet from the shore. The reason for this is to minimize hurricane damage due to storm surges. The north side of Key West (the Gulf of Mexico side) contains two sections. One is bordered by hotels, restaurants, and piers for charter boats, with private beaches tucked away between the hotels. The other half contains Trumbo Point, a US Coast Guard station. Should a visitor travel a couple of blocks west of Duval Street, they would run into a US Naval Air Station. Likewise, if someone strolled a couple blocks east of First Street, the eastern border of Old Town, they would find themselves in non-historic Key West. The eastern, non-historic half of Key West features modern construction, and that's where the major hotel chains, the Key West International Airport, medical offices, movie theaters, major supermarkets, and other contemporary properties are located.

Naturally, one of the first places I took Nitro to was the Key West dog park. The city did not require membership, so we could walk in any time. It was about the same size as our Cary dog park and featured two sections for the large and the small dogs. Key West is dreadfully warm, so their dog park was never too crowded. The park was about half a mile from Mom's house, and Nitro would typically drink only a slurp of water and then rest before we reveled in the balmy walk home. Key West is a dog-friendly island, and we noticed that nearly every bar or shop has a dog bowl full of fresh water by their front door. There was even a "dog beach" next to one of the more popular restaurants (Louie's Backyard) on the island. This beach was thirty feet wide at most, and I took Nitro there a few times to cool off and romp about in the water for a change of pace.

One primary draw for those touring Key West is the mile-long stretch of Duval Street running north to south near the west end of the island. Duval Street is a long strip of bars, artsy shops, restaurants, museums, gift shops, playhouses, churches, and more bars. The bars feature fresh seafood dishes, live music, and are nearly always full of delightful, sun-kissed patrons sipping colorful drinks overflowing with speared fruit and paper umbrellas. There is a "touristy" section near the cruise ship pier that features overpriced doo-dads and knick-knacks in shops that also sell off-color (and hilarious) tee shirts. Other popular destinations include the Key West Aquarium, the Butterfly Museum, the Mel Fisher Museum, Truman's "Little White House," and the famous buoy marking the southernmost point of the continental United States (Hawaii is farther south).

Many adventure tours are available, and folks can charter a fishing boat, rent wave runners, go parasailing, snorkeling, scuba diving, or even take a helicopter tour of the island. The most popular type of adventure tours are the drinking cruises hosted on catamarans and refurbished schooners since these feature entertaining emcee's, ample libations, and unforgettable scenery (sunset cruises are all the rage). Stepdad Bill summed it up best years ago when he succinctly told me, "Key West is a country club for misfits and people who *really* know how to have fun."

When Nitro and I returned to the house, Mom's friends Matt and Kitty were visiting. I had shared many dinners with

Mom and stepdad Bill and Matt and Kitty over the years. They were longtime friends and unpretentious characters. After pleasantries were exchanged, including several wags and smiles from Nitro, Kitty pulled me into the kitchen and whispered, "What is really going on with your mom?"

First of all, she wasn't being sneaky by a damn sight. Secondly, I had just walked in and did not know what had, or had not, just been discussed. I grabbed my phone and held it up briefly to convey the International Sign for "call me later." Simultaneously, I wrinkled my forehead during a wide-eyed nod to convey the International Sign for "your poorly orchestrated interrogative cannot possibly be answered right now." Out loud, I replied, "Oh the glasses are over here." Unconcerned whether Kitty was satisfied with this response, I prepared a glass of ice water right away.

I had been a caretaker for barely a week, but a few unwritten rules had made themselves abundantly clear. Over time I would share these with friends or visitors that, although truly wishing to help, seemed to stumble through their stilted visits. The two primary points I made to people were: bring food and don't talk about it. I also encouraged people to call, text, or drop a note even if they aren't sure when Nikki wanted visitors. Mom wanted attention, but not a lot of questions. It wasn't an easy situation for anyone, because believing you may be terminally ill is unpleasant no matter how you slice it. One prominent takeaway for me during the early phase of support was to learn the difference between the dirty laundry tourists and Mom's true friends.

After a few days of camping out in Mom's living room, it was time to go see Dr. Lawrence, the oncologist and expert in biotherapy. Dr. Lawrence did not have much personality, and he dispassionately shared that based on Keith Ann's biopsy results, Mom was a suitable candidate for biotherapy using Arimidex and Faslodex. These medications effectively work to reduce the amount of estrogen available to stimulate the growth of hormone receptor-positive breast cancer cells. By taking Arimidex daily in pill form, and Faslodex monthly as a shot, the cancer would (ideally) fade away once it didn't have anything to sustain it. This well received news immediately and completely restored hope for us. After much rejoicing, Mom received her first Faslodex shot and grabbed a scrip for Arimidex. Before we left, Dr. Lawrence made it clear that it could take three to six months to see results, and there were no guarantees. We understood this, but it was significantly better news than what the LKMC team had previously offered. Mostly, Mom was ecstatic to hear any diagnosis that did not result in her demise, or worse, chemotherapy.

I didn't expect to be managing a caretaking tour this early in Mom's life (she was only sixty-six), but here we were. Despite how indefinite the outcome was, we finally had a plan and some idea of how long recovery might take. The next action item was to hire a third-shift in-home nurse. After that, I needed to complete a return trip to Cary so I could gather extra belongings more conducive to a three-month stay. I needed my file box to manage bills and file income taxes, and I also wanted to talk to my dad about stopping by my house to bring in the mail and help make the house appear "lived-in" for a while. Dad liked hanging out at my house anyway since he lived alone in an apartment nearby without cable television. He was also a big fan of polishing off leftovers in my fridge, ice cream in my freezer, and whatever else he could scavenge from the cabinets (my friend Chris called him "Catfish Bill"). Living one town over from my dad was like having a seventy-year-old teenager living in the house.

It was a profound situation that we faced. Either Mom was going to get better in the next few months or we were going to lose her. One of the main reasons I looked forward to hiring in-home nurses was to meet others who had experience in managing these critical circumstances. I hoped that Francesca would speak candidly about her experiences, and alleviate some of the anxiety and doubt Mom was enduring. During the next visit from Carol and Fran, we were able to capture Francesca's cell number from the geriatric grapevine. We were then relieved to hear that Francesca had availability and would be able to meet the next day. I quietly wondered to myself whether her previous client had passed away or recovered.

Meeting Francesca proved to be a pleasant encounter and a huge leap in the proper direction as far as acquiring insight and fostering hope. She was empathetic, respectful, and shared many tips, tricks, and gadgets to improve ergonomics and mobility during cancer treatment. She advised us that oncology medicine is only a fraction of what is needed for recovery. Maintaining a good outlook was key, and the way to do that is to thoroughly take care of yourself. Exercise, posture, and nutrition were most important, and Francesca offered several strategies such as skin and hair care, massage, candles, music, better lighting, and a number of other improvements we hadn't even begun to think of.

Francesca instilled confidence during that first meeting, and Mom was more than happy to bring her on board. Francesca then recommended two more in-home nurses to round out the staff. She proposed that we have three nurses, each working two nights a week, and Francesca would work three nights a week. We then arranged for Carol and Fran, Dennis, Tom Luna, and a couple of Mom's neighbors to perform daytime visits with Mom while Nitro and I sped back to Cary to secure my house and gather my "three-month tour" kit.

Nitro and I returned home by driving the 958-mile trip in one sixteen-hour day. We didn't bother with motel overnight since Nitro likes to stay up at night yelling at all the unscheduled noises. We powered through the ambitious drive thanks to my reliable 1999 Honda Compact Recreational Vehicle (CR-V) and a few Monster energy drinks. The fourteen-hour campaign actually took sixteen hours after adding a couple of rest stops and traffic delays that were encountered around Miami, FL, Savannah, GA, and Fayetteville, NC. Even so, traffic through the southeast was a breeze compared to traveling I-95 through New England, that's for sure. Once home, Nitro was quite content to be in his own house again, and going to sleep after the arduous drive was not a problem for either one of us.

The next morning, Dad dropped by to check in (his modus operandi was to raid the freezer and then turn on Judge Judy). We talked a little bit about the Nikki situation, and he assured me he would have no problem making my house look "lived-in" for the next few months. He asked that I keep him apprised of the situation and then mentioned he would visit Key West later in the year. I liked that idea, since Mom and Dad hadn't seen each other since my college graduation in Auburn, Alabama, in 1993.

Nitro and I missed all our dog park buddies and made sure to arrange a few dog park trips during our short stay home. It was cool to see all the familiar faces, and in a park that wasn't hotter than a billy goat with a blow torch. Ninety-nine percent of my clients and friends were empathetic and understanding with regard to what I was up against as a health surrogate. There was one client, however, who felt compelled to complain that she would have to find another pet sitter. I said, "Rachel, do what you gotta do, but this may be the last few months of my mother's life. I need to be there."

She seemed to grasp what I was telling her but replied, "What are you going to do about your business? How will you make money? Are you moving to Key West?"

Before I replied, I remembered to be thankful that folks thought I was such a reliable pet sitter. I responded to her nosey and narcissistic questions by simply stating, "Don't worry about those matters and I'll be back before you know it."

While recovering from the exhausting drive back to Cary, I gathered additional clothing, my checkbook, a few good books to read, and several charging adapters. After our short and snappy homecoming, Nitro and I were ready to pilot the CR-V back to Key West. The return trip ended up taking a whopping seventeen hours. There was a third-shift construction operation this time and some weird nighttime speed limits along Route 1 in the Keys. We didn't encounter this last time since we traveled during daylight hours. Apparently, Key Deer are a protected species, and as you travel Route 1 through Big Pine Key, Cudjoe Key, and Lower Sugarloaf Key the speed limit is reduced to twenty-five miles per hour at night. It's a good thing, too, because we encountered several of the small Key Deer (they are about the same size as Nitro) as they crossed the highway. We finally arrived at Mom's house around midnight. Nitro and I tiptoed past Mom and Francesca, who were both snoring in the living room, and then quietly crept up the stairs to the guest bedroom of our tropical home away from home.

The next few weeks of in-home care and biotherapy resulted in a refreshing and most welcome improvement in matters as Mom rallied. The nurses, led by Francesca, clearly had a magic touch, because Mom, along with her entire living area, appeared brighter, cleaner, and healthier. The alternate nurses included Debra, a single mom who had just served in the Navy for four years, and Gretna, a professional and caring woman originally from Jamaica. Although I was confident the biotherapy medicine was contributing, it was abundantly evident that companionship was the real superstar during this phase of treatment. The nurses were personable and encouraging, and as Mom grew to know them, the reassurance and camaraderie displaced despair and inspired a positive mindset. The improvements were small, but the sum of these details was crucial to the healing process. Francesca encouraged Mom to wear clothes she hadn't worn in a while, and she opened curtains, lit candles, or played guitar. Debra was especially good in the conversation department and shared stories about raising her boy, Kevin, which I know Mom particularly adored. Gretna excelled at physical therapy and was the best cook on the crew. All the nurses loved Nitro, who likewise loved the extra attention and food preparation going on morning and night. Menu items featured foods that were rich in potassium, magnesium, and iron, since they are so revitalizing and improved Mom's bloodwork results.

The nurses also maintained a regular schedule (another one of the "secrets" to caregiving). Francesca pointed out, "Nitro learned right away when it's Nikki's dinnertime. It's as if dogs can tell time!" I laughed but couldn't resist pointing out that dogs have no sense of time. This is counter-intuitive to be sure, since dogs obviously know when we wake up, eat, or return from work. That, however, is called circadian rhythm: physical, mental, or behavioral changes that recur naturally on a twenty-four-hour cycle (distinctly noticeable during those outworn, yet dogged, changes in daylight savings time).

Debra asked me if Nitro was a good swimmer. I said, "He sure is. He's a natural," and told her all about the Lake Crabtree swim club days we once reveled in. She then told me about a boxer she once had that hated the water.

I said, "They are definitely one of those breeds that aren't built for swimming. Bulldogs, pugs, dachshunds, and Pekingese don't like to swim either, but they can if they must. Those flat faces or stubby legs make swimming (and life) comparatively difficult."

"What about Newfoundlands? I've seen them working near the docks, not around here but up north. They swim with mooring lines and are good at rescuing drowning victims. Are they great swimmers because they have webbed feet?" Debra asked.

"They certainly have webbed feet, but so do many breeds. The remarkable thing about Newfoundlands, aside from being huge, strong as hell, and bred to swim, is the ability to use a lateral component to their doggie paddle. They don't employ a full breast stroke, but you would swear they were trying to," I replied.

Sometimes Debra would stop by on her day off to bring her son Kevin to visit Nikki (and Nitro, if he was around). Kevin was an outgoing and enthusiastic young fella about seven years old who loved to pet Nitro and give him treats. One time he shared with us that he knew all the colors in the rainbow. Kevin explained that it's easy to remember because Roy G. Biv stands for red, orange, yellow, green, blue, indigo, and violet. We were all vastly impressed.

A little later, Mom revisited this topic and asked me if Nitro could see colors. "I've heard dogs were colorblind but always wondered, why do people say that and how would we even know if they were?"

I said, "Dogs can see in color, but they don't see 'Roy G. Biv' like we do. They only see yellow, gray, brown, and blue since dogs developed their senses as nocturnal hunters. Their eyes have adapted in such a way that they have a special light-reflecting layer behind their retinas to see well in the dark and to catch movement."

Mom caught on right away. "Ah, so this is a rods and cones thing," she replied.

"Right. Rods are the cells that spot movement and work in low light. Cones work in bright light and control color perception. Dogs have more rods than cones in their retina, whereas people have more cones. So, a dog's color vision is like that of a person who has red-green color blindness. Dogs also have differences in brightness discrimination and visual acuity."

"You're so smart, Eric," Mom bragged.

I laughed and said, "Somebody smarter than me wrote that on the internet. Those vets and researchers are the smart ones. I'm just a pet sitter with too much time on his hands."

I appreciated talking to the nurses and, as always, was so proud of my Nitro by how quickly he made friends wherever we went. The nurses, aside from miraculously pulling Mom away from death's door, bestowed precious time that I used to recharge each evening. The nurses arrived daily at 7:00 p.m. and the first thing Nitro and I did was take our evening walk. I would then update key characters like Aunt Edie, my friends Stephanie and Chris, or one of Mom's friends who cared to know how she was faring.

It was challenging to maintain an air of optimism when there was still so much uncertainty, and we found ourselves taking turns asking the same impossible questions: When will the cancer be gone? How long will treatment take? Will she be completely cured? Will the cancer come back? Despite having decades of combined experience, none of my friends and relatives really knew what to expect, but at least we had seen improvement with Mom's mobility, mood, and appetite in the initial month of therapy and care.

After a good walk with Nitro, I would bring him back to help with Mom while I went out to see a movie or maybe stroll around Old Town to ponder about nothing or everything as I weaved between the island visitors delighting in Key West. Nitro preferred the nights when I would simply retire to our guest room early to escape with a good book or a PlayStation adventure. As mid-April approached, I spent a couple of those evenings tackling taxes for my first year as a small business owner.

For some reason, people love talking about tax deductions. Admittedly, claiming deductions does reduce the tax burden on a small business, but they also require time and effort to prepare. Particularly for new small business owners, the impulse to maximize deductions becomes an intoxicating contest that may lure proprietors to the brink of sensible practice. Resisting the urge to spend money on training or supplies, just because they are tax deductible, becomes a real struggle. One excellent strategy is to find indirect expenses that don't require out of pocket spending and the primary way to do this legitimately is through a mileage deduction. All those two-mile trips I made each day added up to 8,000 miles annually. When multiplied by the Department of Treasury's deduction rate of $0.585 per mile, that's $4,680. However, to do this for more than one year, one must establish their home as a business location. This declaration is also useful to prorate utility bills used in an assigned home office area as a deductible business expense. Then again, this becomes a little less exciting after an irksome receipt search and tiresome tally yields a utility deduction that is barely one hundred dollars per year. I wouldn't say I was thrilled about taxes this year, but learning that the value of my small business transcended proceeds and purpose was somewhat satisfying.

In late April, Mom's friends Steve and Joan visited from Bethesda, Maryland. I had known Steve and Joan since the 1980s, and Steve had worked in the same tax firm as stepdad Bill since the 1960s. My fondest memory with Steve and Joan was when we went on a Bermuda cruise in 1994 with Mom and Bill, Aunt Edie, and my grandma McCausland (Mom's mom). For their current visit, Steve and Joan stayed at the Eden House of Key West (about one block from Mom's house). These genuine friends helped to further inspire us with numerous enriching exchanges during their four-day visit. During one of our sit-downs, Steve and Joan asked me how I liked being a small business owner. I said, "I love being out of the rat race and managing an entity outside of the corporate world is truly a better fit for me. In fact, I just sent off my tax forms and deductions to my accountant in Cary."

This was Steve's wheelhouse of course, and he replied, "Oh? Have you established your home as a business location?"

"Yes!" I proudly replied.

"You do know that establishing a home office changes things with regard to capital gains tax when you sell your home," Steve stated.

"No," I responded, as the joy slowly drained from my face.

Steve was smiling as he continued, "Yeah that's one of those hidden costs business owners encounter in the long run of things. Generally, the sale of a home will be exempt from paying capital gains tax, unless the home was used to run a business. The way you set up your home office and claimed operation and occupancy expenses will affect how much capital gains tax will need to be paid when the home is finally sold."

Although this was news to me, I wasn't too surprised. Reality had unmasked yet another expectation in my world. The ludicrous irony made me chuckle and I thought of the non-business owners I knew that unnecessarily maintained deep deduction envy. Steve and I continued to talk shop about several other matters including IRS audits. Steve said, "The Treasury Department definitely spends time and resources reviewing the activities of LLCs, but don't worry as long as your deductions do not exceed fifty percent of your revenue. LLCs that are donating things like cars, boats, and small aircraft are much more likely to be audited than a one-man pet sitting operation."

Steve had a lot of experience in this arena and completely understood how compelling tax deductions were to people. We talked about deducting cell phone and internet bills, and that even though I used those services mostly for personal use, entities cannot do business without them, therefore they are accepted a deductible expense. Steve mentioned a few examples that surprised me such as when home business owners included trash removal services, cleaning services, homeowner's insurance, HOA fees, or the cost to install and maintain a security system.

Steve wrapped things up with, "Tax deductions will save a few hundred dollars each year, and they feel like a clever way to beat the system through hard work and entrepreneurship. Just remember that Uncle Sam is always a few steps ahead of you. Tax breaks indeed help to start and maintain a small business, but the government scoops their share eventually. The Treasury expects citizens to be confused by that Gordian Knot they call the tax code, and they accrue much of their revenue from hidden fees and interest penalties." Steve and Joan were simply the best and, as usual, time seemed to fly by while they shared stories, provided encouragement, or doled out financial wisdom. I always hated to see them go.

After a second month of biotherapy, a CT scan, and bloodwork, Mom's oncologist told us the same thing he said after the first month: "Let's wait and see what the next scan and bloodwork reveals." Now, considering that we had not received quantitative (or qualitative) results from the previous scans and tests, we weren't sure what to expect on the next go-round. Mom was generally feeling better, so that was a good thing, but we were rather taken aback each month with every "Let's wait and see" report. As Dr. Lawrence maintained an emotional demeanor that would put a World League Poker Champion to shame, Mom continued to abide the monthly routine as the caretaking team kept on trucking. This went on for six months.

By the end of six months, Mom had clearly improved on nearly all fronts. Her freedom of movement, desire for food, cognizance, and general mood were leagues above where she was the previous spring. I wish I could say it was a continuous, albeit slow, improvement over time, but it was not. By the third month of treatment, the nurses and I began to notice a pattern. After Mom rallied, she became overconfident and medically noncompliant. Another crisis would follow, which then led to another rallying phase until overconfidence re-entered the cycle.

It took time to identify these cycles because the first few crises were new problems. After a few months of biotherapy (Mom followed her biotherapy program, it was the diet, physical therapy, and prescription support regimens she would stray from), Mom was well enough to understand that if she recovered from cancer, the nurses, attention, companionship, and her only son, would all abandon her. This led to something that none of us on the treatment team expected. Mom would prioritize attention over recovery and surreptitiously self-sabotage to invent new crises.

In response to this, the nurses and I developed checks and medical controls to ensure Mom wouldn't take too much of one medicine or not enough of another. In those early months, it was extremely difficult to distinguish manipulation from irrational behavior due to her illness since evidence for both was present. Sometimes we even caught Mom orchestrating fabrications to neighbors so they would bring unwarranted medication. Those neighbors (much to their surprise) were soon pressed into service as part of the "checks and balances" system.

This surreal, sad, and stressful supervisory tour was rife with paradox, misgiving, and frustration. The nurses aspired to keep Mom comfortable, but respecting those wishes would sometimes fly in the face of recovery. We were never sure whether that next crisis would be the end for Mom, and the vagueness maintained by the oncology medical office didn't help matters at all. The clouds of doubt wrought intense feelings of depression, denial, and anxiety. It seemed like mission impossible on many days.

Meanwhile, "Remember to take care of yourself" was the mantra my friends and family frequently offered. It was a fine sentiment, but also something that is quickly filed under "easier said than done." Caretaking develops as a profound mind game when feelings of guilt enter into the equation. As the unendurable and inappropriate reality of parenting my parent manifested itself, I spent a significant amount of time reflecting on how my parents had raised me. Of course, this included a fair share of yelling, punishment, or taking things away, but knowing this did little to mitigate stress during the year.

Finally, after the CT scan, bloodwork, and appointment of month seven, it suddenly happened. Dr. Lawrence decisively reported that Mom's cancer markers were down and she would be fine. He recommended she keep taking Arimidex tablets daily, but she would no longer need Faslodex shots, bloodwork, or scans. He said to return in a year for a checkup but otherwise biotherapy was complete. Just like that. Mom had gone from, "You're going to die this weekend" to "Let's wait and see" for seven months, and it all ended with an abrupt "It's all good. Thank you. Come again." Relieved, speechless, and a little annoyed, we left the oncology office and went straight to Wendy's for a couple of cheeseburgers and Frosty desserts.

Since the recovery news arrived right before the holidays, Mom and I decided I would stay for another month and return to Cary in the new year. After I left, Mom would keep Debra on staff to visit a few days a week to provide companionship and help with things Nikki still wasn't able to safely do by herself.

Francesca and Gretna moved on to clients that required full-time care. The last month of 2013 proved to be the most restorative time of the year as Mom was able to return to a semblance of normalcy.

Her favorite outing was to visit Tom Luna when he bartended at the Aqua Bar during their Friday happy hour. They played beloved oldies on the jukebox and served appetizers while Mom "danced" in her chair and sang along with catchy hits from the 1960s. Carol and Fran joined us each week while we listened to the theatric Tom Luna convey hilarious stories about crazy customers and tourists in Key West. We also ventured out to a couple of shows, one at the Waterfront Playhouse and another at The Barn to see Dennis in a production featuring original dance routines that he had designed.

Mom began to finally run errands on a regular basis again, although those grocery store trips still conjure bittersweet memories since she was so pushy and forgetful. Mom liked to bump people in the aisles with her shopping cart when they got in her way. I wasn't sure whether to be embarrassed or to laugh out loud at these absurd collisions. Mom would say, "Oh, excuse me," but the nudges were so blatantly passive-aggressive, she should have just said, "Move it, buster!"

Other times we'd be in the check-out line about to pay, and she would precipitously wander off and blurt out, "I forgot to get soap," despite having no fewer than eighteen of those pump-style bottles of liquid soap in the house at all times. For some reason, Mom hoarded a short list of things including light bulbs, toilet paper, band-aids, batteries, and dish sponges. One of my regular duties was to donate these surplus items to neighbors, the Salvation Army, or whoever I could find to take them.

One day, out of nowhere and in the middle of the holidays, Bridgette Lacy, a reporter from the *Raleigh News and Observer* called me and asked to do an interview. She explained that she was reaching out to people who had started their own small business in the wake of the 2008 recession. I was thrilled to field this call and agreed to have a phone interview with Bridgette right away.

The main point Bridgette made in her article was that unintentional entrepreneurs were on the rise, as North Carolina remained stuck in higher unemployment, the third-highest in the country in July 2013 (three years after my own horror show in 2010). About 70,000 unemployed North Carolinians had been cut off from extended federal unemployment in the previous month, and they wouldn't all be able to find work. Interestingly, Bridgette had also spoken with Fred Gebarowski, the director of the Small Business Center at Wake Technical Community College, and the same gentleman I had consulted with in 2011. Fred told Bridgette in his interview that, "Working for one's self also has become more attractive as wages are depressed and the cost of healthcare is rising."

Bridgette's article pointed out that entrepreneurship doesn't look bad when you compare it to working for an employer who has combined several positions into one. She went on to describe how workers need to be prepared for tough terrain, and that employers are not as loyal as some have been in the past. Yet they have the upper hand since there are more job seekers than positions to fill, which drives down the wages workers can command.

Bridgette wrapped up the article with the observation that, for many people, it boils down to preference. "Do you prefer the stress of drudgery or the stress of risk? The answer changes from person to person." Being included as a source for this article was satisfying since it brought closure, and I was glad to hear so many other folks had started their own businesses and restored some balance to the universe.

About two weeks before Christmas, Mom, Nitro, and I were finally able to experience that visit from my dad that he and I talked about earlier in the year. The caretaking tour had been a peculiar journey, and we had many stories to share with ol' Billdad. There was that very special morning on which Mom woke me up at 3:00 a.m. to tell me we were going to be late for the doctor's appointment (she thought it was 8:00 a.m.). Then there was the time she tried to open a big bag of plantain chips, but it exploded in her hands and chips went everywhere. Nitro loved that story, too, since he was the one who happily snarfed up scores of spilled chips that night.

The coup de grâce, however, wasn't winning the battle with cancer, it was the end of Mom's thirty-year shun on microwaves. Francesca had brought one of those rubber hot water bottles that was microwaveable and (somehow) convinced Mom that she really needed to buy a microwave. She did, and for what seemed like one month straight, Mom microwaved popcorn, hot tea, leftovers, and whatever else she could fit in there. Despite all the scary moments and the manner in which fate had imposed its own version of the Schrodinger's cat experiment onto our year, Mom had recovered and was bursting with pride and delight as she shared her recent experiences with Dad. Those first months of treatment unhurriedly crept into an onerous eight, but I felt like Nitro and I had helped save her life, so it was totally worth it.

Nitro's first vet visit Nov 2009

Rosie enjoying the dog park

The mighty Finn

Greta and Nitro in Lake Crabtree

The 4 o'clock gang at Godbold Dog Park

Misha wishing Nitro a happy birthday

Remy the husky

CHAPTER 5

Golden Rules

"Anybody who doesn't know what soap tastes like, never washed a dog." — Franklin P. Jones, writer and humorist from Philadelphia, Pennsylvania.

After an arduous oncology grind that had lasted most of the previous year, it was a huge relief to be back home in Cary. Nitro was much happier and relaxed at home. I mean, he was always a calm and stress-free guy, but I could tell he missed his preferred observation post on the couch and the convenience of the doggie door. We needed to go to the dog park right away, and not purely to resume our beloved pet sitting adventures. Billdad was back in the habit of dropping by unannounced, stealing snacks, and constantly defragging my computer. Filling the house and yard with several dogs was the best way to encourage a Billdad retreat. Most of the dogs were okay with him, but the old man had just turned seventy and was seldom in the mood to dodge half a dozen dogs weaving between his old knees or out the front door. There was always a chance Jackson or Tucker would be in the house, and neither one tolerated Billdad. Jackson, a German short-haired pointer, belonged to Dru, and Tucker was a Chesapeake Bay retriever belonging to Lara. Those eighty-pound, red-brown dogs did not abide unauthorized access to Camp Ewald.

My return to pet sitting needed to employ tactics so ingeniously contrived that even Hannibal (the Barcid) would turn green with envy. Stage one was a public service announcement to the dog park social media page. Stage two was to re-establish myself as a regular who attended the park at 7:00 a.m., noon, and, of course, Nitro's all-time favorite: the four o'clock block. I wondered how many changes had occurred since Nitro and I had left. It had been a long eight months since the park's unauthorized pet sitter and maintenance man had gone missing. I also hoped everyone was pining for ol' Nitro, the "Mayor of the Dog Park." Channeling the spirits of Peaches and Herb, Nitro and I reunited with the 7:00 a.m. crowd during many cold mornings in January to see what our 2014 homecoming had in store for us.

It was fantastic to be back in the land of happy puppies and waggy tails where many familiar faces greeted us. Justin and Kaiser, his long-haired, rake-hating German shepherd were there. Crystal visited with her risible redbone hounds Zeus and Apollo. Teacher Dave and his dog Sadie were still morning regulars, although people were calling him "Creature Dave" now because he was volunteering at Saving Grace pet rescue in Wake Forest. Several people asked how my mom was doing and, although tempted to rattle on with the sensational details, I simply reported that she was en route to remission.

There were several new parishioners in the early morning crowd including an amusing red-haired lady named Emily who unremittingly ran after her beagle-bulldog mix named Casper. I believe the term for this type of mix is beabull, but I referred to Casper as a bagel because he was kind of round. Casper loved to steal toys, leap on the benches and tables, and generally just tear all over the place. That guy loved the park.

There was a friendly fella with a Scottish accent named Ian who brought two Australian shepherd mixes named Sadie and Ashley. Sadie was mostly white but had a black face, and Ashley was mostly black with white speckles. Although their ancestry was unknown, one thing was for certain: those two liked to fight each other. A lot. When this happened, Ian would roll his eyes and say, "There they go again." Ian instantly loved Nitro and would go out of his way to scrutchle and pat Nitro to give him praise.

Ken and his incredibly lanky German shepherd named Strider were also new characters, and, as I had hoped, his dog was named for the Tolkien character readers know as Aragorn. Strider had a unique habit of gathering tennis balls and placing them in a neat pile somewhere in the park. He would guard the pile for a minute, then go hunting for more plunder. Ken often talked to Stu, who had a black lab and pug mix (a bluggle?) named Domino. Ken and Stu became fast favorites because they both liked *Lord of the Rings,* and Stu, like me, was a fan of videogames, specifically strategy games like *Civilization* or any game set in Middle-earth.

Bobbie and Morgan, a mom and daughter team, brought their puppy lab mixes Gretta and Gwenn, who Nitro chased endlessly. Bobbie was a nurse, so I inevitably found myself bending her ear with stories about Mom and her nurses from the previous year.

One of the first things I spotted upon returning to the dog park was that some people were still bad about picking up their poo. Although many found this to be annoying and horrible, I had long ago accepted that poo just happens. It isn't necessarily willful neglect, either. Dogs poop fast, and piles are difficult to find in leaves or after sundown. Even so, all the familiar sights and sounds of the park brought us comfort, and I loved to see that Nitro behaved as if we hadn't missed a day.

I spoke at length to the morning crew to learn the good news and ascertain how some of the missing attendees were doing. The morning regulars shared that several folks had moved, rescued a new dog, or had fenced their yards. The most compelling sample of scuttlebutt was the news that an enemy pet sitter named Wayne had been trying to take over the park in my absence. Wayne (whom I nicknamed plagiarismo for a short while) was a four o'clock regular I had met the previous year. He visited the park with his Rottweiler mix, Gleason, and a wire-haired terrier named Teddy. Wayne, suddenly and suspiciously, began his pet sitting business approximately four-hundred milliseconds after I left for Key West. Perhaps he had been planning to do this for some time, but I looked forward to talking to this impostor as soon as possible.

As far as the first few weeks of noontime visits, it was a bit of a mixed bag because the regular noontime group had apparently disbanded while I was in Florida. Nitro and I played it cool during lunch hours and took our time familiarizing ourselves with the new assortment of visitors. I struck up a conversation with one personable couple, Jared and Michelle, who were attending with their Akita-shepherd mix named Ruxon. Nitro and Ruxon were getting along just swell, and when Jared said, "We've heard of you, you're the dog guy," I was relieved to learn the good word was still out. Ruxon became my first "back in the saddle" regular and several more soon followed.

On a number of days during the lunch hour, I ran into Ismail and his yellow lab, Misha. He introduced me to Lindy and her dog, Ellie (also a yellow lab). I usually chuckle whenever a dog has a human name and this one indeed struck my funny bone. Yellow labs, regardless of color, categorically adored each other. Their owners caught on to this and, frequently around 1:00 p.m., I would see the regular group of Misha, Ellie, Haiku, William and Kate, and Cody.

Haiku's mom was a quiet Indian lady named Venita who smiled a lot and enjoyed watching playtime. William and Kate's mom was Donna, a Lifetime Fitness instructor and an exceptionally outgoing and positive person. Cody's dad, Phil, liked to take the floor and tell stories about all sorts of things (I strongly suspect Phil had a PhD). Ismail talked only about the New York Giants and how terrible they were, but he was able to cheer himself up by joking that the dogs were having a "lab convention." The group found this play on words to be funny the first time, but soon began to wish the New York Football Giants were a much better team while Ismail perpetrated his overused wisecrack daily.

The superstar of the noontime group was Ed the corgi, who had a dynamo personality just like his owners, Sherri and

Scott. That entire trio kept us in stitches. Some days they would enjoy the small-dog side, and on other days they would visit the "big dog" side; but Ed the corgi was well-received wherever he went. Scott was a pretty easy-going dude, and I wasn't surprised when he told me that the best benefit to owning a dog was the reduction of stress. Sherri approved of this notion and said, "I mean, let's face it, life is like a bowling ball; it's full of holes and hard all over. Everyone needs a dog!"

I completely agreed since adopting dogs into our home brings us optimal companions, vigilant guardians, and perpetual playmates who improve our lives relentlessly. The first thing we appreciate is how they love us unconditionally. I remember Nitro on our first day together when he curled up with me on the couch. He had only known me for a couple hours, and the "best friends forever" journey was already underway.

"Dogs have an innate ability to get you out of your head and live in the moment," Scott offered. He was totally right, and this superpower of theirs is contagious and decidedly effective. I even loved to play the anthropomorphism game where I used the "dog voice" to narrate any situation.

"Absolutely," I replied, "and keeping your pet active keeps you active, too. Walking or running with your dog is something they will never grow tired of." Any Fitbit addict will attest that their daily step-count doubles after they add a new best friend. Hiking and swimming are particularly fun, but dogs are ready to do anything. Skateboarding, surfing, and biking are all fascinating to puppies (the jury is still out on rakes and leaf blowers however).

Whether I was paying bills, arguing with my impossible stepmother, hiding from solicitors, or caring for a sick relative, Nitro had my back. He loved me more than he loved himself. How dogs are able to effortlessly soothe our minds and hearts is still a total mystery to me. They are priceless, precious, and transcendent all at once as they infuse our daily schedule with enthusiasm and love. Dogs change our lives as they snuggle into our travel plans, peer preferences, and sometimes, even our sense of purpose.

The four o'clock gang, thank goodness, hadn't changed a minute while Nitro and I were gone. Ellie and Rosie, Diane and Jasper, Bob and Rex, Jane and Bailey, Kelley and Lily, and Dog Park Doug with big Boomer were there each day like clockwork. George and Petunia were there, too, and the first thing he said to me, as he chortled shamelessly, was, "How is Doggy Style going?"

A number of new four o'clockers had joined the gazebo gang including Terri, a real estate broker, and her black and white maltapoo (a Maltese and miniature poodle mix), Henry. Pam religiously arrived at four o'clock sharp and beamed with glee as she waved and greeted everyone she knew (or didn't know). Her dog, Bimmer, was a well-behaved basset hound that spent the entirety of each visit exploring the park and leaving messages for subsequent explorers. Dog Park Doug, as quickly as he could, barged in to my introduction to Pam with, "Eric! I bet you don't know what 'Bimmer' means."

"It's the nickname used to refer to BMW cars and it's been around since at least the 1970s," I replied, only slightly annoyed by his imposing interrogative. I then parried with, "I bet you don't know how to spell Bimmer. In fact, I bet you don't even know what BMW stands for."

Dog Park Doug had apparently been on Wikipedia the night before because he instantly replied, "Bavarian Motor Works!" However, he admitted he wasn't sure how to spell Bimmer. I explained that enthusiasts referring to BMW motorcycles wrote "Beemer" or "Beamer" back in the 1940s through the 1960s when motorcycle racing became popular in the United States. However, when referring to BMW cars, the convention was to spell it "Bimmer," so as to distinguish them from motorcycles. The only reason I knew all this was because I owned a BMW motorcycle during my college years, but I did not concede this insider information as it would have spoiled my moment of victory.

Dog Park Doug and I interminably endeavored to one-up

each other in the "Did you know?" department, but the master of the one-upping game was Myrtle, a gregarious lady originally from Chicago. Myrtle visited the park with Jambalaya, a Great Dane with a merle coat. Myrtle didn't care how many pets you had, how much your dog weighed, or how many cars you owned, because she always had one more. She was the best, and you were not. To her credit, she was the one who taught us that Chicago is not called the "Windy City" just due to the weather. The nickname also derived from the bloviating and boastful nature of its denizens.

Newcomers to the four o'clock block included Samantha, who brought Angel, a brown lab mix who loved to play fetch with Rex. Angel chased and barked at Rex in a manner that reminded us of Finn. Tyson was a friendly lab mix and his owner, Shannon, loved the afternoon group so much she cackled constantly. Most members referred to her as "laughing lady" since that was easier to remember.

Speaking of Finn, he and a couple other notables were missing from the afternoon group. Greta (Nitro's girlfriend) and her family were in the process of moving to Arkansas, and Stephanie and Finn had already moved out West to take a new job. Jen, Greta's mom, had provided a heads-up that they had not yet been able to find a pet-friendly apartment. They asked if I would watch Greta for a few months as they settled into their new jobs and shopped for a new house. I told her that was a splendid idea and Nitro was equally thrilled.

Before I did anything, however, Dog Park Doug, still steamed from the BMW debacle, double-dog-dared me to scrutinize the best dog breeds. I already knew that choosing a best friend is an intriguing and baffling contest since there were so many breeds to ponder over. Going online to complete superlative searches like "best family dogs" or "smartest dog breeds" is a worthwhile place to begin, but one must be mindful of exceptions, mixed breeds, and at least half a dozen other subjective details.

"What do you mean by 'best'?" I replied to Dog Park Doug

and his fuzzy query.

"Well, which breeds are the smartest? Mr. Smarty Pants," he retorted.

"I would say border collies, Australian shepherds, and German shepherds are usually at the head of the class. That's what most dog experts will tell you."

"How do *they* know?"

"Well, they use several factors to determine intelligence. Things like word comprehension, problem-solving capabilities, responsiveness to training, communication skills, memory, and the ability to predict human behavior. The most intelligent dog breeds score high in all these categories, but just know that the smartest dogs are typically the most impassioned and intense as well."

"Hmm. Interesting," Dog Park Doug said. "What about the dumbest dogs? I had an Irish setter once, and he was about as sharp as a bag of wet mice."

Dog Park Doug was killing me with his rapid-fire questions and folksy metaphors. The truth is, most dogs are intelligent, and dogs that rank lower on the intelligence scale are those who make a willful decision to do their own thing. Dogs ranking even lower on the scale may be overwhelmed by scent, predatory, or other innate drives.

"Well," I began, "mastiffs, basset hounds, and beagles receive the short end of the stick with this tag. Scent hounds are on this list because they are so obsessed with the next scent, they may be harder to train. Keep in mind though, many dogs are simply stubborn, like bosses, parents, or people that drive slow in the passing lane."

Dog Park Doug then asked, "Well, which breeds are the most popular?"

"Oh, by far, in the US at least, it's the Labrador retriever, and not just because they are so friendly, tolerant, and loyal. They are enthusiastic and versatile, and that's why you see them bred and trained for hunting, showing, dock diving, or tracking. They shed a lot, though."

NITRO: A DOG'S TALE

This discussion went on for some time and everyone in the group had an opinion about their favorite breed or type of dog. Dogs who are best with children included the cavalier King Charles spaniel, Bernese mountain dog, Alaskan Malamute, Boston terrier, golden retriever, Irish setter, and pug. Next, we talked about dogs with low grooming needs. However, even the dog breeds that score well in the low-grooming division, like the beagle, boxer, Great Dane, Weimaraner, and Italian greyhound, are still going to press hair onto your black pants. Those short stubborn hairs on seat cushions or in the dryer's lint trap are proof of that.

Myrtle busted in on the conversation with, "Oh, my Jambalaya doesn't shed at all, and she's the smartest dog in the world, and she's the tallest and heaviest dog I've ever known."

Stunned by the outburst, the group managed the non sequitur by briefly glancing at one another before Bob calmly, if not heroically, countered with, "What do you guys think the most active dog breed is?"

The Siberian husky, Dalmatian, springer spaniel, and border collie were eagerly mentioned. Those breeds are great for runners, hikers, spelunkers, or tomb raiders. As far as large dog breeds, the top-rated in that class included the Saint Bernard, Great Dane, Newfoundland, great Pyrenees, and mastiff. These huge companions will ensure your food budget and sleeping arrangement will never be the same. Even their drool is epic, whether you are measuring volume, yarble distance, or slimability. Myrtle gave me the dagger eyes, however, after I mentioned that ginormous dogs tend to not live as long (only eight to ten years) as compared to medium or small breeds that may live to be twelve or even sixteen years old.

I wrapped things up by informing Dog Park Doug and friends that the American Kennel Club website has an online breed selector. Their ingenious questionnaire is designed to choose a breed based on preferences and living arrangements. They begin by asking if you are new to dogs and then cover pertinent circumstances such as living space, activity level, number of children (or other pets), and your tolerance for shedding or barking. After the short test, a chart displays breeds that meet the input criteria. The page includes photos, personality details, popularity, size and weight data, grooming requirements, life expectancy, and more.

I loved having these academic discussions about the varying proclivities of different dog breeds, but everybody knows brown dogs are the best. Brown dogs don't have to be brown of course, and I'm referring to the mixed breeds you find in shelters or rescue organizations. Nitro was a brown dog, and Nitro was the best.

It only took a few weeks for Eric's Pet Sitting to regain 50 percent capacity. Nitro and I were happy to be back in action, but we still had plenty of room in our schedule. While experimenting with off-peak visitation times to meet new dogs, I finally ran into Wayne (the usurping pet sitter) at the park. He opened with, "How many ya got today?"

"Four," I replied.

He said, "I have five."

Oh. This game again. I parried with, "Well, I've got two more at home."

Wayne said, "I've got three more back at the house."

Laughing, I said, "Okay, you win this round." We then spoke for a while as the happy and zany knuckleheads zoomed, played, and zoomed some more. I was a little guarded at first because I didn't know how territorial or competitive Wayne might be. Even so, I was optimistic since he was at least twenty years older than I was. Besides, most pet sitters are not inherently selfish or cutthroat personality types.

Fortunately, the parley went well since we both knew pet sitting requests at Godbold far exceeded our combined capacity. We agreed to work the crowd as cooperative dog walkers as opposed to dueling pet sitters. Wayne had already picked up a couple of my regulars during my absence and, although that didn't truly bother me, I still looked forward to the satisfaction of stealing a few of my preferred customers back. We also shared observations on problem clients and a few tips and tricks on how to handle relatively troublesome charges.

Although we decided there were plenty of clients to go around, I sensed that Wayne, as a relatively new pet sitter, had a gung-ho attitude and wished to prove himself by gathering as many clients as possible. I also sensed that I wanted to let the air out of his tires for copying me and moving in on my territory. I would never do anything so overt, but I did look forward to recommending suboptimal clients to Wayne as soon as possible. That way, while he was distracted with those charges, I could add the more harmonious and happy hounds back onto my roster. Despite our amicable exchange, I suspected the enmity between us might very well roil endlessly beneath the false smiles worn at the park.

All in all, there was still one thing for sure and two things for certain: we both needed to keep away from the complete kooks. One wacky example was Antoinette (and her husky, Natasha), who could not wait to tattle on owners or impose her version of the park rules of engagement. However, Natasha was so busy beating the crap out of the nearest dog, we seldom suffered Antoinette's counsel very long.

There was another fella, a morning regular named Jeb, who popped in with a ball-obsessed black lab mix named Yosef (as long as no one went after Yosef's ball, no one got hurt). Jeb was a car salesman and a good one. I heard that he had sold at least twenty new cars to dog park members just in the last year. I tried to avoid Jeb because it was apparent he had been hounding me to piggy back off my pet sitter network in order to sell more cars. When we did cross paths, he would badger me about having dog park dinners to gather as many dog parkers as possible so he could work his magic. He was an excellent manipulator and, despite knowing his game, I found him to be a funny character and actually enjoyed talking to him in little doses.

Prickly characters were persistent to be sure, and thanks

to the internet, conventional boundaries were transcended when kooks and keyboard warriors exacted their evil genius upon the dog park social media page. During the Key West tour, I had stayed on as Admin for the dog park group page, and I added people who I didn't necessarily know in an effort to grow the online presence while giving strangers the benefit of the doubt. Upon returning in 2014, I became aware that several of them didn't even go to the dog park, and a few had even thought they were joining the Cary, Indiana, dog park page!

Our Godbold dog park page had been gaining traction for a few years, and membership to the actual dog park was mounting as well. I discerned many of the newer characters had joined the page just to promote their (sometimes dog-related) business or e-commerce site, but that wasn't why Kelley and I started the group. There were also a few pet sitters that joined the group, and they liked to spam the page with plugs for their businesses; but those numbskulls operated twenty or more minutes away from Cary. Although I was tempted to remove them from the group, nobody knew them, so they were not a threat to my expanding pet sitting empire.

Mostly, it was the hoax and urban legend boosters, the "save all the dogs" crusaders, and worst of all, the "Surprise! Here's a picture of a starving or a severely injured dog" violators who annoyed me the most. I didn't necessarily remove every offender, but I certainly deleted posts that did not align with the spirit of the page. I then made the group private in an effort to keep the chowderhead traffic to a minimum.

One thing I couldn't stop were the trolls and flame warriors who legitimately belonged as members of the park, but who for some reason felt they had to vehemently contest every pet food recall or any reasonable recommendation shared to the page. Those exchanges were exasperating, predictable, and, admittedly, sometimes mildly entertaining. All I could do was just laugh at myself as I grasped that this was exactly why the Town of Cary didn't maintain a social media page for the dog park. Town officials already had their hands full with the frustrating and outspoken know-it-alls who attended their town meetings.

On the opposite end of the spectrum, there were several parkgoers who had more charisma than they knew what to do with. Dan the jewelry salesman was probably the best example of this as he was epically personable when he brought his lab mixes, brindled Lily and black Basil, to the four o'clock sessions. I watched Lily and Basil on a number of occasions when Dan and his wife vacationed or attended jeweler conventions. I can't say whether Dan sold as much jewelry as Jeb sold cars, but he did a good job of staying engaged with folks, and he regularly made sure there was a heaping stack of photo-degraded, crinkled, dog-eared, and mud-stained business cards jammed into the dog park bulletin board.

As 2014 continued, I maintained a slow, but continuous loading of my schedule. One interesting dog was a ginormous Rottweiler mix named Grizzly, who was wary of strangers and enforced a strict dress code. If you wore a hat, carried a leash, or even liked to tie a sweater around your waist, Grizzly barked and growled in protest. Although daunting, he was a big bluffer and never lunged or attacked anyone. His owner, a pleasant and smiley lady named June, approached me one day with a huge grin and bright face and asked, "Are you a pet sitter?"

"Yes," I replied, amused by her leading question. It was more of an exclamation really.

"Do you walk dogs or just take them to the park? We need someone to walk Grizzly because he's a little fussy at the park sometimes," June said, as Grizzly gave me the side-eye.

Eager to fill my schedule, I agreed to a meet and greet at Grizzly's house a few days later. June's husband, Scooter, was at the house and Grizzly growled and lumbered ominously as I entered and then plopped down on their couch like I owned the place (I've watched a lot of Cesar Milan shows and, surprisingly, most of his tricks actually work). Grizzly, stupefied by my seamless snubbing, approached me to check me out. It took him a few minutes, but as Scooter and I talked, Grizzly warmed up to me, and before we knew it, he was on the couch making pleas for pets and checking for treats.

"You're a natural," Scooter said.

"I wish I had started pet sitting twenty years ago," I replied.

We set up a situation where I would walk Grizzly two days a week, and later we would talk about taking Grizzly for doggie day camp or park visits. I saw that Scooter and June also had a dog named Lolly, a bichon frise that, interestingly, wore doggie diapers. Scooter rolled his eyes and said, "That's June's dog, you don't have to worry about him."

After saying my farewell to Scooter, Grizzly, and leaky Lolly, I returned to my house to check on some of the new charges. I had recently added Remy, the new superstar of the four o'clock tribe who was a beautiful, frisky, and mischievous husky (aren't they all?). People who didn't know Remy thought he was a girl because he was so pretty. Remy LeBeau, named for Gambit from the X-Men, was about one year old and his favorite playmate was Misha, the white yellow lab. Ismail, Misha's dad, also loved Remy and incessantly pestered Tina, Remy's mom, to be in the dog park at his request. I'm sure Tina regretted sharing her phone number with Ismail since he plagued her daily with texts like, "We're already at the park, and Remy is late for the lab convention!"

One thing led to another, and Remy and Misha became regulars with my doggie day camp. This was great in terms of income and reputation, but it also meant Ismail now had *my* phone number.

Eric's Pet Sitting had been filling up fast when I added the most unforgettable, fantastic, and farcical new client named Gizmo. He was a labradoodle of great renown because he darted around the dog park faster than a ray of light. His mom, Catherine, approached me in the park one day and asked, "You have quite the following. Can you take Gizmo three days a week? He's just too much for us at home all the time." I agreed and soon discovered that Gizmo was one of those dogs that would play *all* day. He was so wild that he wore everyone out. This included Nitro, all the other charges, and even myself. I eventually coined the phrase, "We've been Gizmoed," to capture our mood at the end of every Gizmo day.

I also added Uecker, another white labradoodle, who, like Gizmo, was utterly insane. Then there was Rocco, a ginormous Rottweiler mix similar to Grizzly; but unlike Grizzly, Rocco was super friendly and happy all the time. He was also a maniac. Rocco was so high energy and so huge, I was more exhausted than he was after our joint jarring jaunts.

As I strove to have those last few slots in my sitter/walker schedule filled, I once again faced the "how many is too many" perplexity and encountered some peculiar dogs. There was Lita, a black-haired Akita mix, who went completely nuts when a motorcycle or bicycle passed by. She had an unpredictable, explosive, and psychotic energy around dogs, too. I can handle dust-ups and mishaps because dogs typically telegraph their intentions, but there was absolutely no managing the escalations with Lita. I watched her for a few days only and then had to tell her owners it wasn't going to work out. My go-to explanation, so as to not hurt anyone's feelings, was to admit that since I managed a small pack, I had a limited number of energy match-ups. I would then recommend the big box doggie day camps since they had so many more dogs. Even when owners knew how exceptional their dog could be, they still liked to feign surprise at my assessment and recommendation.

I've mentioned before that pet sitting is not hard work, but both the capacity conundrum and the "how crazy is too crazy" question *will* sting you from time to time. From my observations at the dog park, I generally knew when a dog operated on the fringe of ethical behavior. However, part of my reputation was based on being able to manage the scrappier dogs, so I developed a one-week-trial method to determine whether things would work out. I empathized with owners who had high-maintenance dogs because those dogs need love, attention, and exercise just like the rest of us. I empathized less so with owners who were deceptive about the matter.

Thankfully, most owners knew that their dog was nuts and were forthcoming regarding the predicament. One client I walked regularly, a speckled, gray cattle dog mix named Sam, attended the park for many months in 2014, but it became clear that Sam was a little too dominant to be around other dogs. His owner called me one day to ask if I could walk Sam on a regular basis and I agreed. Perhaps I should have set up walking sessions with Lita instead of firing her, but Lita would explode for too many random reasons. Sometimes, as I agonized whether a new charge might be too much, I mischievously recommended them to my arch nemesis, Wayne.

One remarkable four o'clocker was Abby, who put Finn to shame in the barking department. This red-brown hound could knock the shingles off the skate shack. She never barked at anything in particular; she just wanted the whole world to know she had something to say. Her owner asked me to pet sit one weekend and, although tempted to send them over to Wayne (I had long since memorized his phone number by this point), I agreed. Abby did very well during her weekend stay and (thank goodness) she apparently saved up all that barking just for the dog park.

Fortunately, the last few slots in the EPS schedule were filled with ideal charges. Chewy became a new regular for several months. Chewy received bonus points for having a Star Wars name, and for looking just like a mini-Nitro. Chewy was good-spirited, energetic, and regularly full of beans so we were happy to add him to the day crew. The icing on the cake was when Jen followed up with her moving situation, and Greta began staying with Nitro and me in the late spring. Nitro loved having Greta around as a full-time playmate and partner in crime.

After a few years of going to the dog park for four to six hours a day, you begin to notice patterns. Not only the patterns of attendance that coincide with the seasons of the year, but the visitation synchronization as dogs of similar names, breeds, or other traits gravitate to one another. These like-minded owners nearly made me refer to 2014 as the "Year of the Bellas," because I met no fewer than five Bellas, and one of them (little Bella) became a weekday regular at EPS. Park regulars who grew to know the duplicate Bellas developed nicknames so we knew which Bella we were talking about. There was little Bella, speckled Bella, spaniel Bella, barky Bella, and bouncy Bella. Little Bella was about thirty pounds, tan, and was some sort of hound and lab mix. She was rather bizarre and would eat anything. I knew this because she regularly urped up unexpected debris such as business cards, small plants, or leather bookmarks. She took counter surfing to a whole new level and could grab items off desks, dressers, or end tables.

This year also brought an inordinate number of big-headed dogs. These were rare mixes that had the body of a corgi or basset hound attached to a ginormous German shepherd or Labrador retriever head. The notables in this department included Delta Brees (black lab and basset), Lucky (yellow lab and basset), and Smidgeon (German shepherd and corgi). Greyhound tracks seem to emancipate their racers in discrete sets because we encountered greyhound groupings from time to time, too. Some of them still had their prey drive and attended the park wearing a muzzle and (more than once) I witnessed those muzzles do their job as a newly adopted greyhound whizzed toward a small dog visiting the large-dog side. Most of the greyhounds had been weaned from the rabbit reflex however, and two notables in this department were Blitz and Blaze. Their owner, Dr. Puryear, was a well-spoken professor-type fellow and, clearly, his lectures had worked wonders. Maybe that's why Nitro was so well behaved, because I talked to him often!

Dog park members who grew up in England also flocked together. The most outgoing and notable Brits included Melanie and Jen and Dave. Melanie brought Doodle (a black lab mix) and Lucy (a hound mix), and Jen and Dave brought a pair of plucky Australian shepherd littermates named Bailey and Gemma. Brits are fun to talk to and love razzing Americans because we're "dumb, fat, and like to shoot everything." Native Carolinians are used to this sort of talk since New Yorkers had been telling us this for years. The trick to maintaining levity in these circumstances was to provide humorous pushback while reminding these transplants that they moved here for a reason. Although Dog Park Doug didn't help matters when he asked one of the Brits what they were doing for the Fourth of July.

"That never happened!" Jen exclaimed, unwilling to admit defeat from those puny peasants of yesteryear. "Brits have been independent since the dawn of recorded history."

I knew she was kidding, but I also knew a few people within earshot may have truly believed her. Unable to contain myself, I replied, "Well, except for those years Britain was a Roman province, until around AD 410 when the Romans left to handle the Huns. Once the coast was clear, however, the Picts, Angles, Saxons, Jutes, and Frisians overran Britain, and it took them at least four-hundred years to sort things out."

Jen was not amused. Her husband, however, was smirking.

Then I added, "I bet King Egbert of the House of Wessex would have declared an Independence Day in AD 802 but the great Danes kept the House of Wessex busy for a few hundred more years."

"Okay, okay Mr. History buff. Point taken," Jen capitulated.

Feeling compelled to change tack, I offered a trivia question: "By the way, do you know the difference between a Dane and a Viking?"

Dog Park Doug, spring-loaded from his previous gaffe, answered first with, "They're the same thing, right?"

"Basically. Vikings were coastal raiders from Scandinavia who used longships to plunder their targets. The remarkably annoying Vikings who traveled inland and stayed in Britain were called Danes. It's kind of like the difference between

Yankees and Damn Yankees," I answered, recharging the air with levity.

The bottom line is that England does not have an Independence Day, but they celebrate themselves throughout each year for a great number of reasons, like when the king or queen has a birthday. The list of critical holidays that resemble an Independence Day in England probably begins with the Battle of Hastings Anniversary from October 14, 1066, when William the Conqueror of Normandy became king of England and they grew independent from Danish rule.

On June 15, 1215, the legal charter for the Kingdom of England (the Magna Carta) was signed. This gave citizens (some) independence from a king who had too much power, and by 1265 England had their first Parliament. Oak Apple Day was celebrated on May 29 for a time after 1660, when the Stuart Monarchy was restored. This signaled independence from eleven years of rule by Oliver Cromwell and his Rump Parliament while England was a Commonwealth.

Then there's May 1, 1707, the date the Acts of Union went into effect. That's when England and Scotland became Great Britain. Later, the term "United Kingdom" became official on January 1, 1801, when the parliaments of Great Britain and Ireland each passed an Act of Union, uniting the two kingdoms and creating the United Kingdom of Great Britain and Ireland.

In any case, all the jabs were in good fun, and I liked to dig back at the Cockney rhyming gang by reminding them they've had ten civil wars, eviscerated citizens for carrying the wrong prayer book, and commemorated the day Guy Fawkes almost blew up Parliament. That usually shut them down for a bit. At least until the next scandalous US news story broke.

Since my return from the Keys, I was a little rusty in the "letting nonmembers into the park" department. Customarily, I let people in so they could take the park for a test run. Online reviews for Godbold revealed that people who visited the park for the first time were not usually aware of the membership requirements. About 90 percent of those visitors I let in did just fine, and later on I would see those former first-timers and their dogs as regular members of the dog park. However, on some days I would detect a "not a good dog park dog" approach the entrance (when you get the vibe you just know).

There were also those who lied about forgetting their pass. Deciphering pantomimes often sufficed, but I was at the park frequently enough to recognize the cheapskate freeloaders since they were repeat offenders. Eventually, after witnessing a few mishaps and having grown weary of the insulting fibs, I changed my philosophy on this issue and just pretended not to see approaching interlopers. If they caught me near the entrance gate, I would politely tell them they needed to go to one of the several municipal locations that accepted vaccine paperwork and dog park membership payments.

Although rare, some park attendees were actually foster parents. My favorite foster to witness was Onyx, a black and white pit bull mix that Susan brought to the park. Onyx was especially batty, but her most sensational move was to jump the fence between the small dog and large dog areas. She didn't harm any of the small dogs, but it was entertaining to behold the exasperation of the small-dog owners when a large dog leapt over and crazily ran about (any dog over ten pounds was considered large to them).

After speaking to Susan and some of the other foster parents I gathered that becoming a foster volunteer can be a marvelously cooperative and rewarding adventure. Fostering may be a good idea for folks who aren't sure what kind of dog is right for them or who are currently "between dogs." Foster parents may also be people who have lost their once-in-a-lifetime dog and have decided the fostering lifestyle is the way to go. Although foster dogs are more likely to have an interesting or traumatic history, volunteers are only expected to provide custody for a few weeks. Susan volunteered for a local organization called Second Chance Pet Adoptions, which had been operating in Wake County since the 1980s.

Susan approached me and asked if I knew anyone who

might be interested in becoming a foster volunteer. I wasn't ready to be a foster parent, but I enjoyed discussing any topic that involved dogs.

"How expensive is fostering a dog?" I asked Susan.

"Well, the foster group pays for food, flea and tick medicine, veterinary care, and some supplies. You typically won't have to make a large financial commitment to a foster group," Susan replied.

"What exactly is a 'foster fail?'" I inquired.

Susan laughed and said, "That frisky turn of phrase is delivered tongue-in-cheek to simply mean that a foster volunteer has agreed to adopt their temporary foster pet."

"What about the candidate who already has a dog, and needs to see if a foster dog will get along with their first dog?"

"Well, some rescue groups have specific programs for that type of scenario. They'll have you pay a deposit, usually a few hundred dollars, and then you have a week or two to try things out. If the dog acclimates well, your deposit becomes the adoption fee. If you choose not to adopt the dog, they will only keep $50 of the deposit."

"Are potential puppy parents able to foster any dog they want?"

"Sometimes, but the application process used to match foster volunteers with pets is designed to help the rescue group meet their needs before yours."

I had heard several stories about foster groups who maintained immensely stringent requirements for guardians. The word on the street was to study online reviews because organizations that feel that *nobody* is good enough to adopt or foster their dogs can waste your time with their application process. Regardless, this was fascinating stuff. Having been a long-term dog parker, I knew at least two fosters that had been with their foster parents for years. I then asked, "What is the longest time you may need to foster a dog?"

"Their entire lifetime," she replied.

"Wait. What?"

Amused by my surprise, Susan said, "There are a few reasons why this sometimes happens. A foster dog that is terminally ill, or otherwise has a costly medical condition, may be unpalatable to potential owners. An additional reason is that some dogs are just too quirky and unmanageable, and therefore difficult to re-home." She gave Onyx a knowing glance as she went on, "Depending on your foster agreement, this could lead to a situation where a foster volunteer keeps their foster dog for years."

Fostering was beginning to sound just like adopting a dog. If truth be told, you never really know what you're going to get when it comes to animals. Many foster dogs have anxiety and fear, particularly if they grew up homeless. Some will act out by barking, being destructive, or showing aggression. The advantage to fostering is that it's a provisional arrangement, but I could not imagine being able to give a dog away. Susan pointed out that it's easier to see them go if they've already destroyed your screen windows or stripped the linoleum off your kitchen floor. Besides, some foster volunteers are able to stay in touch with their former charges, and a new foster always comes along.

Fostering sounded like it would be ideal for the person who loves dogs but does not become attached too easily. Dog lovers who want to help but who are not able to foster can donate money or time, since the need for volunteers is unending, and foster groups regularly hold events to promote their forlorn and furry friends.

By the time summer arrived, I was operating at full capacity again. During a holiday week, when the whole world needed pet sitting, I begrudgingly steered a few clients to Wayne, my archrival. I made sure to tell them, "He's nowhere near as good as I am, but he's a responsible pet sitter." To be totally honest, I had come to recognize that people liked Wayne just fine and that was actually good to know. As the Fourth of July holiday was approaching, I ran into Wayne at the dog park, and he seemed a little more anxious than his usual self. He approached me and asked, "Are you all booked for the Fourth?"

"Yes," I replied, wondering if he knew how many folks I had given his number to.

"Me too," he said. Then, shaking his head he added, "Do you ever take vacations anymore? How do you do it? Holiday demand is through the roof, and between the holidays there's too many requests to even free up a weekend."

"I know exactly what you mean," I said, "especially when clients want two weeks of overnights, that's a lot of money to turn down. Not to mention, it's difficult to say no to friends."

Wayne and I spoke at length about the ludicrous levels of insistence pet sitters had to manage. It was somewhat cathartic to share experiences with my frenemy who I more or less "worked with" since we operated out of the same dog park. Sheree was the only other established pet sitter that came to our park, but she had her own limited list of ideal clients, and the former pet sitters I spoke with had never truly graduated from the "trying things out" stage. This chat was a good follow up to the previous talks I had with Wayne because it confirmed we indeed did not have to battle to the death over who would win the lion's share of clients.

After talking about overbookings and how to say "No" to clients, Wayne asked me, "What is your take on the pet sitter logo quandary I keep reading about on the NAPPS forum?"

"I haven't been on there in a couple weeks. What's going on?" I asked.

"There's a few sitters out there that refuse to wear or display their pet sitter logo when they go to houses because thieves casing neighborhoods will know the owner isn't home."

I had to stop laughing for a minute before I was able to reply. "Well, some sitters are a little too full of themselves and those forums can certainly end up being a place to crusade about one thing or the other. Personally, I wear my EPS shirt and I also have a magnetized logo on my car when I go to client's homes. Half the time when I walk a dog, someone in the family is home anyway. Not to mention, burglars don't like dogs!"

"Right," Wayne agreed, "and when you try to mention neighborhood watch or house language, the pundits won't even acknowledge you."

"I also do a lot of those noontime walks. In those instances, the owners are home in the mornings and evenings anyway," I added.

It was good to know Wayne and I were on the same page most of the time. The pet sitter logo reveals only a small part of the picture, and besides, what is the likelihood that Harry and Marv are casing the house from their Oh-Kay plumbing van the *exact* moment you drive up to a client's house? Some of those pet sitters out there are just weird.

When I was in Florida, Dog Park Doug had apparently received a lot of "amazing facts" emails and one afternoon he presented a sample of ambiguous anecdotes he had just been agonizing about. Reading from a printed copy of the egregious email, he began the inquisition with, "It says here three dogs survived the sinking of the RMS *Titanic*. First of all, what does RMS stand for?"

"Royal Mail Ship." I answered.

"What? It does not," Dog Park Doug contested.

"It does. Would I lie?" I jested.

"Ok, I'm looking that up later, but it says a Newfoundland, a Pomeranian, and a Pekingese survived the sinking of the *Titanic*. How could that be possible?"

"That sounds about right, but I think it was two Pomeranians and a Pekinese. The Newfoundland story is apocryphal," was the best I could do on this one. Ellie, Jane, Bob, and Diane had joined the summit of suspicion, and Diane already had her smart phone out.

"It says here," Diane began, "that Lady, a Pomeranian, was taken aboard Lifeboat Seven with Margaret Bechstein Hays. Sun Yat Sen, the Pekingese, belonging to Myra and Henry S. Harper (the Harper's magazine people), survived by boarding Lifeboat Three. Another Pomeranian was smuggled onto Lifeboat Six by Elizabeth Jane Rothschild, and it even says here that the crew initially refused to take the dog!"

"What about that Newfoundland?" Dog Park Doug asked.

Diane, searching as fast as she could, came up with, "There's a story that describes a Newfoundland named Rigel, who belonged to First Officer William Murdoch. Rigel withstood the freezing North Atlantic waters and barked to gain the attention of the *Carpathia*'s crew, which helped the rescuers locate the lifeboats. However, there is no record of Rigel, even in survivors' accounts."

"Hah! I knew half of these were urban legends. I can't wait to go home and tell my wife that I was right," Dog Park Doug said.

"Well, you should probably tell your wife that *Diane* was right," Jane giggled.

Dog Park Doug pretended not to hear that and next offered, "It says here that greyhounds are the fastest dogs on earth, and can run up to forty-five miles per hour!"

This one I knew about, thanks to previous parleys with Professor Puryear. "That's true," I began, "but I believe the current world record is held by a whippet named Reas. Keep in mind that when you search for the top ten fastest dog breeds, there is significant variation among the results. After greyhounds and whippets, the fastest dog breeds listed most often included saluki, vizslas, Afghan hounds, Ibizan hounds, Jack Russell terriers, Dalmatians, Doberman pinschers, Weimaraners, pharaoh hounds, and border collies."

"How in the world do they even know how fast the dog is going?" Ellie asked.

"They use those radar guns. You've seen them at baseball games to clock the pitches," Dog Park Doug proudly answered.

"Well, who woulda thunk it," Ellie replied.

"Okay, what about this one?" Dog Park Doug was on a roll. "It says the US has the highest dog population in the world. But that doesn't make sense. Wouldn't China, India, or Russia have more dogs?"

"I know this one, too, because I got a little carried away

during my pet sitting market research. The US has about ninety million dogs, and that equates to 274 dogs per 1,000 people. So, if you know four people, one of them has a dog, if they don't, you are the dog." Through the face palms and head shaking, I continued my deadpan delivery with, "The US has the highest population *density* with respect to dogs, but China has more dogs. About 100 million I believe. Statistics can backfire on you if you aren't careful how you express the superlative. For example, France ranks in the top five of the most dog-friendly countries, but it is nowhere near the top five with regard to any measure of dog population. Australia, Portugal, and Canada are also top dog countries, as far as population density."

"That makes sense," Dog Park Doug replied. "These statistics, or superlatives, whatever you call them, can be confusing. Like this one that says there are seven-hundred breeds of purebred dogs. There's no way there's that many."

It was Bob's turn now, and he chimed in with, "I used to work for the American Kennel Club, and they only recognize about two-hundred breeds. However, the International Canine Federation recognizes three-hundred and sixty dog breeds, but that total includes the two-hundred breeds on the AKC register. There are unofficial registers out there, but even if you include mixed-breed and extinct breeds, there are probably less than six-hundred dog breeds."

"I don't trust the internets," Ellie said. "And that Google is always listening to what I say. They show me ads on my phone or computer about things I've only talked about."

"No one is safe," Diane added.

Dog Park Doug had one more, "About one million dogs in the US have been named as the primary beneficiaries in their owner's will. This can't be right. How is this even possible? Is Boomer going to open his own checking account if I die?"

The gang laughed at that one right before I said, "Although this factoid is clumsily worded, it is probably referring to one million dogs that have been provided with an Estate Trust. Hold on, let me do some math for a minute and I can answer this one."

As I was rapidly searching probate statistics and punching some numbers on my calculator App, I could already hear Bob, Jane, Ellie, and Diane discussing the next topic. The clock was ticking, but before they got too far, I was able to announce, "Okay, according to the internet, only 40 percent of Americans (that's about 130 million people) have made a will. Statistically speaking, about 36 million of those people are dog owners. So, if only 3 percent of those owners have set up an Estate Trust for their pet, that would be about one million dogs. It could be true!"

At the tail end of our fact-finding session, Ellie, Jane, Myrtle, and Diane were absorbed with an oft pondered and markedly idiosyncratic interrogative: What is the best dog food? Understandably, humans want the best for their furry kids, but it didn't take long for the group to remember just how overwhelming pet food analysis can become. Indubitably, there isn't a catchall in the pet food department, but that wasn't going to stop this brain brawl from happening. The four o'clock gladiators jockeyed endlessly to be the smartest dog parker to have ever lived, and I was one of them.

Seasoned disputants knew that when considering dog food, they needed vital information such as protein, fat, carbohydrate, and fiber ratios. Quality of ingredients, kibble size, product availability, and price would all have to be deliberated as well. Of course, age, breed type, allergens, weight-loss requirements, and specific health conditions were pondered, too, along with deciding whether wet, dry, or raw food was the optimal choice. I wondered if our dogs appreciated the agony, analysis, and penny-pinching we go through so they have the finest food that engenders a long, healthy life. After all, a longer life means more time to eat wood chips, food wrappers, acorns, and barf.

I tuned in to the tête-à-tête just in time to hear Myrtle say, "Choosing the wrong puppy food, like one that contains too much calcium, could cause permanent bone damage and hip disease for large breeds like my Jambalaya. And she is the largest Great Dane in the entire history of Great Danes."

The next remark was from Ellie, who never listened to Myrtle anyway. She added, "Compared to kibble, the best wet dog foods contain more protein, fewer carbs, and no cancer-causing preservatives. Plus, they're easier to chew, which makes canned foods a smart choice for puppies, smaller dogs, and seniors."

Diane then parried with, "A raw dog food diet has more notable benefits including firmer stools, improved digestion, a healthier skin and coat, reduced allergy symptoms, and better weight management." And I wondered if any of these guys were even listening to each other.

Dog Park Doug, the germophobe in the group, had at least heard this last statement. "Well, you gotta watch out for bacterial contamination. Raw meats are teeming with *Salmonella* and *E. coli!*" he blurted.

"That's true. Although the risk of food-borne disease is low for dogs since their digestive system is shorter and more acidic, it isn't for humans preparing meals," Jane concurred.

Bob then added, "You know, preparing homemade meals for your dog is a wonderful way to bond with them and keep them happy and healthy. However, if you never make a homemade meal for your spouse, she'll notice." As usual, Bob had us rolling on the mulch, laughing out loud. He went on to say, "On the days you do decide to extend this language of love to your spouse, it is highly recommended you prepare an altogether separate meal, and not simply offer her a portion of the daily dog rations."

These discussions never changed anyone's mind, but it sure made us hungry. The dialogue continued into the parking lot as the group left the park. It finally ended as the last car door was shut and the park goers began their respective drives home. The dog food topic was frequently discussed in online forums and social media, and the engineer in me ensured that I spent way too much time researching pet sustenance. Web pages such as the Dog Food Advisor and Consumer Search (great for researching home, tech, and fitness products too) are extremely useful because they categorize and explain nutrition in a professional and relatable manner.

The real trick with excellent pet food is discovering which product isn't cost prohibitive or hard to find, since vets and specialty stores change their stock over time. Many top-rated foods are three to six dollars per pound, while most regular grocery store dog food is less than two dollars per pound. Dogs in the information age benefit from the internet since online stores like Chewy, Amazon, and Dog Food Direct offer promotions and discounts to make top-rated foods more affordable. Because so many dogs I had known lived a long time eating inexpensive grocery store foods, I habitually bought Nitro the four-star, one dollar-a-pound brands I found at my nearest Harris Teeter. Nutro, Rachel Ray, and Iams may not be the BEST, but dogs like them. Besides, let's face it, our little angel babies are already eating slugs, mulch, toads, or poop every chance they get.

Well, thanks to Nitro, we did it again. We restarted the pet sitting business despite a long sabbatical. I knew the need for pet sitting would in no way subside, although Nitro and I did have to spend several weeks reacquainting ourselves to the new members of the various gangs of Godbold. Honestly, this had been the best year for us because it was like reliving glory days. The four o'clock gang, Sunday night dinners, the social media page, and our pet sitting roster had all been restored into our regularly scheduled program. Now if we could only convince the Town of Cary to finally fix that dang muddy mess around the large-dog's water bowl, life would be perfect.

CHAPTER 6

Willpower

"I have found that when you are deeply troubled, there are things you get from the silent devoted companionship of a dog that you can get from no other source." — Doris Day, American actress, singer, and animal welfare activist.

Upon attaining nearly five years of enjoyment at the dog park, I observed the Town of Cary finally make a move to attend to the muddy mess around the large-dog water bowl: they put up a sign. The unavailing notice provided guidance on how to dump muddy water onto the ground, away from the water bowl area. The placard also included instructions on how to temporarily shut off the water while emptying the bowl. Dog park members instantly recognized this "solution" to be an absurd, ludicrous, and insulting sham. There needed to be drain at this location because the dogs mucked up the water bowl too often and in too many ways to render the Town's futile directives a viable solution. Imagine buying a home without a drain in the kitchen sink. Instead, there would be a sign reading, "Empty water into the bathtub or yard, and try not to dirty too many dishes." Everyone ignored the meaningless marker, of course, and the problem continued. The Town's position was that too many owners allowed their dogs to splash in the water bowl. The problem with that hypothesis was that splash-back wasn't the primary cause of the Godbold river. Big dogs muddied the bowl simply by drinking, and many of them dropped dirty tennis balls into the water bowl, too. The other flaw was that the autofill feature sometimes allowed the water to run constantly and overfill the bowl. If you "jiggled" the bowl for a moment, the fill sensor would recognize a full bowl condition and stop the flow of water, but few dog parkers knew to do this.

Despite these problems, most park members understood that the Parks Department had bigger fish to fry. After all, Cary has 100,000 citizens and dozens of parks and miles of medians to maintain while dog park membership consisted of only a few hundred people. Our park didn't even allow children. However, Fredo (Jackie's dad) could not abide the mud-spattering injustice to continue any longer. Fed up and refusing to be ignored, Fredo focused his passion and organized a grassroots effort for dog parkers to meet with Town of Cary representatives in an open forum. Not unlike Socrates grumbling about the youth of Athens, Fredo made speeches, waved hands, and gesticulated interminably until he finally provoked an assembly. I wish I had a nickel for each time Fredo claimed "The squeaky wheel gets the grease!" All four-hundred dog park members were invited to meet with the Town's representatives, but only four showed: Fredo, Flip-Flop John, Jeb, and yours truly. Fredo was disappointed that so few members were in attendance; but the low turnout was probably for the best. Besides, how many people would actually take off work for a weekday afternoon dog park meeting?

The lynchpin topic was the installation of a drain beneath the large-dog water bowl, but Fredo also wanted the Town of Cary to perform spot mulching between the regularly scheduled mulching events in the spring and fall. His request evolved into an interesting (and somewhat heated) discussion about the dog park budget. Fredo alleged that the Town acquired mulch for free since they regularly gathered and shredded tree debris from Cary properties throughout the year. Fredo also pointed out that dog park members pay for their park passes. Therefore, the Town should pay for anything in the world that he desired.

Statler, the Public Works Director, drew attention to the fact that Cary maintains a cost capture system and that mulch isn't provided to the parks for free. The equipment, materials, and labor required to shred, store, transport, and place mulch around town all incurred costs. Moreover, the funds gathered from dog park memberships also had to be applied toward overhead lighting, weekly trash removal, fence maintenance, tree and shrub trimming, administration, and other expenses such as pass cards, lanyards, and poop bags.

Statler went on to clarify that the total annual income from the membership fees was only $32,000, but the Town's operation and maintenance cost for the dog park was $36,000 per year. For some reason, this made Fredo furious and, as he crashed his fist onto the picnic table, he hollered, "That's a bunch of malarkey!" While Jeb and I held Frank back, the sales expert (and brains of our ragtag outfit) Flip-Flop John, took over, and negotiations resumed with more judicious competence.

Waldorf, the Parks and Recreation Manager, acknowledged our concerns and disclosed that additional remedies were in the works for Godbold. The Town already had plans to repair the gaps, leans, and scour around the dog park fence and post foundations. He described how they would remove the bushes on the inside perimeter of the fence, since the roots were heaving the posts and the enclosure itself. They also intended to repair the outer entrance and exit gates, so that they would close and lock properly. As far as the drain that we requested, Waldorf reported they would look into it and get back to us.

Additional considerations were discussed including the installation of Wi-Fi, an extra gazebo, and more benches. Engaging corporate sponsors or facilitating fundraisers for the dog park were both considered as ways to offset costs without raising membership fees. It was agreed that, in the meantime, park members could donate plastic lawn chairs to provide additional seating. Overall, it was a productive meeting, despite Fredo's abrasive outbursts. Afterward, I reported the meeting minutes to the dog park social media page, and member feedback conveyed relief and appreciation that a

NITRO: A DOG'S TALE

communication bridge had finally been established.

Following the park summit (now referred to as "Mulchgate"), Fredo lobbied to complete the legwork to have porta-johns and poop bag dispensers installed around town. However, Fredo had demonstrated a propensity for taking credit from those who had carried out his drudgery. I carefully and considerately remained unavailable to Fredo and his relentless relegating since Nitro and I were content to remain busy with pet sitting. I had become rather adept at evasive maneuvers since there was seldom a shortage of characters to avoid in Godbold.

Shortly in the tracks of Mulchgate, lazy bones Nitro and I were at the park with "Gate Watcher" Misha, who was waiting for Ismail to pick her up following another long weekend at Camp Ewald. As I was watching the pups, "Filibuster Frances" nearly cornered me unawares. Frances was a lawyer and had mastered the art of gabbing without pause or relief. Gathering my wits, I executed a "diatribe and dash" by feigning an incoming call before becoming entangled in one of her unendurable soliloquies. Subsequent to dodging that bullet, I was relieved to see Dave, the real estate agent formerly known as Preacher Dave, enter the park with his dog Sadie. He deliberately (and covertly) avoided Frances so we could meet up in left field to shoot the breeze.

After articulating the 411 on 919 Realty Group, his new real estate business, he asked if I had considered expanding my pet sitting business. I told him that business was so good that Nitro and I had been running around town like our feet were on fire and our drawers were catchin'. Sometimes I envisioned heaps of glimmering gold as excitement flowed like a roaring wind when I considered walking twenty dogs per day to achieve the coveted "six figure pet sitter" milestone. However, I knew this sort of victory might be shorn of gladness without considering a few particulars up front.

I explained to Real Estate Dave that there were diminishing returns associated with hiring extra dog walkers.

Adding a helper to double the number of clients from six to twelve per day would only increase my income by a factor of 1.4. I wouldn't be doubling my salary, since the cost of wages, health insurance, Medicare, social security, unemployment insurance, and workers' compensation would fly right in the face of that expectation. Newly recruited sitters increase liability, responsibility, and risk as well. Worse, hired walkers would sooner or later figure out they could walk the dogs without my agency, and it would be only a matter of time before they stole clients and struck out on their own. This wouldn't necessarily happen with every hire, but it's definitely part of the pet sitter expansion cycle.

Real Estate Dave, undoubtedly wondering if he should have just talked to Frances after all, asked, "What about hiring an independent contractor instead of adding employees?" Real Estate Dave was no dummy, and the employee versus independent contractor (IC) debate has been raging in pet sitting forums across the nation for decades. Determining which are more economically viable is a function of the needs of the business entity and the laws in their state.

I shared that ICs seemed like the way to go, since you don't have to manage their health insurance, Medicare, social security, unemployment insurance, and workers' compensation costs. Unfortunately, it isn't that simple, because the IRS uses a right-to-control test to determine a business's tax liability, and each state has tests to evaluate a person's status under workers' compensation and unemployment insurance laws. Economic realities tests may make it more difficult to classify a worker as an IC because the IRS examines how the worker may be economically dependent upon a business.

Understanding the difference between these two choices begins with the fact that an employee is covered by federal and state employment and labor laws, and they use their social security number on their W-2 forms. Employees earn an hourly rate or salary, and are paid on a regular schedule. An IC is not covered by employment and labor laws (pending right-to-control tests), and they use a taxpayer ID number on their W-9 forms. ICs report payments using Form 1099, and are paid pursuant to contract requirements once an invoice is processed.

Grasping the differences between employees and ICs is all well and good, but I avoided that entire hornet's nest by remaining a one-man band. It didn't matter which expansion scenario was cheaper since they both posed a threat to my peace of mind. Real Estate Dave responded with, "Sounds like you have put some thought into this. You'd rather manage dogs than people. I don't blame you."

Real Estate Dave was right again. A decision to add employees and expand the number of charges per day would not match my original business plan, so were I to decide to hire employees, the original plan would have to be amended. Moreover, expanding a small business to include a business manager for my LLC (so I could actually spend time with the dogs), would also require changes to my Articles of Organization.

The last point I made to Real Estate Dave was that pet sitters who walk six dogs per day do not walk the same six dogs each day. To achieve six dogs per day, you must care for at least fourteen different dogs per week. Growing to the point where you visit thirty pets a day can easily correspond to seventy different households each week. That equals seventy addresses, keys, alarm codes, and owners to manage, not to mention those third-party folks like teenagers, grandmas, and other unfathomable creatures that occupy client homes. Besides, most of my clients wanted their dogs to be with me and Nitro, not with just any dog walker.

It was also true that whether my daily maximum was three or thirty, client demand invariably had a way of exceeding capacity. I was still a long way from mastering the art of saying "no," but one device I used to let them down easy was to offer a list of other established and recommended sitters. The crucial measure was knowing that too many dogs in my charge diluted the quality of service, and dogs always deserve the best.

I enjoyed talking to Real Estate Dave. He was a legitimate listener who offered conscientious advice, and we both subscribed to a "light a candle and don't curse the darkness" attitude, which was useful because Wayne, my arch nemesis, had just entered the park.

"How many ya got today?" Wayne called out.

"Two hundred and seventy-six," I called back, citing the total number of people who had ever asked me to pet sit.

Wayne laughed out loud (having no idea that at least sixty-four of that number had been redirected to him). Wayne's big news today was that he had finally launched his own website. "Outstanding!" said I, "it restores my faith in humanity when old timers embrace the internet."

Wayne just kind of shook his head at that and remarked, "Well, those web hosts have made it so easy that anyone can do it. I gathered sound designs by looking at numerous competitors' websites. Speaking of which, have you noticed how many sitters carry a dozen or more emblems for pet organizations? Surely, you aren't one of those egomaniacs?"

"Well, I am," I answered, "but I only have two emblems displayed. One for the NAPPS organization and one from Pet Tech first aid trainers." I knew what he was talking about because some pet sitter sites boast badges from every pet sitting organization in existence, even though you only need one membership to obtain insurance. Pet sitters may also display crests from the chamber of commerce, the Better Business Bureau, the SPCA, the Humane Society, and anyone else that will take their money (each badge costs about $100 per year).

"Right. Why would anyone spend so much money on unnecessary memberships? It reminds me of those vainglorious email signatures I've seen," Wayne remarked.

"It does seem that way since that business development strategy impresses conceit to you and me. But it's an effective way to improve their visibility within online search results since pet sitters cannot know which organization or search engine a pet owner might use," I pointed out.

"Hmm, I didn't really think of it that way. What about the whole hullabaloo on overnights? Do you advertise overnights on your site?" Wayne asked.

"No, because there's a law that states that if you charge people money to keep their dogs or cats at your house, you must register with the North Carolina Department of Agriculture as a kennel facility. If I did that, the Town of Cary would probably shut me down," I explained.

"I hear you. But what about all those people on the Rover and Care websites? They advertise overnights online. Doesn't the Department of Agriculture enforce the rules with them?"

"Apparently not, because there are tens of thousands of people in North Carolina on Rover and Care who do occasional overnights for pets. It's essentially an unenforceable law because there aren't enough agents to inspect all those part-time pet sitters," I surmised.

"It's a dumb law. Why don't they just allow people to pet sit for their neighbors? Can't they distinguish the difference between a sleepover and a kennel?"

"I agree," began my diatribe, "but I think the law is in place to prevent folks from taking in forty or more pets and then stacking them in crates in a garage. Locations like that operate beyond the fringe of ethical practice, and had they been inspected by the Department of Agriculture, those animals wouldn't be at risk. But you're right, they don't draw a line between reasonable and responsible pet sitters and kennels. Instead of an honor system, they've made the law 'one size fits all.' I'm sure animal control receives complaints when a resident is keeping dozens of dogs in their yard. There are already laws regarding noise, poo pickup, leashes, and dangerous dogs. If the kennel rule doesn't get you, one of those will."

This was a great topic to discuss since this was the primary reason a number of potential pet sitters I knew didn't follow through to become full-time in-home sitters (that and the pee-stained carpets, smudgy cars, hairy sofas, and shredded pillows). In-home sitting was also a greatly contested topic in online pet sitting forums because, depending on where you operated your business, it was commonly illegal to "run a kennel out of your house."

Most professional pet sitters did not like the unprofessional part-timers they heard about on the Rover and Care networks. Although those networks serve to facilitate a connection with established and recommended pet sitters, they are also a place where tire-kickers or other types of noncommitted sitters could be looking to make money. I didn't get too worked up over all of this, however. Sure, there were teenagers in my neighborhood who "stole" business from me but they were only temporary pet sitters and I was constantly booked anyway.

Wayne wrapped things up by saying, "Well, at least I'm respecting the spirit of the law. That's good enough for me."

One day, in late February, I arrived for the four o'clock dog show a little earlier than usual. Ellie was there with Rosie, but no one else we knew had arrived yet. Ellie opened with, "So, how's it going with your daily menagerie of pets?"

"Overall, it's going swell," I declared. "I mean, it's totally just a bunch of monkey business, but in the wake of twenty years in the rat race, it feels wonderful to be appreciated."

"Good for you," Ellie replied, "but I bet you still have headaches. Work is work."

I smirked at that and then admitted, "Sometimes. I mean, I've got a ton of client's keys on my key chain, and I receive at least twenty robo-calls per day. Once you register a business, your phone and email are all out there. It can get annoying."

"But don't you get tired of giving all those dogs a bath each day?" Ellie asked.

"Oh no. I just keep a few towels in my car, and dirty dogs mostly dry off from all that running around. Don't get me wrong, my windows are completely besmirched with nose prints and hair is everywhere, but I don't bathe them. There's really no need, or time!"

"I don't know how you do it. It would drive me crazy," Ellie confessed.

Little did Ellie know; I was already crazy. I knew what she meant though. From time to time, I would fall into moods that could conceivably be described as burnout. I wondered how long I could handle being a full-time pet sitter. Also, the dynamic of the park community had noticeably changed since 2010 as people moved away or stopped coming to the park for other reasons. The most common reason was that many older dogs outgrew the park. Other people gradually lost their tolerance for a muddy and poopy park, or they adopted a second dog so they could make their own yard muddy and poopy. I also knew that several former members signed on with Camp Bow Wow or other doggie day cares in town. The members who left were replaced by hundreds of new members, but my operation was at capacity, so I was no longer hungry for new charges like I had been a few years ago.

The other casualty of time proved to be the charm of managing the dog park social media page. Influenced by five years of mundane questions, complaints, or other frustrating exchanges, I regularly became afflicted with Admin fatigue. An example of this followed a rash of vehicle break-ins in the Godbold parking lot. This was nothing new and, unfortunately, these crimes of opportunity occur frequently in Cary, particularly in the parks where people leave their car completely out of sight.

Parkgoers who chose to leave valuables in their car (to prevent destruction by the dogs) suffered burglaries and broken windows in broad daylight. Over time, longtime park regulars learned not to leave valuables in their cars; but we also noticed that when a car break-in wave began, it persisted for weeks regardless of our efforts to raise awareness. Dog parkers talked about each new break-in, online and in person, daily. Cary police knew about the problem, but even when they camped out in the Godbold parking lot, another vehicle break-in would happen the minute they left.

The frustration for me, as I watched all this unfold, was that in one week, for four days in a row (a new record), group members posted their break-in stories on the dog park social media page. Clearly, group members liked *posting* to the page, but weren't big on *reading* the page. I needed to remember, however, there were only three hundred social media members, and obviously, only a scant few checked the news feed. Furthermore, there were at least six-hundred dog park members and an unknown number (probably thousands) of citizens who visited the skate park, basketball courts, and the tennis courts daily. Evidently, I was naive to believe that social media could ever make gains toward solving a crime problem.

Despite my feelings that the group page wasn't effective at doing the job Kelley and I had originally intended, I stayed on as Admin; but knew it wouldn't be for much longer. In the meantime, I enjoyed the dog memes and optimistically looked forward to posting a positive update to Mulchgate in the near future.

Then, toward the end of March, when I was enjoying a boisterous and bloomy spring day in the dog park with Nitro and friends, I received a call from Debra (Mom's caretaker in Key West). Debra reported that Mom had to be medevaced from Key West to Miami for emergency surgery. Debra didn't have a complete diagnosis, but she and I both strongly suspected a recurrence of cancer. It had been sixteen months since Mom had been given the all-clear from Dr. Lawrence regarding her breast cancer. I canceled my charges, loaded up my CR-V, and leashed up ol' Nitro to join me on the marathon drive down to Florida.

Following a day of driving and a night of rest at Mom's house, I arranged for Mom's neighbor Robby to check in on Nitro while I traveled to the hospital in Miami. The Miami hospital, about two hours from Key West, was easy to find. The difficult part about this visit was receiving the news from her doctor: Mom had aggressive bladder cancer that necessitated chemotherapy and additional surgery (he had removed a mass from her bladder already). When I went to visit my crabby and agitated mother, she demanded that we bust her out of the hospital right away. I didn't like that idea, but it was her choice to make. Just like it was her choice to tell her doctor, the nurses, and anyone else we ran into, to go pound sand as I wheeled her out of the institution.

The drive home to Key West was somewhat awkward while we made small talk and avoided discussing what was on both of our minds. This wasn't my first rodeo however, and I knew that once Mom had time to cool off and recharge at home, she would be able to tackle treatment talk.

Nitro was delighted to see us reappear in his Key West house, and by the end of the second day we had settled into a routine with Debra, Gretna, and daily visitors. Mom then decided she would consider treatment options. She agreed to see an oncologist, but it wouldn't be Dr. Lawrence since she needed chemotherapy and he was a biotherapy specialist. We met instead with Dr. Morley at the Key West Chemotherapy Center on Roosevelt Boulevard. Dr. Morley was energetic, positive, and friendly, but he had his work cut out for him because skeptical Nikki did not rightly wish to be there. Dr. Morley's leading point was that she would receive a booster of vitamins and supplements to alleviate the usual side effects of chemotherapy. Mom suspected this was a heap of hogwash but begrudgingly agreed to begin a chemotherapy regimen anyway.

It did not go well at all. The night subsequent to her first chemo infusion found her in a sedated zombielike state. Debra and I weren't sure what to do. Mom was conscious, but unresponsive. We had expected fatigue as a side effect of the chemo, but this was distressing and something Debra had never seen. After an hour, Debra and I took Mom to the hospital as a preventive measure. While at the hospital I called Aunt Edie (Mom's sister) with a status update. Edie wasn't sure what to make of the excessive weariness I described, but she did enlighten me about one fact: Mom had gone for a checkup five months prior, and the oncology center had reported that Mom's cancer markers were up. They had recommended she make an appointment for a CT scan, but according to Edie, Mom's response to this was, "Screw them!"

Near to three nights in the hospital, Mom arrived home again having recovered from her chemo-zombie trip. A few days later, we met with Dr. Morley to discuss what happened. Mom did not bandy words as this unpleasant encounter began. She told Dr. Morley that she did not trust him and would never have chemotherapy again. Dr. Morley insisted that she continue chemotherapy or the malignancy could eventually lead to kidney failure. I will never forget the resolve displayed by my mother at that moment when she told him, "I don't believe you."

After Mom gave Dr. Morley a piece of her mind, we spent the next few weeks managing as best we could while Debra, Gretna, and Nitro helped out. Mom was still awfully frail and struggled with mobility issues. She was also plagued by anxiety, and despite numerous attempts by the caretaking team, we could not ameliorate her fits of nervousness. Debra suggested an antianxiety medication, but Mom adamantly refused. Mom had unremittingly been anti-medication, and the chemo debacle only steeled her resolve on the matter. The only medications I had known her to take (aside from gin and tonics) were the biotherapy pills she took in 2013. Mom's conviction was that prescriptions begat side effects which only led to more scrips. The irony, of course, was that her refusal to reduce her anxiety compounded the strain on everyone. I had expected we would be in the "just keep her comfortable" phase by this point, but, like so many platitudes, that was easier said than done. At least things couldn't get any worse.

Until they did.

In early May, Aunt Carol (Dad's sister in Charlotte) called me to convey that my dad had been admitted to the Wake Med hospital in Cary. My response was, "Wait. Why? What?"

"He isn't able to keep anything down. He is also suffering from fatigue and, well, the concern now is that it may be heart failure," Carol reported.

"This doesn't sound right. Did you know anything? Had

he mentioned anything?"

"He has been seeing a cardiologist, but I just assumed things were going okay."

"What, what does this mean?" I was not processing this very well at all.

"They are doing tests now, and I'm going up there tomorrow. I will update you as soon as I know anything." And then Carol added, "I think you should probably come back to Cary, too."

"I'll let Mom know and will get back there in the next couple of days," I offered.

"Okay. Can you call Doug?" Carol asked.

"Yes. I'll let him know what's going on."

"Okay."

The story was rather vague, but Billdad preferred it that way. Mr. Top Secret Security Clearance invariably kept his cards close to his chest. In fact, whenever Dad went to New Jersey to "work on his sailboat," Brother Doug would point out that another Al-Qaeda VIP had been assassinated. We knew Dad was too old to be a clandestine operative, but Doug's levity precisely conveyed the mystery surrounding our father. If he were experiencing critical heart failure, we wouldn't know anything about it until he was on his deathbed. Even then, he would just tell us, "I'm fine. Everything is fine. Now get back to work."

After speaking to Aunt Carol, I told Mom the news. She began to cry. Nitro went over to her and rested his muzzle on her knee. She then began to sob uncontrollably. "Oh, Nitro," she began. A few minutes passed, then Mom wiped her eyes, looked at me, and said, "You should go and see your father."

"Okay Mom, I'll get back as soon as I can," I promised.

As Nitro and I endured the epic drive back to North Carolina, I had plenty of time to make calls and catch up with a few folks. The key player I needed to reach out to was Brother Doug. He wasn't completely sure what Billdad's prognosis was (none of us were, really), but he reported that he was heading to Cary as soon as possible. I also reached out to Aunt Lise (pronounced Lee-ZUH), and she revealed that she would fly down from Vermont in the next day or two. Lise, a librarian at Norwich University in Northfield, Vermont, is Dad's youngest sister and only eight years older than I am. We have a long history of talking things over, and calls to Aunt Lise seldom lasted less than one hour.

One person I did NOT call on this trip (or any other) was my wicked stepmother Leslie, whom I had not talked to since she and Dad divorced in 2007. I never had a glowing rapport with her since, to put it graciously, we didn't have good chemistry. The bad chemistry probably began when she sold my belongings that I was unable to take with me when I started college at Appalachian State University. That was in 1987, the same year Dad and Leslie were married. Another disharmonious moment was the day she told me that Fang (my seven-year-old black lab and the first dog I ever had) mysteriously "ran away" about a year into my college career. Over the years I struggled to get along with Leslie as best I could, but it just never panned out for us.

Leslie was Dad's second (and last) wife. After Billdad and Mom divorced in 1980, Dad moved to North Carolina to accept a teaching position at Wallace O'Neal Day School in Southern Pines. This worked for him on two fronts since Southern Pines is near Fort Bragg, where he also served as an Army reservist for many years. I went to live with him and the rationale for this was that teachers' offspring were not required to pay tuition at this respectable private school. One weekend a month I would fly as an "unaccompanied minor" from Fayetteville, the closest commercial airport to Southern Pines, to National airport in DC, which was only a few Metro rail stops from Mom's house in Bethesda, Maryland. I also spent summers with Mom, and this custody arrangement lasted from seventh grade until I graduated from high school.

However, I attended O'Neal for only two years and then transferred to Pinecrest High School (also in Southern Pines) in the ninth grade. Likewise, Dad only taught at O'Neal for those two years I was in junior high. In 1982, Dad began working for the Environmental Protection Agency in Research Triangle Park, and thanks to the Ewald driving gene, he didn't seem to mind commuting forty-five minutes to work each day.

After I graduated from high school, Dad married Leslie and they started a new family straight away and moved into a house they had built in Apex, North Carolina in 1988. He finally retired from the EPA (and the Army Reserve) in 2006, and about a year into retirement, he divorced Leslie. In the middle of 2007, he rented an apartment in Apex so he had somewhere to sleep following a daily pattern of visiting my house, defragging my computer, and eating all my food.

Succeeding the long ride back to Cary with Nitro, I arranged to meet with Aunt Carol and Aunt Lise before visiting Dad in the hospital. We met for breakfast at the IHOP on Kildaire Farm Road, just a couple of miles from the health center.

"Did you know anything about his health condition?" Carol began.

"No," I responded, "but I have seen that he becomes winded easily. When he visited Key West, and this was just a year and a half ago, we went for a walk, but he couldn't make it to Duval Street, which was only five blocks away."

"I knew he was working on a program with his cardiologist," Lise offered, "but I wasn't aware of the details."

"None of us were," Carol pointed out. "I thought he was doing okay."

"It's not like Mr. Security Clearance would tell us anything," I quipped.

"I know," Lise confirmed. "He better not really be in trouble."

After struggling with all the uncertainty, and a few ginormous piles of pancakes, we wrestled in vain to fasten the lids on our to-go cups of coffee. Then, while Carol and Lise argued (they each insisted on paying the bill), I texted Brother Doug to let him know we were on the way to the hospital. He responded that he was also on the way, and upon our arrival, we found Brother Doug in the hospital parking lot and we all entered Dad's room together.

Dad was awake and in an inviting mood, despite appearing fatigued and underweight. Never one to waste time with small talk, Billdad promptly and plainly stated that his heart was failing and there was nothing the doctors could do. In the wake of the shockwave of this unexpected news, all four of us began to offer sympathies, ask questions, or blurt out a few choice profanities simultaneously. Dad raised his arms to shush the cacophony of our incredulous outcries, and then calmly said, "There's nothing that can be done. I've come to terms with this. Why don't you just sit down."

We sat down. Brother Doug was visibly upset. Lise appeared calm but concerned. Life had interminably been one "What the hell?" moment after the next, so I'm pretty sure I was wearing my "What the hell?" face. Carol was pissed, and I imagined her thinking: "Doctors are chowderheads. How do we ever abide the incoherent rambling of those sots?"

Dad described how he and his cardiologist had been working on a program during the last few years, but he simply had not reached the goals that he needed to. None of us were happy to hear this, but the remarkable fact was just how calm and collected Dad remained. He went on to say that he had informed the Connecticut Cousins (George, Henry, and Ginny) and they would be visiting soon. I wasn't particularly close with the Connecticut crowd, but Dad had visited them often during summers and holidays while he was growing up. George, Henry, and Ginny are the children of my great-Aunt Floss (Grandad Ewald's sister's given name was Florence).

Brother Doug and my aunts went to visit Dad each day for the next several days, sometimes at different times, but Brother Doug and I usually stopped in together. One time I brought Nitro in to visit, and Dad really enjoyed seeing him. There were some highs and lows during that week, but overall, I had to hand it to ol' Billdad as he maintained great poise with the many visitors he received. He was not typically a talkative man, but he was the ringleader that week as he recounted funny stories about the old days, particularly when the Connecticut Cousins were present. Dad shared the details of his numerous misadventures (usually involving motorcycles, trespassing, and a lot of drinking) with those New England kids back in the 1950s.

One day, after several riveting and unbelievable tales of Dad's youth, the Connecticut Cousins went back to their hotel, and as Brother Doug and I were about to leave, Dad motioned that he needed to speak to me alone. I suspected that he needed to talk about his will, which he had prepared at least ten years ago. I had both my parent's (separate) wills filed somewhere in an archived file box since I hadn't expected to look at them for at least two more decades. He reminded me that I was designated as the sole executor of his estate, and he proceeded to convey pertinent instructions on how to take care of his apartment, accounts, and property. The pragmatic portion of this discussion was brief since he only owned a truck and two boats. He had saved most of his energy, however, to discuss two important people: his ex-wives.

First, he diplomatically and considerately recommended that I bury the hatchet with the old battle-axe (wicked Leslie) during the probate process. He knew Leslie and I hadn't spoken in years, and he wanted me to keep the past in the past as I was about to become the gatekeeper for his pensions and life insurance. I assured him I would do so, and then he added, "I know you will. I also know that no truce with Leslie lasts very long, so hopefully it will take less than a few months to administer paperwork for her."

He next told me that I should resume caretaking duties with Mom. He knew he didn't have much time left and there wasn't anything I could do for him, but Nikki needed her son to help her in Key West. Finally, he requested that I take his ashes to Button Bay, Vermont, to perform a water casting in Lake Champlain (where he and Mom would go for summer picnics during the Middlebury College years). I loved hearing that story and pledged that I would take care of that. We went over a few other items, like how to find his sailboat in New Jersey and other such details before I said the last thing I would ever say to my dad: "I love you Dad."

I had a lot to think about as I traveled to Key West again with Nitro. This year was not getting any easier. Mom had been "terminal" for two years now, and I wondered what was going to happen next. Sometimes I questioned whether doctors really knew anything at all. I turned to look in the back seat at Nitro. Maybe he had answers. Nitro just looked at me with adoring eyes. He didn't understand medicine or English, but he knew what loyalty and love were and that actions speak louder than words. All things considered; Nitro's presence served as the best remedy anyway.

Nitro was an excellent passenger and navigator. He slept on the back seat since he was too big to fit in the front seat comfortably. The back bench bestowed ample room to stretch out, and he wouldn't stir unless he sensed the car slowing down or perhaps heard the crinkling of a bag of plantain chips. This was the third era of painful uncertainty I had undergone with Nitro. The consolation and ardor embodied by his company was undeniably transcendent. During that long drive in the middle of May 2015, I experienced an epiphany. I suppose it may have been a caffeine overdose, or too much MSG from those gas station eggrolls, but I was overwhelmed by the notion that "A dog is a man's best friend" would never again be just a cliché for me.

Although we arrived late in the evening, Mom was awake and greeted Nitro from her super recliner in the living room. She was so happy to see us again and could not wait to give Nitro a couple of cookies for being a good boy. Debra was there, too, and after Nitro checked her for treats, he followed me up to our room so we could rest from our grueling journey. It did not take long for the Sandman to knock us out as the window-mounted air conditioner droned and drowned out the sounds of inebriated tourists in the streets below. My mind swiftly cruised into slumber as the phantom traffic lines rushed over the backs of my eyelids.

The next morning, I corralled Nitro outside for a few minutes, then sat down and told Mom about Dad's diagnosis. She was saddened by the news and told me, "Your dad was an impossible husband, but he is an honorable man and a father who loves you very much." Later that morning, Mom and Dad talked on their flip phones for at least an hour. It was reassuring to know they were there for each other at the end, after all this time.

As Mom concluded the call, I wandered back into the living room. "Your dad and I had a nice talk," she announced.

"Good," I uttered, "did he make fun of Obama?"

Mom laughed and answered, "No, wise-guy, we talked about what matters most: love and family. Despite our disagreements, we did the best we could as parents."

"I know you did, Mom. You guys were always there for me. Dad was always yelling, but he was there."

Mom smiled. "He was not easy to live with, but he was proud of you."

"Thanks to you, I always knew that. Thanks, Mom. For everything."

We sat in silence for a little while. I assumed Mom was reminiscing about the Middlebury days, while I thought about the early years of my life. Back then, Mom and Dad were happy together and I cherished numerous fond memories with family, friends, and neighbors. I remembered our Bethesda neighborhood and what a safe haven it was, and all those trips to Massachusetts and New Jersey during the holidays to visit my aunts and grandparents. As a forty-six-year-old who had suffered many fools and seen the unkindness humans do to others (and to themselves), I was especially grateful to Mom and Dad for the numerous blessings I had growing up. Perhaps we didn't have a normal life, but by now I realized there was no such thing. There's just life.

During the silence, Nitro continued to hold the world

down. He was snoring quietly as he basked in the sunbeam that landed in the middle of the living room floor around this time of the morning. The quiet was broken as the Key West Conch Tour trolley crawled by and its loudspeaker bellowed: "In Key West, conchs are people born in Key West. You're not considered a conch by simply living in Key West; but if you've been a local for at least seven years, you may be considered a 'freshwater conch' in some circles."

Mom and I looked at each other and smiled. Despite the circumstances, at least I was able to be here. The caregiving program this time around was a little different from how events unfolded in 2013. Aside from having only Debra or Gretna come over for the twelve-hour night shift, the main difference was that Mom did not continue with any cancer treatment. She did, however, host her favorite visitors, like Carol and Fran, or Tom Luna, Dennis, and some others. Aside from a couple of visits each week by Linda, her physical therapist, Mom cared to do little else.

Gradually, the anxiety she experienced accumulated into upsurges of fear. These incidents became so woeful, we usually ended up in the emergency room to have her looked over. Each time, the emergency room doctor told her she was experiencing high blood pressure and a panic attack. Her bladder cancer was still a threat, of course, but it was her "mind playing tricks" that caused the bouts of distress. Noting a pattern in the episodes of anxiety, Debra deduced that Mom subconsciously wanted to go to the hospital because they used Ativan in the IV during those visits. Debra, knowing that Nikki loathed prescriptions, astutely pointed out that Mom was essentially already prescribing herself Ativan. We then made an appointment to see Mom's primary care physician, Dr. Molliver, who promptly wrote her a scrip for lorazepam, which worked immediately and kept her even-keeled and comfortable.

In the early afternoon of May 22, 2015, while walking with Nitro in Old Town Key West, my phone rang and Aunt Carol's number displayed on the caller ID.

I took a deep breath and answered, "Hello?"

"Eric," Carol began, "your dad just passed away." I stopped walking for a moment.

"Were you able to be there with him?" I asked.

"Yes. Yes, Lise and I were there. He went to sleep and, and he went peacefully."

"I'll drive back tomorrow. I love you."

"Love you too. We can talk about the details when you get here."

After we hung up, I walked around Mom's neighborhood for a while as ol' Billdad sailed over an ocean of fond memories in my mind.

When Nitro and I returned to Mom's house, I shared the bad news and Mom started to cry. Overwhelmed with the weight and sadness of the situation, all I could muster was, "One of Dad's last requests was to spread his ashes over the water in Button Bay."

This made Mom burst into a passion of weeping. Nitro went over to console her, and during a minute of pats, she whispered, "Good boy, Nitro." Several minutes passed before we talked about what I needed to do as far as making arrangements in Apex. We then spoke for a long time about Dad, his parents, and his sisters, and we shared a great many pleasant memories. It was heartening to process my grief in person with Mom that afternoon while Nitro comforted us both. After a while, I assured Mom that once arrangements were settled in North Carolina, I would return again to Key West. Early the next morning, Nitro and I climbed into the CR-V for the long trek back to Cary.

Aunt Carol was a huge help once I was back in North Carolina. She wasn't an estate attorney, but lawyers network well, and her advocacy facilitated efficiency. Carol was by my side as I managed responsibilities at the funeral home; and she then pointed me in the right direction regarding the probate process in the Wake County Courts. I developed a plan of action; my first duties were to arrange a memorial, reconcile Dad's properties and accounts, and clear out his apartment.

Going through Dad's apartment was physically and emotionally exhausting. One striking memory from that three-week process was the discovery that Dad had kept a number of drawings and other creations that his children made for him over the years. It revealed a sensitive side to the grouchy, nose-to-the-grindstone, and serious dad we had known. He even kept a lumpy, lopsided, and otherwise poorly crafted pencil holder I made for him out of clay in the seventh grade. It was as big as a grapefruit, but only held one pencil! Good ol' Dad.

About two weeks after he passed, we held a memorial at Saint Paul's Episcopal Church in Cary. As it was determined that I would assume the style of eulogy speaker, I crafted a speech remembering Dad as a devoted parent, a career military man, and a lifetime biologist. I also shared that although he was sullen and stern, he had a twisted sense of humor that we appreciated and enjoyed on those rare occasions he chose to be offbeat. He wasn't a paragon of patience, but he was a parent who improved with age, and when he did share his wisdom, it disclosed intelligence delivered with an equal measure of eloquence.

Once the funeral home, clerk of court, memorial service, and apartment were settled, I was prepared to go back to Key West. I still needed to sell Dad's pickup truck, Zodiac boat and trailer, and that confounded sailboat he kept in New Jersey; but they would have to wait. It was early July when Nitro and I completed our third ambitious drive of the year to Key West to assist with the ongoing mom situation. Debra and Gretna sustained their night shifts while Mom's health, unfortunately, continued to decline.

Around the time of Mom's sixty-ninth birthday, on July 17, we began to notice the lorazepam was no longer keeping her at ease. We immediately made a walk-in visit to her primary care physician, Dr. Molliver, and he wrote out a prescription for OxyContin. The new pills seemed to work, but within a couple of weeks, Gretna said to me, "We should have Nikki speak to a hospice doctor. They are excellent at what they do, and her current prescriptions won't be adequate for long."

I knew this wasn't going to go over well, but Gretna was right, and Debra concurred. Mom had grown to trust her caretakers and loved them as friends. They were both superstar caregivers for their outstanding bedside manner, but they also had the moxie and smarts to deal with Nikki's fussiness. Mom deemed submission to hospice care an admission of defeat that only happened to *other* people.

Sure enough, Mom dug in and fought the notion with her enduring Gibraltar will. However, just like with the biotherapy, the antianxiety meds, the microwave, and a number of other necessities, Debra and Gretna persuaded Mom to have the palliative care physician visit her at home. They elucidated that palliative care and hospice workers both provide assistance in coordinating care that involves symptom relief and emotional, spiritual, and financial support for the patient and their family. Any patients who have a serious, long-term illness are eligible for palliative or hospice care. The primary distinction is that hospice eligibility begins when a doctor has determined that a patient has less than six months to live and the patient has stopped curative or life-prolonging treatments.

Dr. Appleton from the palliative care team proved to be remarkable. He was the first doctor who spoke to Mom candidly while he remaining empathetic regarding her decision not to receive chemotherapy or additional procedures. He convincingly conveyed that Mom's stage IV breast cancer diagnosis from 2013 was a terminal condition. Then, acknowledging that she had done everything she could, he tenderly articulated that the cancer had developed to the point where it was going to end her life. With a quiet air of mastery, he offered to help her pass with dignity and comfort.

Impressed by his manner and honesty, my ornery and obstinate mother agreed to have the palliative care team assist from that day forward. Although Mom sardonically referred to Dr. Appleton as "Dr. Death," his timing and delivery were impeccable. Mom had been tired of fighting ever since the chemo-zombie disaster and she also felt that her previous doctors had never been completely truthful throughout the nebulous era of her cancer treatment. Of course, no one could have foreseen her fate, but Dr. Appleton was definitely the only one who had tendered a straightforward assessment.

Right before the morphine-dosing stage began, Mom sat me down for a talk. She admitted that she had been clinically depressed since stepdad Bill passed away in 2010. She shed light on how she had refused to talk to anyone about managing her grief, and she shared how sorry she was for disrupting my life. She then suggested I return home to North Carolina so I could manage my business and the remaining probate dealings for Dad. I told Mom that she had nothing to be sorry about. Those decisions had been hers to make and her only son was happy to help during this difficult time. We continued our heart-to-heart discussion and ultimately agreed that I would go to North Carolina for a month or so. On the evening of my forty-sixth birthday in July of 2015, I spoke the last words I would ever say to my mother: "I love you Mom."

On the drive back to North Carolina, I remember wondering if depression can actually *cause* cancer. Whether that is physiologically possible or not, I cannot say, but the lesson I derived was that severe depression is no joke. These thoughts evoked the feelings of depression I experienced in 2010, subsequent to losing my job and sense of purpose. I didn't talk to a psychologist about matters at the time, but I had Mom, friends, Nitro, and other family members to talk to, especially Aunt Lise. Aunt Carol had always served as the "family lawyer," but I considered Aunt Lise to be the "family therapist." I called Lise during the drive, and we spoke at length about illness, hospice, loss, and grief. I conveyed to her how shaken and sad I had felt when Mom first developed cancer. I shared that I didn't entirely feel that way any longer. After speaking to Mom recently, and knowing the decisions she had made, and piling on two years of hindsight, I felt oddly at peace. Lise explained, "You've taken a step toward acceptance, but don't be surprised if your feelings change again. Emotions are complicated."

Once we were back in Cary, Nitro and I spent most of our first day back on the couch recharging. Soon enough, however, duty called, and I began figuring out what to do with the thirty-foot sailboat in New Jersey. Nitro and I traveled to Perth Amboy and spent a couple of days cleaning the sailboat and taking photos to use in an online ad. Upon researching values, logistics, and a number of options, I decided it was most cost effective to donate the sailboat to a national organization called Works for Life. This not only promoted a worthy cause but also ensured that this visit to north Jersey could be my last, since the charity organization manages the mobilization effort for donations.

At the close of the New Jersey sojourn, Nitro and I returned to Cary and, although pet sitting was still on hold, I took Nitro to the park right away since he missed all his friends. One conversation led to another and Bobbie and Morgan (Gretta and Gwenn's owners) made an offer to buy Dad's Ford pickup truck. In the ensuing week, I facilitated an exchange where Brother Doug agreed to take ownership of the Zodiac boat and trailer.

The only task that remained for Dad's estate was to schedule the water casting on Lake Champlain. I made arrangements with the funeral home in Apex to have Dad's cremated remains placed in a special container for water casting. Interestingly, these objects are provided in shapes such as seashells, turtles, seahorses, and a number of other (biodegradable) seaborne creatures. I chose the turtle because Dad liked armor, taking things slowly, and snapping at people. Then I let Dad's sisters, wicked Leslie, and my half-siblings know that I would target a weekend during the following summer to perform the ceremony since I wasn't up for an additional thousand-mile drive this year. Besides, September was approaching, and by the time we aligned schedules, Button

Bay would be frozen. Dad would not approve if our last memory was a stranded turtle on the ice over Lake Champlain.

Speaking of thousand-mile drives; on September 2, 2015, Nitro and I were finally on the way to Key West again when Debra called. I clicked on the receiver icon and answered: "Debra?"

"I'm so sorry Eric, Nikki passed away at 4:02 p.m. today," Debra pronounced.

It's amazing how many emotions one can experience in a single moment. Aunt Lise was right. I was sad again, despite expecting (one day) to hear this news. I was also relieved that Mom no longer suffered from the pain and anxiety instigated by her illness. I was mad, too. Mad at her doctors, and mad that I couldn't fix what ailed her. I was sorry I wasn't there yet. I felt guilty and regretful and powerless. As I shoved all these reactions away, I responded, "Nitro and I probably won't arrive until midnight. Do you need me to call the funeral home?"

"No, Eric, just focus on the drive. We will take care of everything here," Debra answered.

"Okay. Thank you, Debra. Thank you for taking care of Mom."

"You're welcome. Give Nitro a pat for me, and we'll talk again soon."

Those remaining hours of travel along the southern Florida highways were replete with a lifetime of memories with Mom and Dad. I attempted to alleviate the profound loss by assuring myself they would eternally be with me. Mom and Dad formed the foundation of who I am and had provided the lessons and tools to cultivate an honorable person who knew right from wrong.

While these thoughts were doing exactly nothing to allay my grief, I noticed Nitro in the rear-view mirror. He was sitting up and looking intently at me. He tried to put his paw on my shoulder, but had a hard time balancing in the car. He then put his little snout on my shoulder. Say what you will about the intelligence of dogs, but when you experience a moment that exhibits the epitome of empathy such as this, it's nothing short of priceless.

It took about two months to go through Mom's house. During the first two weeks, stepdad Bill's daughter (stepsister Stacey) visited from Virginia to help me sort through the prodigious number of clothes, files, and other belongings that Mom had never removed since he had passed. I had known Stacey since 1980, and we consistently got on well. She is two years older than I am, enjoys sports (especially tennis), and became a tax lawyer, just like her father. Working together provided mutual support and tremendous relief as we gathered keepsakes such as photos, travel journals, books, and other special items that we knew had meant a lot to Mom and stepdad Bill. We then donated most of their books and clothes before I held an estate sale to take care of the remaining items including furniture, artwork, kitchenware, tools, and, well, everything else. An estate sale will even reconcile sundry items such as light bulbs, sponges, paper towels, soap dispensers, and every last item you decide to leave behind.

Florida is a little different from North Carolina on the probate front. Florida requires executors to hire an attorney to manage all the paperwork associated with an estate. That was a big time-saver for me, and I used the extra hours to prepare a considerate memorial for Mom and stepdad Bill at the Lopez Funeral home on Simonton Street in Key West. Mom had never held a memorial for Bill, she just couldn't bring herself to do it. Stacey helped with the memorial as well, and we experienced several hours of bittersweet nostalgia as we looked through photos of Mom and stepdad Bill from the 1940s through the 1980s. We scanned a portion of these and posted printed copies of our favorites to display on easels at the memorial.

A few weeks after the memorial I chartered a boat so Stacey, along with stepsister Leslie and stepdad Bill's grandson, Tee Jay, could participate in a water casting for Mom and stepdad Bill. Leslie (not to be confused with my wicked stepmother

Leslie) was stepdad Bill's oldest daughter and Stacey's half-sister. I had the remains for Mom and stepdad Bill placed in a sky-blue seashell, and we motored a few miles out from the Atlantic (south) shore of Key West so they could embark on their final sea voyage together.

By the beginning of November, my work in Key West was complete and Nitro and I made our fourth, and final, trip back to Cary. I looked forward to the splendor of pet sitting, my cozy dog house, and life around our favorite dog park. It took only a few weeks to resume my role as a part-time pet sitter. A fully burdened schedule wasn't prudent since I still had probate work to complete. Besides, several elements had amassed during the year. These included the realizations that part-time sitting was more sustainable and that I no longer felt the need to be the greatest pet sitter in the universe. Wayne, of course, was elated that I decided to reduce my number of charges each week and was happy to steal several of my clients (again).

Another key cognizance was that I needed time to process losing Mom and Dad. I had been so busy with files, articles, and effects, that I now required some breathing room. The last straw, however, was when I received a call from the Town of Cary resulting from a dog park member who had reported me for having more than two dogs in the park. This felt like a kick in the pants, but then again, rules are rules. I didn't need to bring five dogs to the park anyway since I had my backyard and my reputation among those who mattered was still intact. Although I remember feeling "betrayed," it was probably one of those folks who go to the park once, complain, and then never go back again. Even so, the two-dog rule tattling and the changes in the dog park membership community completely aligned with my new vision for EPS to be a part-time endeavor. I also finally resigned as Admin from the dog park social media page.

Prompted by this arduous year of stress and heartbreak, taking a few steps back from things to simplify life became an apt adjustment. It had never been my job to be the welcome committee or maintenance man in the dog park anyway.

Although those callings were well received and fulfilled a sense of purpose, times had changed. I hailed a new season of backyard shenanigans and more time at home with Nitro (who was not opposed to that at all). The final word on 2015 is that the Town of Cary, at long last, installed a drain under the large-dog water bowl, and this made a lot of people happy. Other items like extra gazebos, additional benches, and corporate sponsors hadn't materialized, and unsurprisingly, nobody seemed to notice.

CHAPTER 7

Change Is

"Dogs do speak, but only to those who know how to listen." —
Orhan Pamuk, Turkish novelist and recipient of the 2006 Nobel
Prize in Literature.

My path to an early retirement began in the early months of
2016 while I was maintaining my new part-time pet sitting
schedule and visiting the dog park only once per day. New ideas
for the future crept into my mind as I perused my e-reader
and Nitro and his friends played (or napped) in the backyard.
Nitro, who was turning seven that year, loved our new schedule
because I was home nearly all day until we went to the dog park.
He was usually ready for the next lie-down by then, and he had a
singular habit of snoozing in Godbold regardless of how busy it
became. To him, the dog park was, for all intents and purposes,
an annex of our backyard; and after greeting everyone he liked,
he found a nice spot to assume the cozy "donut dog" position.
Dog park regulars found this rare behavior to be quite amusing,
and the other dogs seldom bothered Nitro during his naps. Nitro
was not a dominant dog in conventional terms, but he garnered
respect as an old-timer who preserved a calm demeanor while
enjoying his home-field advantage.

My regular line-up in 2016 included Ruxon and his new
sister, Callie, along with Rex, Remy, and Misha, who visited
two days per week. Angel, Jax, and Grizzly and Lolly came over
one day per week, and I walked Bailey and Sam on two days
each week. I deliberately scheduled this line-up so the daily

maximum number of guest dogs was only four. We were even pleasantly surprised and engaged in much rejoicing when Greta moved back from Arkansas early in 2016. However, Jen and Phil didn't visit the park too often because they had bought a house in southern Wake County (about twenty minutes away). Nevertheless, Greta and Nitro enjoyed playdates replete with side-leaping, chasing and, of course, a little humping. Their playdates happened on occasional weekends when Greta stayed over, or we would meet Greta at the newly opened Jack Smith Park in southern Cary. This equidistant destination was convenient for both parties, and I had been particularly eager to explore the new and improved dog park in town.

Jack Smith Park is similar to Godbold in most ways, but the park designers had value engineered a few of its features. For starters, the new park topography was flat compared to Godbold. This served to prevent the scour and erosion that resulted in the undesirable displacement of large volumes of wood chips during a high intensity rain event. Another noticeable difference was the surface texture of the tables and benches. In Godbold, dogs sometimes caught their claws in the small holes within the weave of those surfaces (it resembled chicken wire fence, but with smaller holes and thicker strands). At Jack Smith, bench and table faces consisted of a slat pattern narrow enough to sit (or stand) on, but large enough so that dogs were unlikely to snag their toenails.

Finally, and most interestingly, the water bowl stations were installed in concrete pads twice the size of those in Godbold, and they featured a surrounding floor drain. Not surprisingly, Nitro and Greta were much too elated by their reunions to notice any of these improvements. Nonetheless, few distractions served to break the monotony of daily existence more than witnessing two hairy, monster-faced, longtime besties engaged in jubilant play. Nitro loved his Greta, and when she was around, all was right in the world.

Jack Smith Park was nice to visit, but the nine-mile drive from my house was too far to include it in a daily routine.

We regularly visited Godbold, where the well-acquainted crew (Ellie, Jane, Diane, Bob, and Dog Park Doug) still honored their four o'clock tradition. On most days we also ran into Lara and Tucker, Samantha and Angel, Tina and Remy, Ismail and Misha, and Justin and Kaiser.

One day, we were talking about how strangely dogs behave and how dogs do the darndest things. Following a few exchanges, Bob wryly said, "Rex doesn't do anything weird, he's a completely normal dog." Bob was obviously being facetious, but I could not resist pointing out that when Rex stayed over, he liked to steal logs from my woodpile and move them to the middle of the backyard. Rex was also a reverse sneezer, and whenever someone came over to visit, he became so excited he convulsed with forceful attempts to inhale through his nose.

"Boomer does that too sometimes," Dog Park Doug reflected, "Why do dogs do that?"

"Doggie doctors say it is caused by a muscle spasm at the back of the mouth," I answered, "but some experts say it occurs when the dog's soft palate is irritated, causing spasms. This harmless but terrifying phenomenon will go away by itself in about half a minute, but presenting them with a treat or rubbing their belly will serve to reverse the reverse sneezing."

"I bet you have a lot of stories about our dogs that we don't know about," Ellie said.

"There's a few," I admitted, "like the way Gizmo pees in food bowls after mealtime."

"That's hilarious," Ismail giggled, "What does Misha do?"

"She likes to visit the bathtub, but only when no one is looking."

"What? She hates baths!" Ismail exclaimed.

"Perhaps, but it's a regular occurrence. Pawprints never lie. Maybe her doggie therapist encouraged her to face her fears?" I joked. It is worth mentioning that dogs are fully cognizant of the behaviors that crack us up. I also told the group about wall licking. The first time I saw this I thought, "Oh I guess some food splashed on the wall." Then I realized how absurd that sounded.

I had a regular client named Brewsky who liked to lick interior walls often, and he would customarily stare at me while doing so. I tried staring back at him, but that just made the whole episode even creepier. Tempted to begin licking a TV remote or a PlayStation controller to one-up the goofball, I decided instead that a treat was a better (and less enabling) distraction.

As a rule, dogs like to eat the most disgusting artifact they can find. However, I once had a Weimaraner named Rueben who preferred to sneak into the tub and eat soap (perhaps that's what Misha was looking for). Even on the trail of five years of pet sitting, I've never known another dog to eat soap.

Jane was next to join in and asked, "Have you ever noticed dogs like to nap in all sorts of peculiar positions? I've seen Bailey look like a corkscrew, Superman, or a Swiss army knife when she's sleeping. I can't imagine any of those being very comfortable."

"I know," Diane added, "Jasper does that too. I'm glad when he feels happy and safe, but the ergonomics of those positions are egregious!"

I then inquired, "Do any of your dogs stare at you when they poop?" This made Ellie guffaw and spill diet Dr Pepper everywhere. "I mean, the whole poop ritual is an outlandish oddity to begin with," I continued, "and I routinely have to pretend I'm *not* waiting for them to poo. But some dogs dump an additional variable into this ostensible occasion by staring at me while they poop. Ruxon is famous for doing this."

"Rosie doesn't do that!" Ellie exclaimed, "But now I think you are just making stuff up."

"No, it's for real," I pleaded, "and doggie psychologists say they do this when they are waiting for a reward for pooping outside, but it's likely that some dogs are just weirdos."

There was no shortage of kooks in our dog park. I mean, the primary reason people even came to the park was to watch the acrobatic zoomies with the hope that their own dog enrolled in the leap-froggy and butt-scoochy scampering. Boundless scurrying, twirling, and hip and shoulder checking ensured a well-rested household each night. This wild and hilarious behavior fostered positive reinforcement, and the merriment even tired the spectators out.

"They are a bunch of oddballs," Jane affirmed, "and one thing I've noticed with Bailey, despite how bizarre she can be, is that I cannot find her reflex spot."

"What's that?" Dog Park Doug asked.

"You know," Jane began, "when scrutchling a dog on their belly, or wherever their 'spot' is, causes a reflex where a singular sewing-machine-leg erupts in rebellion."

"The experts say the dog is actually trying to make you stop, but I don't believe that," Diane added before sealing the deal with, "Besides, it's an excellent way to test that your dog's interneurons, afferent neurons, and efferent neurons are all in proper working order."

"You guys read too much," said Ellie before asking, "but maybe you know why Rosie eats grass all the time?"

"That," I began, "is an instinctive trait which may also be implemented to rectify a fiber deficiency. Also, grass feels cool, and I've even seen dogs eat grass when they're thirsty."

"Well riddle me this, professors," Bob began, "Why does Rex turn around seven times before he decides to lie down?"

"There are a number of details associated with this crowd-pleasing vestigial behavior," Samantha answered, "Circling before lying down serves to check their surroundings, clears the bedding zone of snakes or insects, and pats down the grass to make the ground more comfortable. It is likely that all the berth banding could also be a way to mark ownership."

"That actually makes sense," Bob conceded.

"Okay, I'll buy that one, but why does Boomer kick after he poops?" Dog Park Doug asked, "I've heard different reasons for this. Is he trying to hide his poop?"

"No," Diane began, "dogs kick after pooping to mark their territory with scent from their paws. They have sweat glands in their feet that make pheromones, and scoop-kicking soil following elimination is their way of signing their work. Also, kicking around the freshly soiled soil spreads the dog's scent, thereby accentuating the mark."

"That makes SCENTS to me," I shamelessly replied, and then laughed at myself for at least ninety seconds. As our riveting discourse continued, we discussed butt-dragging, dreaming, and humping. Butt-dragging, although humorous, could also be a sign something is medically wrong. However, most of the time it is because dogs are trying to pass one of the many outlandish objects they liked to consume (i.e., a Lego block or carpet fringe). Dreaming dogs are entertaining to watch since they seem to be chasing somebody (or running for their lives), and they make a suppressed barking sound as their legs twitch.

Naturally, no dialogue on dog behavior was complete without a treatise on hump attacks. Head humping, side humping, reverse humping, or the famously apprehensible coup de grâce of humping, air humping, were all discussed. Most of the time, dogs use the hump attack to initiate play, and park regulars found it irresistibly hilarious. Humping is also a dominance move, however, and not everyone is in the mood for that. Dogs are an unusual bunch and, like humans, they do bizarre things for more than one reason. Unlike humans, they do not spend a lot of time wondering why they do what they do.

Nitro was rather normal as far as dogs go. Although as a puppy, he liked to steal my flip phone and take it to the backyard. He didn't chew or shred the pilfered item (it was sometimes a shoe or pen), he just stole it. It was particularly vexing when leaves covered the backyard, making the item nearly impossible to find, and he never stashed doodads in the same place either. Also, Nitro liked biting at falling snowflakes, which is something I hadn't seen other dogs do. The most inexplicable (but endearing) Nitro trait was how he maintained the bearing of a sagacious old soul, and this curiously hypnotic power made for one superbly soothing companion.

Thanks to encouragement by William and Kate's owner, Donna (a four o'clock irregular), I also began a gym habit in 2016. It was slow-going at first, but several peers had shared their Fitbit experience, and once I jumped on that bandwagon, there was no turning back. The first day I wore a Fitbit I logged 12,000 steps. Word on the street was that 10,000 steps is the accepted daily goal, so I was pleased to know my current lifestyle was exceeding *someone's* standards. However, my obsessive and competitive nature craved more daily steps, and the Fitbit opened a door of opportunity to finally use my OCD powers for good instead of evil. As I increased my activity-level over time, I felt healthier, slept better, and even shed a few pounds. I found that walking briskly produced more steps each minute, so I tried something I hadn't done in over a decade: I ran. I could not run far due to my unexceptional conditioning and old legs, but the virtual coach was always with me to provide encouragement and count those steps. Each day became an exciting opportunity to beat my previous record, and before I knew it, I was able to run in 5K events again and maintained a daily goal of 16,000 steps.

One funny and unexpected occurrence in 2016 was a resurgence of replies from emails I had sent during my 2010 job search. Former coworkers, human resource managers, and job recruiters were finally reaching out to me with new job opportunities. While the revelation that the environmental consulting market was making a comeback was reassuring, there was no way I would have gone back. I had been reveling in the autonomy of being my own boss for far too long, and besides, reading in my backyard while enjoying the companionship of furry friends was idyllic and never grew wearisome.

I did, however, make it a point to respond to these sluggish proposals. Despite how dejected and depressed I had felt when no one had called me back in 2010, I proudly and politely told the inquirers that I had started my own business and was not interested in their offers. Then, I cracked open a Monster and an absorbing novel as I swung lazily on my backyard hammock. All that was left to do, as the cool breeze and dappled sunlight washed my worries away, was enjoy the satisfaction of knowing I had exacted the best revenge on those corporate cronies and their ludicrously tardy replies.

Easily the most memorable event of 2016 was the water casting for my father in Button Bay, Vermont. I coordinated the event so Dad's sisters, my wicked stepmother Leslie, and all three of my half-siblings could meet near the quiet bay on the eastern shore of Lake Champlain on a Saturday morning in mid-July. The weather was perfect as we gathered on the rocky shoreline, uttered a few words, shed a few tears, and lowered the turtle effigy into the calm, clear water.

Afterward, we enjoyed a picnic lunch in the Button Bay Park grounds and shared our favorite stories about Big Bad Bill. This took a while since there are so many yarns about Billdad, the stubborn adventurer and master of unfinished projects. We had long lost count of the number of times Dad had disassembled another perfectly good car or boat, only to leave the operation unattended (and the garage unusable) for years. Each season of procrastination came to an end when the crafts were sold as-is so Dad could fund the next scheme (or one of our many hair-raising and death-defying escapades).

Throughout my formative years, I accompanied my father on dozens of journeys to destinations such as Cape Lookout in the Outer Banks or one of the National Forests in North Carolina. We very nearly perished in several picturesque woodlands including the Uwharrie, Pisgah, and Nantahala Forests. In between those tests of survival, we sometimes set out on cross-country skiing, sailing, or deep-sea fishing trips. While those types of excursions may sound harmless, Dad always found a way to nearly kill at least one of us, regardless (like the time we almost drove off an icy mountain road near Stowe, Vermont). The details of those trips and how (or why) we flirted with disaster so many times will be covered in my next novel; suffice it to say, Dad liked to "push the envelope" and never took the easy route. It is possible he was channeling Teddy Roosevelt, or perhaps he was designing ways to dispatch me for the insurance money. In any case, the pinnacle of these adventures was, without question, our two attempts to conquer Whiteface Mountain in the Wilmington Wild Forest of upstate New York.

The first attempt was in the summer of 1981, while Dad and I were enjoying a stay at grandma Ewald's summer home on Saranac Lake, New York (only a twenty-minute drive from Whiteface Mountain). The Whiteface Mountain summit trail is a paltry ten miles in length, but the elevation gain is about 3,600 feet, so it has been assigned a difficulty rating of "hard" by most websites that rate and rank trails today. Dad and I didn't have the internet back then, of course, but that would not have mattered anyway. The hike began splendidly as Dad and I enjoyed the fresh Adirondack air and scenic vistas from various lookout spots alongside the mountain. After a few hours, Dad was huffing and puffing a little, but he was determined to master the mountain. Billdad was only thirty-seven years old at that time and was in pretty decent shape since the Army Reserve required physical training for all active personnel, regardless of age or rank. However, during the last thirty-minutes of our seven-hour trek, our delight turned to distress as a sudden storm rolled in and swirled about the top of Whiteface Mountain.

The whiplash thunderstorm that turned our sunny, seventy-degree day into the afternoon from hell featured biting cold winds, stinging rain, and even hail. I had been hiking slightly ahead of Dad, so I turned back to see how he was faring and became worried when I noticed he was leaning against a tree, appearing exhausted. I went to help, but he just hollered at me to go on to the Ranger Station and he would catch up shortly. Praying that I would not be struck by lightning or blown off the mountain, I scurried ahead through the storm clouds. It took me several minutes to reach the Ranger Station (essentially a small wood cabin) at the summit. No visitors remained in the mountaintop shelter, but thank goodness two park rangers were still on duty, presumably to help any poor souls caught in the storm. I reported that my dad was not far behind me, and one Ranger said, "Well, we'd better help him the rest of the way."

We scrambled out into the freezing thunderstorm and found poor Dad face down on the rocky peak several hundred feet from the Ranger Station. He was still conscious, but he was shivering and in a bad state so we helped him up and brought him to the cabin. Dad had to be taken down the mountain in an ambulance because he was at risk for hypothermia, but he soon recovered.

The very next summer, ornery Billdad, in true dad form, insisted that we climb Whiteface Mountain again and "do it right this time." So, in the summer of '82, Dad's grudge against the mountain ensured that, once again, an ambulance would deliver him from the summit of Whiteface. This time, Dad had suffered a diabetic episode induced by over-exertion. Although that was the last time we climbed the Whiteface Mountain summit trail, Dad and I braved numerous "what doesn't kill us makes us stronger" vacations throughout my teenage years. Those memories may be bittersweet, but I will say this: Dad did his job because he instilled confidence in his son; being raised by Big Bad Bill conferred courage that serves me to this day.

Back in Cary, as 2016 wound down, pet sitting part time continued to provide the exact recipe for an ideal work/life balance. By the time 2017 was underway, it was clear that new dog park members greatly outnumbered the old. Even so, I primarily preferred to remain an incognito pet sitter who cared for just enough dogs to keep me engaged, but not so many as to totally drive me bananas. New members who did not know me very well noticed when I brought different dogs to the park, and it became a guilty pleasure of mine to see their puzzled expressions. Short-timers sometimes asked, "Wait, where is your husky?" or "Criminy, how many dogs do you own?" and I would just smirk a little as I delivered vague responses. Remy, the handsome husky, was easily the most asked about, and I had known him long enough to answer questions without actually revealing that he was not my dog. I only brought two dogs to the park at a time, of course, because I suspected the anonymous tattletale who ratted me out in 2015 probably still remained at large.

Longtime dog park members who knew me recognized

that I preferred to swim in a sea of anonymity and helped to preserve my secret pet sitter identity. This year was interesting because I perceived what seemed like an unusual number of new dog park members who just came and went, never to be seen again. Granted, I was not going to the park as much as I had in the old days, but even when I made morning, noontime, or off-peak visits, attendance was low compared to the golden age (the first few years) of my pet sitting endeavor. It had always been apparent that the dog park was not for most people anyway. Peak membership was never more than several hundred, and that is only a drop in the ocean when compared to the thousands of dog owners in town. Part of the reason for this margin was that many vets and trainers recommend against dog parks. I knew also, from personal observation, that many new members did not become regulars (or ever return again) because the brouhahas were too much to handle. Strangely, a significant number of dog owners are extremely poo averse as well (there are at least two dozen abandoned piles of poo in Godbold no matter when you visited). By far, the number one reason dog owners would not join the dog park was the forty dollar per year membership fee.

I never quite understood what some people expected from the dog park. Certainly, there is risk, but you can also be bitten, run over by a bus, or abducted by a UFO just by walking down the street. I have to say, though, that the epitome of short-sightedness was indubitably demonstrated by those who brought food into the dog park. Naturally, they were mugged straight away; and although some took this in stride, others scowled and complained as the dogs jumped all over them. Those were exactly the types of folks who "came and went." In any case, 2017 was a year when the number of longtime dog parkers I knew continued to slowly decrease, and so did the pool of new regulars. As the overall attendance dwindled, I tended to spend even more time in the shaded privacy of my very own backyard dog park.

All the same, it is worth pointing out that conspicuous

park visitors (nonmembers) still popped up now and again. "Photo bandits," as I liked to call them, would visit the dog park on some days in an attempt to drum up business for their photography studio. These small business owners were mostly well-received since they understood how to entertain the dogs and capture vibrant photos. Then, on the heels of leaving an obnoxious pile of business cards in the bulletin board cabinet, they went about their business never to be seen or heard from again. Singular visitations occurred on occasion as well. One Saturday afternoon, during a skate park event, two Red Bull girls raided the dog park. Those two caricatures clambered out of their car (ludicrously fashioned to resemble a giant-sized can of Red Bull), donned a couple of outrageously oversized backpacks (also shaped like puffed up cans of Red Bull), and then stormed right into the dog park. They then proceeded to hand out free cans of Red Bull to the dog parkers, patting the dogs as they went, before going on their merry way.

The most rare and remarkable visitors were local news reporters. Their visits typically trailed in the wake of some scandalous story related to dogs. The reports may have been about kennel cough, peaks in shelter populations, or even the extremely rare case of rabies. If nothing too outrageous had happened for a while, news crews certainly knew how to turn up the heat on the "leaving dogs in a hot car" issue. In the late spring of 2017, there had been an upsurge in dog flu reports around Wake and the surrounding counties, and one afternoon a crew from a popular local news network visited the park to sow panic with news of an impending endemic.

The reports around town had been that a large number of dogs were showing symptoms of canine flu (referred to as canine infectious respiratory disease complex, or CIRDC). CIRDC refers to a syndrome of diseases that can be caused by several different bacterial and viral pathogens. These pathogens are often highly contagious, and synchronic infections are common. Bordetella (kennel cough), distemper, and canine flu fall under the umbrella of CIRDC, as do several other afflictions. Most dogs are already vaccinated against Bordetella and distemper, yet as fate would have it, spikes in cases of CIRDC happen from time to time. Public health agencies use the acronym CIRDC during outbreak events because of the shared symptoms for these conditions. Clinical signs of CIRDC are typically mild and self-limiting, resolving after about a week. Dogs will exhibit indicators such as coughing, sneezing, and ocular or nasal discharge, but energy and appetite will usually remain normal. Dogs who exhibit fever, lethargy, decreased appetite, or more severe manifestations likely have secondary bacterial infections.

As the news team perpetrated their visit, there were about half a dozen dogs with their owners in attendance. Real Estate Dave was there with Sadie, as well as Donna and her black lab mix, Fritz. An actively playful pup, Fritz came over to Eric's Pet Sitting occasionally for vacation visits. He was mostly black, but looked like he had walked through a pan of white paint. Karl and Colleen, an outgoing and friendly couple originally from Canada, were there with Tucker, an old golden retriever who preferred people and didn't run around too much. Finally, there was Vicki, an intelligent, composed, and relatively new park regular with her two dogs Guinevere (a husky-lab mix) and Reeses (a hugely enormous black Irish wolfhound mix).

The news crew was composed of a cameraman named Gus and a female reporter named Roxanne. Congenial Colleen, with her husband Karl, let the news team in the park and the dogs took several minutes acclimating themselves to the interlopers and their terrifying media gear. Dogs definitely notice when someone enters the park without a dog and, generally speaking, they don't like it. I've never seen anyone attacked or bitten, but dogs rush suddenly and suspiciously toward these types of trespassers and bark in protest. I imagined the dogs were saying, "Hey, you forgot your dog! Why would you do that? Go back and get your dog!" It didn't help matters that Gus was lugging a backpack and a bazooka-like camera rig. Once everyone settled down, Roxanne (wearing clothing she most certainly was going to regret wearing to a dog park) began asking whether we had heard any reports of dog flu.

I am not a big fan of news reporters since I associate them with sensationalism, rage farming, and the gross misuse of confirmation bias. However, I was grateful that a local news team were giving dog owners a heads-up on a health concern. I joined the question-and-answer session with the intention that my canine business acumen might thwart efforts by this agency to frighten a large number of pet owners with click-bait. Life always seemed better when area residents remained calm and informed between headlines.

"Have y'all heard about the canine flu going around?" Roxanne asked.

"Yes. Yes, we have," I answered.

"Are there less people coming to the park in the wake of this outbreak?" was Roxanne's next heavily loaded interrogative.

"Some folks lay low when they hear about canine flu in the news," Real Estate Dave began, "but clinical diagnosis of dog flu is based on a recent history of exposure and physical examination findings. Determining the actual cause requires the application of specific diagnostic tests, and results can be difficult to interpret. Not to mention, the bloodwork, radiographs, and extensive tests are cost prohibitive for most dog owners."

Thank goodness for Real Estate Dave because he nailed it. We could see Roxanne's eyes start to glaze over about halfway through his response. Before she recovered, Vicki articulated, "In other words, the exact cause of a local outbreak may remain unknown in the short-term. Pathogen-specific diagnostic assays can be performed from samples obtained with a nasal swab, pharynx swab, tracheal wash, or a specimen from the lungs. However, samples collected after pathogen shedding, or at a location peripheral to the source of infection, could result in a false negative. Sample degradation, recent vaccinations, or infections that aren't producing symptoms may also lead to false negatives."

Roxanne was briefly bewildered by Vicki's vaccination vernacular. However, she was a trained professional and recovered faster than a Terrelian Jango Jumper. Her subsequent interrogative was delivered in a mere moment: "Aren't y'all worried about canine flu spreading throughout the region?"

"Not too much," Donna offered, "since the risk is higher for large numbers of dogs housed together in animal shelters, boarding facilities, or day-care facilities that create conditions that are conducive to the spread of canine flu."

"Right," Vicki added, "most agents are transmitted by inhalation of respiratory droplets, although fomite transmission, from items such as clothing, bowls, or furniture, can take place."

"Hopefully those big-box doggie day cares are doing their part," I declared, grabbing my opportunity to disparage corporate giants, "in terms of disinfection and overcrowding prevention, since those work to reduce the risk of illness."

"Besides, we have our Bordetella, distemper, and other vaccinations up to date," Karl stated as he patted old Tucker.

"Will vaccines stop a worldwide dog flu pandemic?" Roxanne prodded.

"Vaccination is a vital prevention strategy," Real Estate Dave responded, "but additional precautions must be taken because immunization does not protect against all infections. Vaccines are available for common pathogens such as canine adenovirus, distemper, parainfluenza virus, canine flu, and Bordetella."

"That's true," Vicki added, "and with the exception of distemper, these vaccines do not produce sterilizing immunity but rather decrease the severity of symptoms and extent of pathogen shedding. No commercially available vaccines are available for reduction of clinical signs caused by canine coronavirus and canine herpes."

"By the way," Real Estate Dave put in, "did you know that coronavirus, when viewed from an electron microscope, has a ring of projections that appear like a coronet, that is, a small crown made of ornaments fixed on a metal ring?"

"Oh, no, I did not know that," Roxanne admitted before asking, "what kind of treatment is there for dog flu?"

"Treatment of dogs with uncomplicated signs of canine flu involves supportive care at home," Real Estate Dave began, "This can include hydration, nutritional support, oxygen therapy, nebulization, and even carefully striking the chest to dislodge crud. Further irritation to the trachea may be prevented by avoiding a neck lead and removing barking triggers."

"Don't forget," Colleen offered, "expectorants or cough suppressants are sometimes recommended by a veterinarian to provide relief. However, a productive cough works to clear bacteria and may serve to reduce the risk of secondary infections."

"And antimicrobial treatment," Vicki began, "is necessary for dogs suspected to have bacterial pneumonia and should be directed by a veterinarian based on bacterial susceptibility results. The development of pneumonia may exacerbate an underlying distemper virus infection or immunosuppressive disease. Unfortunately, there are currently no labeled antiviral therapies for dogs with canine infectious respiratory disease complex."

"Oh. I see." responded Roxanne. "So, how deadly will this outbreak of canine flu be?"

"Mortality rates are difficult to determine since they depend on many factors including age, vaccination status, and type of infection," Donna said, as she was trying to leash up Fritz for his trip home. I could sense she had nearly had enough of Roxanne by this point.

"Right," said Real Estate Dave, "and the CDC maintains that less than 10 percent of *confirmed* canine flu cases are fatal to dogs."

Subsequent to Dave's last comment, the crowd leisurely dispersed as the group offered polite partings. That night, I viewed Roxanne's (severely abridged) "dog flu" segment online and shook my head in disappointment. All the pertinent and technical information we shared had been edited out of her report. One bit that remained included when Roxanne asked if we were worried about canine flu, and Donna replied, "Not too much." The other clip was Karl's comment about our vaccinations being up to date. So much for regaining my faith in the media. At least the news video did have about ten seconds of the dogs playing, which included one and a half seconds of Nitro circling for a nap.

Thankfully, dog parkers could still rely on their vets and other reliable sources to provide information and prevention measures to otherwise remain unruffled. Not long after the canine flu summit, I ran into Vicki, who was all keyed up about DNA test results she recently received for Guinevere and Reeses. With wild eyes and wavy arms, she was beginning to deliver the news to her friend, Courtney, while a regular we knew as Bronco Bart hovered nearby. Courtney visited the park with Ruby, a lab mix wearing brown and white splotches. Bronco Bart attended the park with his brown boxer named Beauregard. We called him "Bronco Bart" because he drove a Ford Bronco, and spent heaps of money on aftermarket parts for his Bronco, and talked chiefly only about Broncos.

"I finally received the dog DNA tests for Guinevere and Reeses!" Vicki exclaimed.

"Excellent!" Courtney replied, "What did they say?"

"Well," Vicki began, "Guinevere is a—"

"Those tests are just a novelty," Bronco Bart interrupted, "so labs can make money."

"They are called genotype research facilities, thank you very much," Vicki declared, with a dash of disdain, "and the tests are quite popular because they have become increasingly affordable and accurate."

"Yeah," Courtney chimed in, "and aside from ancestral breakdown by breed, DNA test centers may reveal whether a dog has a medical predisposition to a genetic disease."

"Dog DNA tests also can be used to confirm that a purebred dog was, in fact, purely bred," I offered, "and DNA test

NITRO: A DOG'S TALE

reports offer particulars on behavioral tendences, history, and unique traits of different breeds."

"Exactly!" Vicki confirmed. "Anyway, Guinevere is a—"

"What does DNA stand for?" Bronco Bart interrupted, "is that when cells do mitosis?"

Bronco Bart suffered from some form of cryptomnesia and Tourette syndrome because he had a horribly annoying ability to abrasively interrupt without remorse. He would jump to erroneous conclusions and blurt out vague, conflated, or irrelevant questions that were not only aggravating, they were nuttier than a squirrel turd. Any attempt to negotiate (or even decipher) his outbursts was simply maddening. To prevent him from hijacking our interesting discussions with inane questions, we would silently designate one person to draw him aside and change the subject (usually to Broncos). Fortunately, Bernard, Courtney's husband, had just returned from a poo pickup and sensed what was happening. As Bernard and Bronco Bart began to discuss three-inch lifts, granny gears, and locking differentials, Vicki was able to continue.

"Anyway!" Vicki exclaimed, as she let out a big sigh and rolled her eyes, "Guinevere is predominantly a husky-lab mix, but there are more breeds listed in her results. Reeses is, surprisingly, a chow, lab, and shepherd mix. Even though she looks like an Irish wolfhound."

"That's cool," I said, "I should DNA test Nitro. How do those tests work?"

"You can order a test kit from Amazon or Chewy for about a hundred bucks. Then you collect a sample from inside your dog's cheek using a swab they provide. The skin cells in the cheek contain white blood cells with your dog's DNA, in case you didn't know."

"I did not know that! How long before they send results back?" Courtney asked.

"About three or four weeks," Vicki answered.

"Which test did you use?" I asked.

"I went with Embark," Vicki reported, "since they had the

highest rated dog DNA test kit on Amazon. They use a research-grade genotyping platform developed in conjunction with Cornell's College of Veterinary Medicine. Embark compares dog's DNA with over three hundred breeds, including dingo, coyote, wolf, and street dogs. It also tests for genetic diseases."

"I may just have Ruby tested, but are there cheaper tests out there?" Courtney asked.

"Well, there's Wisdom Panel and DNA My Dog," Vicki responded, "Wisdom Panel is priced a little bit less than Embark, but DNA My Dog is only around seventy dollars."

"What is the accuracy rating on these tests?" I asked.

"Embark and Wisdom Panel dog DNA tests can accurately predict a dog's breed at 90 to 95 percent, and the assessment unveils a dog's breed mix as a percentage breakdown. I mean, they are accurate and all, but breed information is primarily provided for its entertainment value. However, they do foster a superior understanding of mixed-breed dogs that will be useful as you socialize and train your dog. Disease gene information is nice to have, but I would only act upon that in consultation with my vet," Vicki summarized.

"Dog DNA tests divulge which genes a dog may carry, but not display," Courtney astutely affirmed, "and knowledge of dominant and recessive genes could enable breeders to compare results from sires and dams."

"That's a valid point, and it's good to know, too, that although top-rated dog DNA testing companies make every effort to maintain a high level of quality control, dog DNA tests are not regulated by the US Food and Drug Administration," Vicki concluded.

I had never DNA-tested Nitro because it seemed so obvious that he was a German shepherd mixed with a Labrador. As I strolled away from our riveting conversation, I overheard Bernard telling Bronco Bart, "No, no, no! Riboflavin is completely different. Are you thinking of ribosomes? Or RNA? That would be another type of nucleic acid." I kept walking but felt bad for Bernard as he was victimized by Bronco Bart's oppressive and infuriating "interrupto-mnesia."

Before we knew it, the end of another year was upon us. I had continued to consider retirement at various times during 2017, but my reduced volume of charges assured exactly the right amount of dog park, reading, dog walking, and workout time. As writing had remained one of my favorite hobbies, I tossed around the idea of starting a weblog about pet sitting since I certainly had enough stories and photos to kick off a blog at any moment. Not to mention, Nitro would be an ideal writing partner given that he was such a quiet, easy-going, and photogenic character.

Regardless, I shelved the retirement idea because operating as the "incognito part-time pet sitter and international man of leisure" was working so well for Nitro and me.

Springtime in North Carolina is pleasingly picturesque. In Cary, there are a variety of blooming trees and shrubberies to enjoy as the dogwoods and azaleas bud and blush the landscape with bright colors. One weekend in March of 2018, as Nitro was eager to spring into action, I remembered that the Neuse River Golden

Retriever Rescue was conducting one of their Montague Pond fundraisers. I hadn't taken Nitro to one of these in a dog's age, and we were both motivated to revisit this timeworn adventure. We arrived at Montague Pond around noon, and there must have been at least one-hundred dogs running amok, splashing about, and smiling excitedly. The dogs were engaged in all manner of swimming, playing, running, shaking, leaping, and fetching in and around the small lake. As soon as I unleashed Nitro, he bolted into the pond, swam for a bit, then turned around and dashed right back to me. Once he shook all the water out of his fur, he charged splashily into the lake all over again.

I weaved my way along the lakeshore, basking in the contagious joy shared by the dogs and their companions. Nitro was almost nine now, but he was behaving just like the puppy I had brought to Lake Crabtree for our maverick swim club so long ago. Today, around the sunny pond on the Montague property, I recognized at least a dozen dogs and people I hadn't seen at the dog park in a long time. Didi the husky was there with her owners, and we spotted Aesop, Loco, Tuoma, Coco, and many more. The four o'clock gang were also there, and they had gathered around one of the picnic tables, so I sauntered over to say hello. On the way, I saw Justin, and then spotted Kaiser, completely saturated, exiting the lake. I had to do a double take because when Kaiser was all wet, his fur stuck to his body, and he appeared at least 50 percent smaller than usual.

I approached the gang of four and greeted them with, "Ahoy-hoy!"

Ellie, slapping the table and wearing a big grin, said, "There he is! Where is ol' Nitro?"

"I have no idea! He's running around here somewhere."

Bob then reported, "Rex and Rosie are over near the dock. Or at least they were."

Diane motioned toward Jasper with a nod and added, "Jasper is right here. He's fine with just letting the young ones have all the fun."

"I have no idea where Bailey is," Jane announced, "but I'm

sure she's giving someone the 'what for' and will be in trouble sooner or later."

"I wish the Neuse River Rescue people did this every weekend," Ellie opined, "Rosie loves this place."

"It wouldn't be the same if they had it every week," Bob uttered as he patted Jasper.

Just then, a man walked by with a large, brown, lab mix. His dog was wearing what we recognized as a "service dog" vest. We stared in silence at the paragon of obedience as he strolled by, indifferent to the surrounding sounds of splashy shenanigans.

"Well, that is a well-trained dog," Jane remarked as her eyes opened wide.

"That must be some kind of test," Diane surmised, "why else would he bring his dog here, and on *this* day?"

I didn't know the answer to her question, but I knew service dogs were remarkable animal companions. They are a class of working dogs who are so special, they have even been included in the laws of the land. Apparently, however, this had been completed in a bit of a hurry because the designation system uses inconsistent nomenclature and leaves many of us out to sea on most of the guidelines. Sorting out the types of dogs who provide assistance to humans, and considering the many awe-inspiring ways that they do so, is not an easy task.

While we all gawked at the service dog calmly walk by, Justin and Kaiser approached the table. Kaiser had shaken off the lake water, so he was all fluffy again, but continued to drip everywhere. "Did you guys see that service dog?" Justin asked, "That guy is awesome."

"We saw him alright," Ellie answered, "but aren't they called assistance dogs?"

"Outside of the states they sometimes are," Justin answered, "but the ADA uses the term 'service dog.'"

"The Americans with Disabilities Act," Diane added, seeing the perplexed look on Ellie's face. "The civil rights law that prohibits discrimination based on disability."

"Oh, okay. I knew that. It was just another memory that I

forgot," Ellie admitted.

"Is a therapy dog a service animal?" Jane asked, looking at Justin.

"Well, not exactly," he responded, "a service dog is trained to assist an individual with a disability. ADA disabilities include both mental and physical conditions, and a condition does not need to be severe or permanent to be a disability. Additional dogs who are associated with special needs include facility dogs, therapy dogs, and emotional support animals. Although there are similarities with regard to their function and behavior requirements, there are distinctions, particularly as they relate to ADA protection." Justin knew his stuff, and he continued: "Owners of therapy dogs volunteer to visit a variety of settings to purposefully cheer people up. Therapy dogs bring joy and reassurance to hospital patients, assisted living center residents, or stressed travelers in airports. Therapy dogs are also used to alleviate stress for victims of traumatic events or disasters, but therapy dogs are pets and not defined as service dogs under the ADA."

"I see," said Jane, "so you can't take a therapy dog just anywhere?"

"Right, the key distinction concerning service dogs," Justin explained, "is they receive protection under the guidelines of the ADA since they are specifically trained to mitigate their partner's legally defined disability. This means that service dogs are legally permitted to have access to a handler's workplace and public facilities where pets are normally not allowed. Special housing accommodations must be conferred to service dogs, as well as cabin access on commercial flights; but those considerations are covered in the Fair Housing Act and Air Carrier Access Act. It's all a bit more complicated than it seems at first, I know."

"Especially when not all disabilities are apparent," I added, knowing just enough to be dangerous, "even to the most observant maître d'. When it is not obvious that a dog is a service animal, only two questions may be legally presented to the handler: 'Is the dog a service animal required because of a disability?' and 'What work or task has the dog been trained to perform?'"

"Not only that," Diane pointed out, "the ADA does not require service dogs to be registered, wear vests, or display ID. The vests were established as a 'best practices' effort to keep grumpy restaurant managers and grabby children informed of the situation."

"This *is* confusing," Bob remarked.

"It is," Justin agreed, "particularly when there are individuals and organizations that sell service animal certification or registration documents online. But those documents do not convey any rights under the ADA and the Department of Justice does not recognize them as proof that the dog is a service animal."

"So, a service dog can go anywhere?" Jane asked.

"Not just anywhere," Justin replied, "For example, at a boarding school, service animals could be restricted from a specific area of a dormitory reserved specifically for students with allergies to dog dander. At a zoo, service animals can be restricted from areas where the animals on display are the natural prey or natural predators of dogs. Also, the ADA does not override public health rules that prohibit dogs in swimming pools. However, service animals must be allowed on the pool deck and in other areas where the public is allowed to go."

"What about churches, temples, synagogues, and mosques?" I asked.

"Religious institutions and organizations are specifically exempt from ADA compliance. However, there may be state laws that apply to religious organizations," Justin replied.

"How do you know all this about service dogs?" Ellie asked.

"I mostly picked it up during my enlistment in the Army," Justin clarified.

While Nitro, Rex, Rosie, and Bailey ran around having the time of their lives, we continued to grill Justin about service dog training, tasks, and breeds. We already knew that service dogs needed to be trained to perform their specific assistance work, and they required additional training so they would not be a nuisance in public. However, we didn't realize that, ADA or no, if your service dog poops on the karaoke stage or starts humping Chuck E Cheese, they can kick you out of there. Service dogs may be a specific breed, a rescue dog, or a dog already in the family. There are even established organizations such as Guide Dogs for the Blind that maintain their own breeding stock to ensure healthy puppies with desirable traits. Service dogs may be trained by charitable organizations, professional trainers, or their handlers, and training is typically completed by the time the dog is two years old. The cost of training varies, but it may be as high as $25,000. The ADA does not require service dogs to be trained with a designated professional or a specific program. Those decisions are left to the owner, and lately, more disabled people have been self-training their own service dogs.

Service dog duties may vary from picking up dropped items and taking laundry out of a washing machine to interrupting self-harming behaviors or providing deep pressure therapy for an autistic person. Service dogs can even call and then open the door for arriving EMTs. Hearing dogs, or signal dogs, help the deaf and hard of hearing by alerting on overhead announcements or people waiting to be noticed. Medical alert dogs are trained to signal the onset of a medical issue such as a seizure or low/high blood sugar, or alert the user to the presence of allergens. Mobility dogs assist individuals who use wheelchairs or walking devices. They can pull wheelchairs, provide momentum assistance, and even help make the bed. Psychiatric service dogs assist individuals with disabilities such as obsessive-compulsive disorder, post-traumatic stress disorder, and many other conditions. Examples of work performed by psychiatric service dogs can include entering a dark room and turning on a light to mitigate a stress-inducing condition, interrupting repetitive behaviors, or reminding a person to take medication.

We were all amazed by the scores of tasks service dogs can perform. Justin provided additional examples such as waking up a handler having night terrors, retrieving medication from a designated location, or nudging an unconscious handler into a recovery position. Some service dogs can place items in a shopping cart, and even pay the cashier. Others assist handlers in and out of bed (or chairs, bathtubs, pools, etc.). If the handler of a service dog loses consciousness, the dog will alert caretakers to an emergency condition or burrow under the legs of their unconscious handler to raise their blood pressure. There seemed to be no end in what they could do, and we learned the most common breeds trained as service dogs are Labrador retrievers, golden retrievers, and German shepherds. Unsurprisingly, breeds like Great Danes and Saint Bernards receive high marks as mobility assistance dogs.

Satisfied that we had learned all we could about service dogs, Diane asked, "What were you saying about facility dogs? I've never heard of a 'facility dog.'"

"Courthouse dogs are an example of a type of facility dog who assists special victims and vulnerable witnesses during legal proceedings. Special education teachers may also use facility dogs to improve interactions with students. Psychologists, physical therapists, or other healthcare professionals handle facility dogs to ease recovery and symptom management," Justin explained.

"That sounds like a therapy dog," Ellie commented.

"Facility dogs are often confused with therapy dogs," Justin corroborated, "however, facility dogs are more highly trained, work full time, and are handled by a working professional. Therapy dogs generally have less training, volunteer part time, and are handled by their owners. Facility dogs are working dogs, but not service dogs, and they are not protected under the ADA."

"And emotional support animals aren't the same as therapy dogs?" Jane asked.

"No, emotional support animals provide comfort just by

being with a person," Justin began, but before he could continue, Bob exclaimed, "Like Rex!"

Bob had us all laughing out loud by the lake with that one. "Very true," Justin admitted, then clarified, "the ADA distinction between psychiatric service dogs and emotional support animals expresses that a service dog would be trained to sense an anxiety attack and would perform a specific action to help avoid the attack or lessen its impact. Since only the mere presence of an emotional support animal provides comfort, it is considered a pet and not a service animal. *However*, state and local governments have enacted laws that allow owners to take their emotional support animals into public places where pets are normally not allowed, and those owners may be eligible for access to housing that is not otherwise available to pet owners."

"What about on airplanes?" Diane asked.

"Many airlines permit travelers to bring emotional support animals into the cabins on commercial flights under specified conditions, like a signed letter from a medical professional," Justin answered.

"And did you know?" I interjected, "Courts have approved animals besides dogs to provide relief to individuals? Bunnies, guinea pigs, horses, llamas, and yes, even cats, can be an emotional support animal. I learned that on the 'no drama llama' website."

"You're such a goofball, Eric," Ellie announced.

"Thanks for the 411, Justin, but I think it's time for Rex and I to find an emotional support meal," Bob stated as he rose to begin leaving the lake area.

"It is getting to be that time," Jane concurred, as the gang began their egress.

Feeling enriched after another one of our "fireside chats," we learned way more than we had bargained for on this trip. I cherished these moments with my friends and their dogs and so recorded the conversations with the express intent to publish them some day. I preferred to dwell on the successes more than the prickly and annoying characters around the dog park, but even the anecdotes of waywardness proved humorous in hindsight. Regardless, it was challenging, out of such a wealth of material, to select the events that were most interesting in themselves and at the same time served to display those cherished behaviors for which Nitro was famous. While I stockpiled my stories, however, the world continued to have its way as it levied heavy tolls onto our contented community.

As my tenure of pet sitting approached the eight-year mark, fate refused to withhold every opportunity to harshly remind us that all good times will come to an end. Those sad moments when a client's best friend crossed the rainbow bridge occurred with unwelcome frequency.

During the latter months of 2018, Ellie lost her Rosie, Diane lost Jasper, and a handful of Nitro's other friends passed away including Angel and even our beloved Greta. Losing a pet is nothing short of a horror show, and I observed my friends handle their heartbreaks in different ways. Diane swore she would never go through it again, while Samantha adopted a new puppy within a few months. Ellie decided she would only foster dogs once Rosie passed. I did what I could to offer condolences since I wholly understood the profound sense of loss they bore. Dogs offer unconditional love, and losing your soul dog is undeniably overwhelming.

Both Diane and Ellie continued to join the four o'clock assembly without Jasper or Rosie, and the support offered by the group proved to be an invaluable component to processing their sorrow. It was around this time when I overheard Jane say, "Grief is the price we pay for love." For some reason, I have found this thoughtful and perfectly articulated expression exceedingly difficult to forget.

It was also around this time when Bob asked me if I would be able to watch Rex five days a week (instead of only two), and if I wouldn't mind picking Rex up and dropping him off at the end of each day. Needless to say, I agreed, but I also quietly wondered if Bob was doing okay. It is not my style to ask nosey questions, but my sixth sense imparted the notion to use my role to perform wellness checks as necessary. Bob lived in a third-floor apartment, so perhaps he was simply having new difficulties with the numerous flights of stairs. Not long afterward, during one of my visits to walk Bailey, Jane asked me if I had perceived anything going on with Bob. I reported that I had recently began to watch Rex five days a week.

"Hmm. We've been wondering about him," Jane said, "and we haven't seen him at the park lately. He still comes out for Monday night dinners, but he doesn't order dessert anymore."

"That is strange," I admitted. Bob loved cake. He talked about it all the time.

"I asked him if everything was going okay, and of course he told me he's fine, but my intuition says otherwise," Jane offered, "I mean, it's his business, but I hope he knows his friends would like to help any way they can."

"I know," I agreed as I desperately sought a benign rationale, "maybe he's just having a harder time getting around. I've noticed he uses his cane more than he used to. I'm sure he'll be okay, but I'll keep an eye out." Bob, now in his late sixties, was no longer a spring chicken.

"I hope so," Jane said, as Bailey started tugging and hollering at me, "well you better do what Bailey says, she's ready to conquer the world and we're just burning daylight over here."

Laughing, I then proclaimed, "Will do!" and walked boisterous Bailey outside toward the neighborhood streets to patrol her province once again.

As the end of 2018 finally arrived, it was not without a persistent struggle to decide when to retire (i.e., to become a writer). The dynamic equilibrium at Eric's Pet Sitting was such that I still had too many dogs to focus on a full-time writing effort without too many distractions. I wanted to retire, but I loved watching dogs, and I just could not do both. While the gravity of the blogosphere sustained its pull, I spent a significant amount of time researching the categories and conditions of contemporary weblogs. There were already tens of millions of bloggers in the world, but that failed to deter my aspirations, because I was the only one who knew how to write exactly what I wanted to read. Surely there would be thousands of dog owners and potential pet sitters who could benefit from my musings?

Having discerned that video blogs (vlogs) had become all the rage; I naturally began my blog research by watching vlogs on blogs. What I gleaned from these investigations is that in order to earn a significant income from a blog, it *must* become a full-time job (as opposed to some kind of easy-peasy passive income generator). Interestingly, I also discovered that an inordinate number of vlogs were dedicated to teaching people how to make money with a blog. To unlock those secrets, all I needed to do was pay and subscribe! Wary of devious promises and resistant to the lure of fast and easy money, I continued researching free websites instead.

Further study revealed that high-revenue blogging requires an investment of thousands of dollars per month to ensure online traffic is diverted to a blog. There are many ways to manage these types of e-commerce sites but, suffice it to say, writing is just a small part of it. The main goal of e-commerce sites is to attract internet users to purchase clothing, food, video games, dog toys, snake oil, diet pills, or whatever else is featured on the site in the form of reviews and promotions. None of this appealed to me as I imagined myself as a casual blogger who provided honest advice about becoming a pet sitter and a small business owner. Above all, I liked the idea of helping those who were underemployed, cared for pets, and wondered if pet sitting might be right for them.

Having guaranteed a way to procrastinate one more year, and satisfied with my research efforts, I hatched a plan to divorce pet sitting *after* 2019. I intended to use the year to research history, since I had also considered blogging about the Ancient and Classical Eras. I had always been fascinated with early civilizations, and understanding the remarkable sequence of events that led to the formation of empires gratified the engineer side of my brain that wondered how things work. Moreover, reading about the foundations of cultures placated my need to delight in fantastic tales of legendary characters. I promised myself that I would definitely decide whether to blog about dogs or history at the end of 2019.

Unfortunately, 2019 began with the news that Bob had developed cancer. His sister, Trish, traveled from Michigan to be his caretaker, and I continued picking up Rex for day camp and returning him to Bob's home each evening. Sadly, Bob passed on Valentine's Day in 2019 and, while this devastated the four o'clock gang, many more in the dog park shared in this huge loss. Bob had been a beacon of good will and humor and never spoke an unkind word toward anyone. Speaking to Bob in the park (or anywhere) was such a pleasure and a treasure since he brightened everyone's day whether he was describing our dogs, delivering puns, or discussing desserts. He was one of those rare people who, no matter how my day was going, lifted my spirits as I approached the dog park entrance. Several people brought up the question about who would take care of Rex, but Bob's sister would only say, "Bob has provided for Rex." I had assumed that Trish would take Rex back to Michigan because I had noticed how much she loved him.

After Bob's memorial service, and much to my surprise,

Trisha asked me if I would be willing to adopt and care for Rex. Unbeknownst to me, Bob's will provided that I was to inherit Rex and I wholeheartedly agreed since it made sense on several fronts; it was also the least I could do to honor Bob. Rex already knew Nitro and my charges, and he had stayed at my house more times than I could count. Rex had always preferred to camp out on my guest bedroom bed, and once he moved in, that room became rightly known as "Rex's room." Rex, who was turning nine years old in 2019, loved his new digs and daily playtime with his old buddies. Even so, I observed that whenever someone pulled into my driveway, Rex became extremely wound-up (way more than what was typical). I deduced that Rex was pining for Bob, and his devotion was heart wrenching to witness as this expression of their bond remained unending.

As time marched on, I reflected on the many changes since Nitro's puppy days in the park in 2010. By the end of 2019, my roster consisted of only a few dogs each week. Remy, Jax, and Ruxon and Callie were my only regulars.

Vacation visitors stayed over occasionally, like Fritz, Ruby, or Guinevere and Reeses, but most of my former charges had moved on in one way or another. Holding to our glory days, Nitro and I carried on with our visits to the enduringly appreciated park at least a few times a week. Now and again, we were treated to a run-in with people I hadn't seen in a long while. They asked me questions like, "Whatever happened to Jan and Bacchus?" or "Do Joan and Vixen still come to the park?" or they might ask about one of the many Bellas or Baileys we once knew. Nitro and I still valued the dog park and it made me smile when I spotted brand-new groups engage and fellowship along with their furry friends. Although I missed the old days that evoked the epitome of community and quintessential business growth, gatherings of fresh-faced puppies with new congregates endured, and this seemed to make Nitro smile too.

Between the moments when I waxed nostalgic, countless hours were spent reading about our world in ancient times. I primarily studied Mesopotamia, Egypt, and the Greco-Roman synthesis, and I was rather surprised by how much I had forgotten in the thirty-two years since high school. One detail I *do* remember, however, was how dull and distant history seemed to me as a teenager. It was only after experiencing decades of a world cluttered with tax codes, political hyperbole, health care conundrums, and crushing debt that I could finally appreciate those earliest societies. I remember too, that previous history lessons conveyed the notion that archaeology was a much more complete picture than it actually was. Refreshing my recollection in the past year conferred a significantly more veritable account of that unfinished puzzle we call archaeology today.

The first insight to strike was a realization that ancient maps illustrate regions using ethnolinguistic labels. Regions were named to consider the prevailing language of an expanse during a given time period. Yet even so, numerous cultures speaking different languages were present in those areas. So, for example, Anatolia (now Turkey) was not a country in the Ancient Age, it was a region where cultures (mostly) spoke languages of the Anatolian branch of the Indo-European language tree. Furthermore, I had considered the Dark Ages to be a singular period in Europe after the fall of Rome. However, there were numerous Dark Ages in history, like the Bronze Age collapse around 1200 BC that affected Mesopotamian, Egyptian, and Near East cultures. There are several reasons why it happened, but even the archaeological experts do not agree on (or even know) all the causes.

I will not go on and on here (although I want to), but I cannot resist sharing that the most famous Cleopatra (and there were seven Cleopatras) was not Egyptian, she was Greek. Although the Sumerians are credited for being the first civilization, I was fascinated by just how many cultures pre-dated the Sumerians. Numerous artifacts around the world date back to the Neolithic Age (about 10,000 to 3000 BC, depending on the culture). Moreover, arrowheads have been found in Africa which date to unbelievable times like 70,000 BC. The oldest wheel (named the Ljubljana Marshes Wheel) was discovered in Ljubljana, the capital of Slovenia, and dates back 5,150 years.

The Sumerians won the civilization race because they were the first to develop all ten criteria that define a complex civilization. Many cultures worldwide had developed the wheel, chariot, sailboat, plow and irrigation; but Sumerians had writing, foreign trade, an increased settlement size, political organization, a class-stratified society, representational art, full-time specialists, large-scale public works, a knowledge of science and engineering, and a concentration of wealth. Sumerians established Uruk around 4300 BC, but cultures growing around the Nile, Indus River, and the Yellow River Valleys advanced all ten criteria as well. However, the evidence proving that Egypt, India, or China had it all together lends itself more toward 3300 BC. Later, the Minoans began around 2700 BC, the Olmecs started about 2500 BC and the Mayans in 2000 BC. It wasn't until after 800 BC that the Greeks, Persians, Romans, and Carthaginians began to develop as complex civilizations.

It was exciting to confirm the differences between the six major Mesopotamian cultures and empires, but I had only glimpsed the tip of the iceberg. I was not truly qualified to be a history blogger, at least not yet. So, as the curtain fell on 2019, I decided that 2020 would be my year to retire. I resolved not to renew my business license and pet sitting insurance since it was finally time to take a swing at my long-delayed writing career. Despite the fact there were seventy million blogs out there, I would add one more, and it was going to be about dogs.

CHAPTER 8

Ultimum Vale

"Dogs come into our lives to teach us about love, they depart to teach us about loss. A new dog never replaces an old dog. It merely expands the heart." — Author unknown.

Retirement! Finally. I promised myself that 2020 would be the year I read the complete works of J. R. R. Tolkien, George R. R. Martin, Arthur Conan Doyle, and Andrzej Sapkowski all over again. However, I was also determined to kick off my dog blog and fill each day with productive activities. I normally sleep only six hours a night, so I crafted an Excel spreadsheet to map useful tasks onto those remaining eighteen hours. Most of each day was smartly booked for writing or researching the dog blog topic of the week. Additional callings included working on the yard, leisure reading, and going to the gym. In between hourly missions, I designated a session here and there to complete mundane briefs like cleaning, paying bills, or going to the store. I had it all covered. Friends and family have razzed me over the years for being obsessive about spreadsheets and checklists, but structure is effective at keeping me focused. After all, it had been my self-induced schedule (and Nitro) that kept me busy and staved off depression in 2010. I designed my agenda in such a way that I continually had something to look forward to after each period of adversity (e.g., dusting or going to the dentist). Admittedly, I seldom followed my timetable to the letter, but by the end of each week, the discipline did pay off.

The first assignment I needed to tackle for the blog was to

organize a few hundred Word files I had written and saved over the years. Many of these documents were already refined since they had either been posted to social media or sent as emails to dog park friends (e.g., instructions on how to begin a pet sitting business). Others needed improvement, and diatribes that were not about dogs were parked in a "wildcard blog" folder on my computer. I also reviewed and organized my four thousand photos of dogs and the dog park to find the best of the best images to use in the blog.

Once I untangled my source material, I signed on with Word Press and decided "Pet Sitter Compendium" was the optimal name for my new project. The first few entries were about becoming a pet sitter from home and starting a small business. Sharing incisive and hilarious observations from the unpredictable dog park after all those years proved to be refreshing, cathartic, and satisfying. The writing came naturally to me, and I told my friends and family about the blog once several posts were up. I'm pretty sure most of them rolled their eyes and thought, "Oh great, another blah blah blog," but I ended up with about thirty subscribers during the first few weeks. It was all very exciting.

The additional plan I had was to write a book about the dog park. I imagined calling it "The Adventures of Eric and Nitro" or "Amazing Dog Tales." The novel narrative overlapped with the blog musings, but it would be more of an autobiographical journey with behind-the-scenes content that clients and pet sitters might enjoy. Of course, you know this because you are reading it now, and my (half-chewed dog park) hat's off to you if you've made it this far. Hang in there, we're almost done.

Retirement from pet sitting did not mean retirement from the dog park. Nitro and I still liked to sneak over there at random times of the day, or maybe later in the evenings when the "Sweat Hogs" hung out (they were not nearly as wild as their reputation alleged). We also made more trips to the Jack Smith Park, which was not only better for acquiring steps, but Nitro loved it, and people didn't know me there. This was important since I still dreaded saying no to nice people who needed pet sitting. Well, to most people. Despite my attempts at keeping a low profile and announcing my superannuation on social media, I was hounded by a handful of clients who could not seem to get enough of Nitro. It was flattering, but I had already been putting off retirement for nearly four years by this point.

Life was rolling along quite well in February when there was suddenly a buzz about a new strain of flu in China. This news reminded me about the bird flu scare in 2000 and the swine flu pandemic in 2010 that—despite raising alarm— turned out to be less severe than seasonal flu. In regard to the latest reports (COVID-19 they were calling it), I figured, "Oh that's just something happening 'over there'" and decided not to fret the flu. Then the reports of COVID-19 began to appear in more countries. I thought, "Well, that's just in *those* countries and I won't be traveling anyway. Besides, America is too high tech and conscientious to let anything happen *here*." In early March, the cases in the US started popping up, and by the end of March the shutdowns began and March Madness took on a whole new meaning.

At first it was the airports, train stations, and locations where large crowds of people tended to gather. Before long, schools, restaurants, and most businesses (including gyms) closed. This was unnerving, but I took a page from the Book of Nitro and remained calm. As you can imagine, corporate media outlets were having a field day. National news invariably reminded me of the boy who cried wolf, but Americans divided into two groups: those who did not believe COVID-19 was truly a big deal, and those who became extremely worried.

I remained skeptical as usual, but then I researched the 1918 flu and was reminded how this pandemic (like the 1918 pandemic) may very well last for two years while tens of millions perished worldwide. Even so, I decided to model my COVID coping plan from Nitro's modus operandi: be cool and lay low. Thankfully, adjusting to COVID-19 was not too much of a

NITRO: A DOG'S TALE

change for me since I was already a work-from-home writer and retired dog walker. As long as I masked up, I could still go to the grocery store, gas station, or pharmacy, so enduring a gym closure was the only real hardship I suffered in the short term.

Meanwhile, there was entirely too much controversy and confusion as the pandemic quickly continued to spread. Hundreds of thousands were stricken ill, and shutdowns led to furloughs, while the general stress level of America (and the world) ramped up rapidly. When data revealed that some countries had fewer cases than ours, pundits argued whether this was due to political leadership, engineering controls, population density, or other factors. Furthermore, we could not necessarily trust the numbers of confirmed cases, hospitalizations, or deaths reported in some countries. Agency credibility was the primary concern, but there was also the issue of whether COVID-19, preexisting conditions, or secondary infections were actually causing fatalities. Experts and laypersons alike were overheard arguing whether people were dying *with* COVID or *from* COVID. Testing for COVID-19 was also a big production since long lines, protection measures, and false positives (or negatives) compounded everyone's stress. Too much was happening too fast and, early on, concern and suspicion were more prevalent than answers.

The Information Age had conferred lightning-speed advances in genetic engineering, synthetic biology, nanotechnology, data science, and artificial intelligence. Heck, I had heard we could even clone sheep. None of this was relevant however, because a new airborne contagion had introduced itself to the world. Expecting that we should have nipped this whole menace in the bud, and exhausted from the ludicrous blame game, I became very disappointed with everyone in general and steeled myself for a long year (or three).

One morning, in early April, while I was minding my own business and writing a riveting blog entry, Nitro padded into my office and nudged me because apparently, it was time for another treat. We walked into the kitchen together and he immediately checked to ensure the cookie box had not disappeared since the last time we were here. I made him sit, and lobbed a small Milk Bone biscuit in his general direction. Nitro snapped it out of the air with striking precision then stared at the box again. I wondered how many treats he would eat if I kept tossing biscuits his way, but I was pretty sure we would run out of boxes before I could find out. As I pitched his last treat for this sitting, I noticed a strange blob on his lower-left gumline. I put the cookie box away and took a closer look, hoping it was just a bit of half-eaten Milk Bone (or mulch shard, or acorn, or whatever). It wasn't. It was definitely some kind of growth. As the thought of cancer began idling uncomfortably in my mind, I knew my next move was to mask up and head over to the vet. I had Nitro gear up in his harness and collar (he normally lounged around the house naked) and we sped over to the Cary Veterinary Hospital right away. No call. No appointment. I intended to simply barge in there like the Kool Aid guy and find out exactly what Nitro and I were up against.

Our vet was just a few minutes away, so I did not have an opportunity to overthink matters too much. Even so, I briefly brooded over how dreadful the year had been thus far and hoped his sore wasn't serious because Nitro was only ten years old. We walked into the vet's lobby and I explained what was going on to the front desk folks. They directed us to Exam Room 1 and informed me that Dr. Moyer would meet us shortly. Nitro, meanwhile, was happy as ever because he knew every room in this joint had a cookie jar. Going to the vet never made Nitro nervous, except for maybe those rare occasions they had to take him to one of the back rooms for a nail grinding or an ear cleaning.

While we waited, I told myself everything would be okay as Nitro was undoubtedly wondering why we even visit this place when we have perfectly good dog biscuits at the house already. Dr. Moyer soon arrived to greet Nitro and ask me how he was doing (Dr. McCann had retired a few years prior, but

Nitro liked Dr. Moyer just fine). It only took a few moments for Dr. Moyer to observe Nitro's gumline before he calmly stated, "We will take a sample of this to confirm but, this unfortunately looks to be consistent with malignant melanoma. We have seen this before in dogs his size and age, and it usually means they have about five months left."

Sweet Mother of Pearl. Not Nitro. Not now.

I asked about surgery and treatment options and Dr. Moyer explained they could not operate on the gums because the outgrowth was attached to the teeth and jaw in such a way that it would just return in a few weeks unless they removed his lower mandible. However, he recommended we visit the Veterinary Specialty Hospital (VSH), an emergency vet hospital in Cary, for oncology services. Needless to say, I made an appointment with VSH right away.

The team at VSH could not see us for a couple of weeks, but fortunately, Nitro's inelegant lump on his choppers wasn't bothering him in the short term. He could eat and scarf treats just fine, and he wasn't horking or worrying over it. I was troubled, of course, because it was plainly growing. I wondered if treatment would work, and whether I even wanted to put Nitro through cancer treatment. How much would it cost? Would he lose his hair? Gah! I hated all of this. I really, REALLY, did not want to be thinking about anything resembling the end for him.

When the day arrived to have Nitro's oncology appointment, I made sure to arrive early and brought his medical records, though I suspected it was a moot effort. His medical history—which was just a collection of vaccines, teeth cleaning, and the surgery to have him "fixed" back in 2010—was most assuredly irrelevant now, but I needed a sense of control. I remembered to don my mask too, since the COVID-19 protocol at VSH required that we pull into their parking lot, call the front desk from the car, and staff members would come out to take Nitro inside. It was a strange new world, I thought to myself, as I looked around the parking lot and saw numerous vet customers wearing surgical masks in their cars. It only took a few minutes of witnessing this bizarre paradigm before I became antsy and began walking around the vet property. It was a nice spring day near the middle of April, and I needed the steps.

Before long, Nitro's new oncology vet, Dr. Miller, called me to deliver her recommendation. She endorsed radiation treatment for the melanoma growth on the gums and stated they had a 98 percent success rate with that kind of treatment. Then she shared that radiographs revealed that Nitro had soft tissue masses in his lungs and they could begin a chemotherapy program to deal with those metastatic lumps. However, the success rate for chemotherapy was only 15 percent. I agreed to both treatments in an effort to do all I could for poor Nitro. It wasn't only that sweet Nitro was a calm and cool character, he was my best buddy, and I loved that furry sandwich thief immensely. I knew he loved me, too, and as long as his cancer (or treatment) did not diminish his quality of life, I would have his back.

The treatment schedule was charted in such a way that Nitro would receive a total of three radiation treatments and four chemotherapy injections. Radiation and chemo were scheduled so that he would not receive two treatments during the same week, and he would also have a week off here and there. The first treatment was a radiation dose and the circumstances resembled dropping off a loved one for surgery. I brought him to the vet first thing in the morning (while adhering to COVID-19 procedures), and I was free to go about my day until they called me shortly after the lunch hour. Nitro was a little groggy and droopy for a few hours afterward, but otherwise he managed his dosage download like a champ.

Just like Dr. Miller promised, the mouth tumor diminished significantly right away. I was so relieved, since the ugly growth had been considered inoperable. We still had a long way to go but the main point I was grateful for was Nitro's ability to maintain merriment between oncology appointments. The chemo treatment routine was similar in fashion to the radiation mornings (at least from my point of view): I would drop him off in the morning then complete half a day of frittering while I waited for the noontime call. Once the vet called, I would drive over to the super flu reduction zone and take blotto Nitro back to the ranch.

I dreaded having to take Nitro to cancer treatments, but aside from the saggy hours following each dealing, he mostly behaved like the same old Nitro. I did notice however, that he was more clingy than usual. Prior to his oncology tour, he always kept me in sight, or stayed only one room away. During his cancer treatment phase, he consistently stayed within just a few feet from me. Dogs know. They can sense when something is off, and in addition to his illness, I'm sure he sensed my unease. I did not expect to lose him at any moment, but I was certainly treating each day as if any of them could have been his last.

Full disclosure: I have not won any gold medals for optimism in my lifetime, but I have learned how to recognize when it is prudent to count your blessings. Winning that wrestling match with my mind was never easy, but it served to lighten my burdens. During that stretch of Nitro's cancer treatment, I thought about how the most beautiful aspects in life are feelings and moments and smiles and laughter.

Nitro had been the constant in these last eleven years while I was making friends in Cary, leaping into self-employment, and cheering mom up in Key West. Nitro even effected a perceptible de-grumpifying influence on ol' Billdad. Making the most out of our moments together wasn't complicated, since all Nitro ever wanted was to be with me. It did not make a difference where we were but, to be sure, an occasional cookie, pizza crust, or some bacon-wrapped shrimp always helped.

Meanwhile, the world continued to deal with (or go berserk over) the COVID-19 pandemic. By the beginning of May 2020, massive unemployment developed as a result of the shutdowns as temporary furloughs became layoffs for millions of Americans. This fostered a suboptimal blend of uncertainty, distress, and despair as transportation hubs, schools, offices, and most businesses remained closed. Being cooped up at home with the entire family may have been fun for a short while, but COVID fatigue set in quickly for most of us. Moreover, the mixed messages broadcast from national and social media continually made matters worse (thanks a lot Information Age!). We could still go to grocery stores, but that apparently became the best place for people to blast each other in a "mask or no mask" debate (while wearing a mask under their chin or dangling from one ear). Some actors gathered to protest business shutdowns, but the wheels undeniably fell off in late May when George Floyd was killed by Minneapolis police.

The unrest that followed lasted for months as racial tensions and COVID stress boiled over in the cities and neighborhoods across America while national and social media outlets did everything possible to exacerbate the situation. The summer of 2020 became a season when an entire cross section of society believed they needed to hit the streets and then hurl screams, pepper spray, bricks, or bullets at the closest neighbor who disagreed with them.

On the rare occasions I tuned in to the news, I half expected onomatopoeia slides (like those famously displayed in the 1960s version of Batman featuring Adam West) during clips of citizens clashing with police or one another. As if the incessantly annoying politicization of science, economy, and crime in the last twenty years had not been enough, the situation now had devolved into some kind of a nationwide, special nightmare edition of the Jerry Springer show. Both sides engaged, and people were forced to sort out truth with common sense and reason as trust in political leaders and professionals of science, medicine, and law enforcement had been eroded by conflicting opinions presented as facts. I decided that I hated 2020 as I pondered whether it was Mark the Apostle or Abraham Lincoln who said, "A house divided against itself cannot stand!"?

It was moments like these when I genuinely missed

my parents because they had consistently offered sage advice during stressful times. I did have friends and neighbors to talk to, and despite having to make significant adjustments as a result of the shutdowns, most of them remained even-keeled during the pandemic. This helped me to affirm that, even though national and social media were cherry picking the worst of the worst, not everyone had lost it. Not yet anyway.

My old college buddy Chris was definitely a bastion of sanity and my most preferred friend with whom to commiserate. He tended to maintain a positive (and frequently hilarious) attitude regarding life's difficulties, not unlike my fifth favorite author, Douglas Adams. Chris had such a way with words that this gift enabled him to summarize any personal or national crisis with an unforgettable one-liner (our mutual friends labeled them "Chrisisms"). His ability to blend the disappointment, absurdity, and profoundness of our world with clever quips made him a hit at parties and Sunday night dinners. We habitually met at Rudino's during football season, but Primo Pizza, D&S Cafeteria, and Asian Garden were all considered excellent off-season choices. Near to the middle of June 2020, with Nitro on board, we met on the outdoor patio of Primo Pizza.

"How's it going kemo sabe?" Chris asked me through his industrial-sized KN95 face mask upon approach.

"Hangin' in there," I replied, while patting Nitro as he looked curiously at Chris, who rather reminded us both of a plague doctor with his oversized air filtration device.

"Haven't seen you in a while! The super flu continues to rage with impunity," Chris observed, "will this reign of terror ever cease?"

"No doubt, but it still isn't as bad as England in the 1500s," I prodded, knowing Chris would appreciate the plague doctor inference—being the Anglophile that he was.

Chris was laughing as he removed his mask, then pronounced, "Well, while England ostensibly has an old-world elegance and allure that is rarely rivaled in America, they have certainly excelled at being brutal."

"To be sure. At least no one has been drawn and quartered in the Town Square lately."

"Or burned at the stake, and that was just for carrying the wrong prayer book!" Chris countered. Our sense of humor had perhaps grown rather twisted over the years, but it was nice to hang out with a like-minded comrade on the first Sunday night dinner we'd had since the lockdowns began. Chris then asked, "How is ol' Nitro doing with his oncology regimen?"

"He appears to be doing as well as can be expected," I replied while accidentally allowing a slice of pepperoni to fall in Nitro's general direction.

"How many more treatments does he have scheduled?" Chris asked.

"Just a few, we should be done in mid-July. His vet, Dr. Miller, said—"

"Is she hot?" Chris interrupted.

I laughed and almost dropped half a slice of pizza onto Nitro (which he would have devoured in 200 milliseconds flat). Chris regularly did this whenever I mentioned meeting a new female. In fact, I deliberately verbalized "Dr. Miller" to keep the answer gender neutral, but Chris knew that trick all too well. The truth is I had never seen Dr. Miller and even if I had, she would have been masked.

"Yes. She's the hottest canine oncologist I've ever met," I lied.

"I knew it!" Chris exclaimed.

"You are still a complete degenerate," I replied.

"I knew that too," Chris admitted, "but please continue."

"Anyway, in a few weeks Nitro will be done with his first round of treatments. Then we wait and see."

Chris knew "wait and see" all too well, and he gave Nitro a friendly pat on the noggin. It became a worthy occasion to change the subject when I asked, "So, what do you think about the state of the nation nowadays?"

Chris took a deep breath and began with, "Was it Peisistratus or Winston Churchill who said, 'Democracy is the worst form of government, except for all the others'?"

I nearly fell out of my chair laughing as Nitro's ears perked up while expecting an entire pizza to fall off the table while it bobbled during my laughing fit.

It didn't (this time), and Chris continued, "I don't know why the whole nation has gone Friday Night SmackDown on us, but I can't take much more of it. Not to mention, the contradictory guidance from public health officials, arbitrary school and business shutdowns, and the absurd policies like beach closings aren't helping. The news is so insulting. I needed something to turn things around for me, so I just watch cooking shows now."

A plot twist, but par for the course with Chris. "Well, I didn't see that coming, tell me more," I prompted.

"I once thought cooking shows and particularly entire networks devoted to food were pointless. But after observing the shouting matches on the news, the cooking shows became welcome visual sanctuaries. I cut down the volume and get lost in the soothing colors, imagining the smells as ingredients blend and bring out each other's full potential."

"You hear that Nitro? Food!" I exclaimed as I feigned another unintentional fumbling of a piece of pizza crust. "I, too, have actually found myself tuning in to the Food Network while channel surfing. The food looks transcendent and I inevitably discover a dish idea or an ingredient I may not have thought of if it weren't for their clever tips and tricks in the kitchen."

"Indeed. And Nitro appears to be finding more 'people food' these days," Chris observed.

"Hah! He hasn't been this spoiled since the Key West tour. Did you know he could eat an entire slice of pizza in one gulp? I've seen it happen."

"I believe it."

We ate in silence for a few moments as my mind wandered through memories of Nitro being a good boy and lifting our spirits during the stay with mom in Key West. Chris and I had both lost our parents in the last decade, and we each lost our mom to cancer.

"Food is love," Chris continued before the silence could become too awkward, "and by the way, have I ever told you why I like D&S Cafeteria so much?"

"Because it's cheap and the hostess is hot?" I launched as Chris chuckled.

"Well, yes, but also because it is my personal temple of Southern cuisine. As soon as I enter, I am greeted by the fragrant ghosts of many moons ago, and I am instantly reminded of gratifying road trips with my mother and grandmother. The food of my youth is there: collard and turnip greens, yams, cornbread, fried chicken, tender country style steak, REAL mashed potatoes and gravy, chicken and pastry, roast beef, and turkey and dressing. As the steam from the food fogs up my glasses, I actually enjoy waiting in line and mentally going over every possible delicious combination I can imagine. Once I sit down, I am reminded that life is indeed worth living because I have the good fortune to enjoy the food that I associate with my youth and my family. I never feel like I truly eat alone and the meals at D&S will always be associated with a time when I felt unconditionally loved."

"That's deep, man," I admitted.

Chris certainly had his moments. In between our complaints and skepticism of issues surrounding the pandemic, he knew how to offer an honest and heartfelt anecdote characterizing what truly counted. We talked for a while longer about music, British history, the upcoming football season, and anything else to take our minds off COVID for a spell. It was a refreshing break from these last few months of chaos. Before long, once Nitro had consumed all our pizza crusts, it was time to head back home. We bussed the table and expressed our farewells as Chris climbed into his Ford Taurus he drolly dubbed, "El Toro."

As we grow older and wiser, we inevitably outgrow some of our friends for various reasons. Although the quantity of friends decreased over the years, the quality of my remaining friends appreciably increased. Chris was remarkable because despite being relatively quiet, he could light up a room with laughter whenever he imparted one of his profound, yet succinct, Chrisisms. His infectious good nature was nothing short of inspiring, and when you needed someone to talk to, he was a superstar friend and listener. I perpetually appreciated his unique blend of empathy, insight, patience, and sincerity.

While the world insisted on becoming more disconcerting daily, Nitro completed his oncology tour around the time of his eleventh birthday (July seventeenth). I was feeling optimistic since his gumline tumor was in clinical remission. However, upon examining Nitro post-treatment, Dr. Miller reported that chest radiographs showed mild to moderate progression of his pulmonary nodules with an additional protuberance. In other words, his lung cancer had worsened despite the chemotherapy. She said to monitor him at home for a month and then bring him back to VSH in mid-August to reassess. My optimism took a hit, but I also knew we had been whistling past the graveyard for nearly four months already.

A couple of weeks later, as I was researching and writing for my blog in the spare bedroom office, I heard a strange clatter coming from the living room. The fireplace tools sounded like they were falling over or otherwise being jangled about. I remember thinking, "It's way too hot to have a fire, what is Nitro doing in there?" I walked into the living room and unfortunately bore witness to Nitro having a seizure. He was on the ground next to the fireplace, kicking the metal tools convulsively and I immediately went to his side to keep him from hurting himself. The seizure barely lasted a minute but I knew it was time to bring him right back to VSH to determine what we needed to do next.

I drove Nitro over to VSH and, along the way, spoke to Dr. Miller on the phone about what had happened. We arrived several minutes later and the vet staff whisked old Nitro inside to complete his next examination. On the heels of pacing around the VSH parking lot for what seemed like an hour, Dr. Miller called me to confirm that the cancer had spread and was indeed the cause of his seizures. She recommended radiation therapy around his brain and an additional program of chemotherapy, similar to what he had undergone from April through July.

I just could not put him through any more treatment. We had already completed a round of chemotherapy, which clearly had not worked. I was not surprised since I knew how small his chances were, but a hammer hit my heart regardless as I realized we were finally close to the end for poor Nitro. I declined the additional oncology medications, but they provided a scrip for phenobarbital to stop his seizures. The staff explained that this barbiturate will make him sleepy and sozzled for the first ten days, but once his system acclimated, he wouldn't act so inebriated.

My job now was to take Nitro home and keep a close eye on him. Once we returned to the homestead, I helped him stagger into the house. He then meandered into the living room for a minute, checked that I was still there, and plopped down for a nap. He slept for about twenty hours a day while on that phenobarbital. I stayed close to Nitro and I remember offering a lot of pats while letting him know I loved him. Whenever he awoke, he would immediately wobble toward the doggie door to go outside to pee or poop. It wasn't easy since he was so plastered, but he managed. As always, he first ensured I was there with him and I must say Nitro was a trooper until the end. Sadly, he did not make it the full ten days that were required for him to "acclimate and be okay," but I was right by his side when Nitro, peacefully and sleepily, lost his battle to cancer on August 9, 2020.

It was particularly difficult to keep it together for the next couple of weeks when the hurt felt most agonizing. While I was no stranger to loss, it is one of those singularities that never becomes easy. Talking with my family and dog park friends helped significantly as I processed and remembered Jane's words from the previous year: "Grief is the price we pay for love." It is so true. I suppose most people find it difficult to find words of consolation for those who have lost a loved one, but anyone who told me, "You were the best dad Nitro could ask for" won the blue ribbon. I rescued Nitro from a shelter so he could enjoy eleven years and one month of hanging out with his best buddy (who serendipitously happened to be the friendly neighborhood pet sitter). In an effort to fight off the sadness, I told this to myself over and over again. Even so, it wasn't easy.

Thanks to reliable old Rex, I was not completely dogless. I imagined Bob was taking care of Nitro now, so I continued to take excellent care of Rex. We went for a lot of long walks during those weeks subsequent to Nitro spiriting across the rainbow bridge. Rex and I both enjoyed strolling along the Greenways through the parks I once walked with Nitro during his puppy phase. The summer saunters around Lake Crabtree and Bond Park served us well as Rex clocked nearby squirrels and I reminisced about puppy Nitro.

Nitro was one of a kind, and I was so grateful he had been with me through all the trials during our era together. I missed his "old soul" personality and how he could sense how I was feeling and offered his paw so I knew he was there for me. Especially during his first year, Nitro's ability to gain rapport with dogs and owners at the park had made my small business possible, exactly when we needed it most. I suppose that sometimes the planets just line up in such a way that a special season solemnizes our lives, and I would say this genuinely qualified Nitro as my "once in a lifetime" dog.

Not long after Nitro passed, I received the keepsake container with his cremated remains along with a nice card signed by Dr. Moyer and the staff at Cary Veterinary Hospital. The card read, "Time will pass and the sorrow fade, but the pawprints in your heart will remain." Nitro's primary vet, along with the oncology team at VSH, had been extremely supportive and gracious through the entire cancer treatment process. As I rationalized the distressing loss, the magnitude, timing, and delivery of their empathy was momentously appreciated.

I would say the bottom line with dogs is how they are able to bring out the best in people. Sure, they are imperfect beings (like us) who become distressed and growl or bite (like some of us). They also do dumb deeds like run out into the street for no useful reason. However, they have an innate ability to rapidly assure an alliance with their companion and, I believe, over the long run, this symbiosis sustains inspiration and joy. Not all dogs are alike, of course. Some have a scent drive, or prey drive, but Nitro had a companion drive and it worked perfectly. Spending days with a partner who follows you, adores you, protects you, and loves you unconditionally fosters confidence, healthy choices, and an active lifestyle. I will eternally cherish the Nitro years and the way he channeled kindness and optimism wherever we went.

In parting, I wish upon all the readers of this story, as you strive for fulfillment in those endeavors you deem to matter most of all, that the love of your very own "Nitro" may become a part of your life. Such a precious gift of loyalty and love is a rare find to be sure. Dogs are just dogs, until they unexpectedly merge with your family and change you. They steal your heart, then affect your daily schedule, peer preferences, travel plans, and sometimes, even your sense of purpose. It is difficult for me to imagine living without a dog to help keep things together (like krazy glue). This lasting bond will be one you never forget. Even once they have gone, they stay; in your memories and in your dreams.

EPILOGUE

Duncan (tan coat, next to his big brother Rex) entered my life on November 17, 2020, exactly eleven years after I rescued Nitro. Duncan is a good boy, and is both similar and very different from Nitro. Duncan is outgoing and friendly with people and other dogs, but unlike Nitro, Duncan has way more hound in the woodpile. Therefore, he is emotional, impulsive, a hunter, and dramatic. I look forward to my adventures with Duncan, because he's a pretty crazy guy. Rex is still with me. He has been teaching Duncan important things like when to counter-surf, how to pee outside, and the best spot to take a nap. Duncan keeps old Rex in shape by frequently leaping on him when he least expects it.

If Mom were still with us, she would say: "Goodbye for now." Or, as Dad liked to say: "Get back to work!"

ACKNOWLEDGEMENT

I would like to offer my sincere thanks to Stephanie Attia for her fantastic help and hard work in reading and reviewing this work and providing me with valuable feedback and support.

Additional thanks my friends and family who provided guidance, encouragement, and inspiration throughout the pet sitting era: Lise Ewald, Carol Ewald Bowen, Jenny Fehlberg, Jane Merritt, Lisa Vartanian, Darren Gilbert, Donna Etheridge, Mike Jenne, Jenn Gooding, Tammy Kahm, Jared and Michelle Wiese, Bobbie Rose, Ellie Loring, and April Anderson.

ABOUT THE AUTHOR

Eric A. Ewald

 Eric Andrew Ewald was born in Burlington, Vermont but grew up in Bethesda, Maryland and then Southern Pines, North Carolina. Later, he attended Appalachian State University in Boone, NC (BS Physics) and Auburn University in Auburn, Alabama (Bachelor of Civil Engineering). Eric is now retired and lives in Cary, NC.

Find out more at petsittercompendium.blog

Made in the USA
Las Vegas, NV
13 October 2023

79041874R00134